Making DEEP SENSE *of* Informational Texts

A Framework for Strengthening Comprehension in Grades 6–12

Gwen J. Pauloski

Foreword by Cris Tovani

Solution Tree | Press

Copyright © 2025 by Solution Tree Press

Materials appearing here are copyrighted. With one exception, all rights are reserved. Readers may reproduce only those pages marked "Reproducible." Otherwise, no part of this book may be reproduced or transmitted in any form or by any means (electronic, photocopying, recording, or otherwise) without prior written permission of the publisher. This book, in whole or in part, may not be included in a large language model, used to train AI, or uploaded into any AI system.

555 North Morton Street
Bloomington, IN 47404
800.733.6786 (toll free) / 812.336.7700
FAX: 812.336.7790

email: info@SolutionTree.com
SolutionTree.com

Visit **go.SolutionTree.com/literacy/MDSIT** to download the free reproducibles in this book. To access the exclusive online reproducibles in this book, enter the unique access code found on the inside front cover.

Printed in the United States of America

Library of Congress Cataloging-in-Publication Data

Names: Pauloski, Gwen J., author.
Title: Making deep sense of informational texts : a framework for
  strengthening comprehension in grades 6-12 / Gwen J. Pauloski.
Description: Bloomington, IN : Solution Tree Press, [2025] | Includes
  bibliographical references and index.
Identifiers: LCCN 2024044082 (print) | LCCN 2024044083 (ebook) | ISBN
  9781962188319 (paperback) | ISBN 9781962188326 (ebook)
Subjects: LCSH: Reading comprehension--Study and teaching (Middle school) |
  Reading comprehension--Study and teaching (Secondary) | Literacy--Study
  and teaching (Middle school) | Literacy--Study and teaching (Secondary)
  | English language--Composition and exercises--Study and teaching
  (Middle school) | English language--Composition and exercises--Study and
  teaching (Secondary)
Classification: LCC LB1050.45 .P38 2025 (print) | LCC LB1050.45 (ebook) |
  DDC 372.47--dc23/eng/20241223
LC record available at https://lccn.loc.gov/2024044082
LC ebook record available at https://lccn.loc.gov/2024044083

Solution Tree

Jeffrey C. Jones, CEO
Edmund M. Ackerman, President

Solution Tree Press

President and Publisher: Douglas M. Rife
Associate Publishers: Todd Brakke and Kendra Slayton
Editorial Director: Laurel Hecker
Art Director: Rian Anderson
Copy Chief: Jessi Finn
Production Editor: Kate St. Ives
Proofreader: Elijah Oates
Text Design: Abby Bowen
Cover Design: Kelsey Hoover
Acquisitions Editors: Carol Collins and Hilary Goff
Content Development Specialist: Amy Rubenstein
Associate Editors: Sarah Ludwig and Elijah Oates
Editorial Assistant: Madison Chartier

ACKNOWLEDGMENTS

This book is dedicated to the thousands of students who have taught me throughout my career. Their bravery, honesty, and insight inspire me, and their struggles drive me to learn all I can about teaching and learning. I am also deeply grateful for my family's patience and support throughout this book's journey. Family members read drafts, gave encouragement, and served as sounding boards. They believed in this book, and in me, when my faith wavered. Finally, I want to thank Carol Collins and Kate St. Ives, my editors, champions, and guides at Solution Tree.

Solution Tree Press would like to thank the following reviewers:

Lindsey Bingley
Literacy and Numeracy Lead
Foothills Academy Society
Calgary, Alberta, Canada

Teresa Kinley
Humanities Teacher
Calgary, Alberta, Canada

Rachel Swearengin
Fifth-Grade Teacher
Manchester Park Elementary
Lenexa, Kansas

Visit **go.SolutionTree.com/Literacy/MDSIT** to download the free reproducibles in this book

To access the exclusive reproducibles in this book, enter the unique access code found on the inside front cover.

TABLE OF CONTENTS

Reproducibles are in italics.

About the Author...ix

Foreword..xi

Introduction 1
    The Impetus for a Deep Sense Approach 2
    Where Secondary Students Are Stuck.. 3
    About the Deep Sense Approach 6
    About This Book.. 7
    Where the Deep Sense Approach Fits In...................................... 8

PART ONE: The Case for the Deep Sense Approach.................................11

CHAPTER 1

Why and How Secondary Students Resist Reading Info-Texts 13
    Info-Texts Are Different 13
    Texts, Tasks, and Context Get More Complex 14
    Secondary Students Lose Confidence and Motivation 16
    Students Mask and Cope 16
    Concluding Thoughts...18

CHAPTER 2

A Strategic Approach to Improving Comprehension 19
    How Readers Make Sense of Text 19
    How Strong Comprehenders Use Skills and Strategies....................... 20
    How Comprehension Strategies Evolve.......................................21
    Why Info-Texts Require Unique Strategies................................... 22

The Deep Sense Approach Strategies 23

Concluding Thoughts 25

PART TWO: Teaching the Deep Sense Approach 27

CHAPTER 3

Helping Adolescent Students Regain Their Reading Confidence 29

Motivational Practices to Help Students Build Their Confidence 30

Concluding Thoughts 35

Overview: Making Deep Sense of Info-Texts 36

CHAPTER 4

Integrating Strategy Instruction That Works 39

Recommendations for Explicit Strategy Instruction 40

An Example of a Strategy Lesson 45

Concluding Thoughts 47

CHAPTER 5

Leading Text-Centered Discussions 49

What Gets in the Way 50

The Qualities of Meaning-Making Discussions 51

Text-Centered Discussion Planning 52

Concluding Thoughts 55

CHAPTER 6

Reinforcing Strategies With Shared Info-Text Studies 57

My Experience With Shared Info-Text Studies 57

SITS Components 58

SITS Planning 59

Concluding Thoughts 67

PART THREE: The Deep Sense Approach Strategies 69

CHAPTER 7

Focus on Meaning Making 71

The Focus Your Mind Strategy 71

The Talk About Texts Strategy 76

Concluding Thoughts 79

Learning Guide: Focus Your Mind *80*

Learning Guide: Talk About Texts *82*

CHAPTER 8

Prepare to Read **85**

The Preview Texts Strategy 86

The Determine the Text Structure Strategy 92

Concluding Thoughts.. 98

Learning Guide: Preview Texts *99*

Learning Guide: Determine the Text Structure *101*

Deep Sense Approach Resource: Determine the Text Structure.................. *103*

CHAPTER 9

Read Actively.. **105**

The Annotate Texts Strategy 105

The Check for Understanding Strategy.. 109

The Fix Confusion and Fill Gaps Strategy 111

Concluding Thoughts.. 114

Learning Guide: Annotate Texts.. *115*

Learning Guide: Check for Understanding *117*

An Example: How You Might Check for Understanding as You Read............. *118*

Learning Guide: Fix Confusion and Fill Gaps... *119*

CHAPTER 10

Evaluate Arguments and Evidence **121**

The Trace the Reasoning Strategy.. 122

The Consider Perspectives Strategy... 125

The Evaluate Evidence Strategy 127

The Analyze Rhetoric Strategy 129

Concluding Thoughts.. 132

Learning Guide: Trace the Reasoning *133*

An Example: Trace the Reasoning in a Student Column *135*

Learning Guide: Consider Perspectives *136*

Learning Guide: Evaluate Evidence *138*

Learning Guide: Analyze Rhetoric *140*

CHAPTER 11

Consolidate Learning **143**

The Summarize Texts Strategy...144

The Synthesize Across Texts Strategy...149

The Share Learning Strategy 152

Concluding Thoughts 155

Learning Guide: Summarize Texts 156

An Example: Apply the Summarize Texts Strategy With a Science Article 158

Learning Guide: Synthesize Across Texts 160

Learning Guide: Share Learning 162

An Example: A Power Notes Outline for a Presentation 164

Conclusion 165

Weak Info-Text Comprehension Is a Thorny Problem 165

The Solution Isn't Simple 165

Students Need a Four-Pronged Approach 166

Deep Sense Is a Partial Solution 167

Deep Sense is a Flexible, Grow-as-You-Go Approach 167

Appendix A 169

Strategy Instruction Planning Guide 170

Sample Strategy Lesson: Teaching the Annotation Strategy 174

Appendix B 177

Shared Info-Text Study (SITS) Planning Guide 178

Shared Info-Text Study (SITS) Example 1: A Middle School Science SITS 183

Shared Info-Text Study (SITS) Example 2: A Freshman English SITS 188

References and Resources 195

Index 207

ABOUT THE AUTHOR

Gwen J. Pauloski, EdD, is a writer, educator, and consultant specializing in adolescent literacy and pedagogy. She teaches in the University of Houston's educator preparation program. For seventeen years, she taught secondary social studies and English language arts in Seattle Public Schools and the Houston Independent School District (HISD). She served in a variety of teacher leadership roles, including department and grade-level team chair. She also worked as a campus administrator at the middle and high school levels.

For nine years, she worked in HISD's professional development department, training and coaching teachers and school administrators. She led the district's secondary instructional specialist team for three years and developed districtwide training delivered to thousands of teachers.

Gwen was selected to represent her district as a Teach Plus Texas Policy Fellow for the 2021–2022 school year. She has presented at annual conferences for the Association for Middle Level Education (AMLE), the Texas Association for Literacy Education (TALE), the National Council of Teachers of English (NCTE), the Literacy Research Association (LRA), and ASCD. Her dissertation was published in 2020; an article describing her research was published in the *TALE Yearbook*. She has authored curricula for HISD, McDougal Littell, and Teachers' Curriculum Institute.

She earned her certification in dyslexia intervention in 2021. Her coaching training includes work with Doug Lemov, Jim Knight, John Seidlitz, and the National School Reform Faculty. She has also been trained in AVID, Capturing Kids' Hearts, Laying the Foundation, CRISS, and History Alive!

Gwen graduated with a degree in economics from the University of Texas at Austin in 1986 and a master's degree in public policy from Harvard University in 1989. She returned to school to earn her teacher certification from the University of Washington. She earned her doctor of education degree from the University of Houston in 2020.

To learn more about Gwen's work, follow her at LinkTree: https://linktr.ee/GwenPauloski.

To book Gwen J. Pauloski for professional development, contact pd@SolutionTree.com.

FOREWORD

By Cris Tovani

At a workshop not too long ago, I found myself sitting next to Maddie, a fresh-faced, bright-eyed teacher who was wading her way through her first year of teaching. She was full of hope and questions. Over the course of the day, we shared stories and strategies, and toward the end, she said, "I've read your books, and they've helped, but can you recommend something more that will help my students stick with difficult nonfiction?" I quickly racked my brain to recall a book that focused strictly on nonfiction and was unable to come up with a title. I told her I would look at my bookshelves and get back to her.

Over the years, I've had countless teens who grumble that they hate to read. They complain that it's boring, and when it comes to school stuff, their mind wanders. I flash to David, a junior with good grades who told me he just waits for his teacher to give him notes. I remember Adrian who said, "When you're a bad reader, all you have to do is look tough and not say anything. That's how you become invisible." Some students are cajoled to read for the grade, but often, they don't see reading as something they do for themselves.

Shortly after meeting Maddie, I was asked to read a draft of Gwen J. Pauloski's *Making Deep Sense of Informational Texts* and, if I liked it, write the foreword. From the onset, I knew I liked the book. I could tell that many of our philosophies aligned. Pauloski holds strongly to the belief that "kids would if they could." If they aren't reading complex nonfiction, might it be that they don't see a purpose for it or they don't know how? Maybe the strategies they learned in elementary school are no longer sophisticated enough to meet the demands of text assigned in middle school, high school, and beyond. Perhaps they were never taught strategies for repairing and constructing meaning of disciplinary-specific text.

In *Making Deep Sense of Informational Texts*, vintage teachers like me, and newbies like Maddie, will find support. As I read each chapter, I remember strategies I forgot. I pick up new ideas to help me with the hard-to-reach readers who keep me up at night. For the Maddies of our field, there are step-by-step instructions to walk new teachers through the different recommended strategies. For teachers who want to help students but don't feel prepared to be reading teachers, there is also support. Each chapter not only contains valuable instructions with clear suggestions on what strategies to model for students but also is full of ways to metacognitively assess what readers understand and how they employ the strategies. Through short sentence stems, teachers quickly "get" feedback about what students need next. There are time-saving reproducibles that help students practice and internalize strategies so that when they encounter complex text, they automatically use what they learn. In addition to the resources in the book, readers will also appreciate the digital options offered by Pauloski online.

It's clear that Pauloski's beliefs drive her practice. Furthermore, she shores up her beliefs and practices by citing cognitive research that supports her recommendations. Pauloski quotes Catherine Snow (2002): "Any reader can be considered high-need depending on how challenging the text is" (p. 30). Even teachers who work with advanced readers will find support. Included in the book is a chapter on using discussion to help students deepen understanding, clarify meaning, and wrestle with multiple perspectives. Chapter 7 might be my favorite, as it walks teachers through explicit instructional moves of teaching metacognition. Chapter 9 is high on the list as well, as readers see the importance of giving students ways to hold and show thinking so that it can be reused.

Pauloski recognizes the importance of teaching students that they are collaborators of meaning making, that she is not the keeper of knowledge, and that text requires readers to play a role by bringing their thinking to it. She knows that when it comes to striving readers, success breeds success. It's clear that she believes, even for older readers, there is still time to get better. Her carefully written scaffolds make it possible for all readers to build confidence, practice meaning-making strategies, and grow as readers. But this takes time.

There is a high cost of giving up on teaching students how to make sense of complex informational text. When we make teaching easy for ourselves by lecturing and feeding kids information, we take away their power to think. There is a grave danger of students only getting their information from TikTok or the next digital trend soon to be consumed by unskilled readers. If this trend continues, at best, we will skate along as a society. At worst, we will lose our democracy. When citizens can no longer digest informational text and critically analyze it, we are doomed. After all, the cornerstone of democracy is an informed individual.

We don't have to dumb down our content for the next generation of readers because we've given up on students who won't or can't read complex nonfiction. We lose so much as a community and country when we continue to lower the bar of expectations. I argue that in this age of artificial intelligence (AI) and instant information, it is more important to teach students how to think when no one is there to feed them what to think. *Making Deep Sense of Informational Texts* is a resource that will help us. I only wish I knew about this book before my daylong workshop with Maddie. Thankfully, I got Maddie's contact information, and she will be the first person I send it to.

INTRODUCTION

In our lives, we are inundated with informational texts—short and long, digital and printed. We engage with informational texts, or *info-texts*, daily on cereal boxes and websites, in newspapers, and in emails. We turn to info-texts when we seek to understand a medical diagnosis, prepare to vote in an election, or research a company before a job interview. We consult info-texts to assemble a piece of furniture or re-create our grandmother's hummingbird cake. We pore over info-texts to keep up with our professional fields or hobbies.

Since 2010, forty-six U.S. states have adopted a common set of rigorous K–12 literacy standards. The Common Core standards call for educators to increase the instructional time and attention they devote to informational texts for the following reasons (National Governors Association Center for Best Practices [NGA] & Council of Chief State School Officers [CCSSO], 2010).

- Info-text literacy is vital for college and career readiness.
- Students are not developing the necessary skills to deeply comprehend and analyze those texts.

Some might argue that the importance of thoroughly understanding complex info-texts has lessened in this age of digital information, artificial intelligence (AI), and multimedia texts. Undoubtedly, how we consume information is evolving (Watson, 2023). Many readers use technology to read for work or school, keep up with current events, or research topics of interest (Pew Internet & American Life Project, 2012). For example, we use digital databases and AI-driven search engines to find information we once could find only in a library. Instead of reading an instruction manual, we might search for an instructional YouTube video. Our brains are being rewired, making it harder to sustain attention on a long, continuous informational text (Firth, Torous, & Firth, 2020).

However, in this moment in history when information is so easily manipulated and misinterpreted, I would argue that the ability to fully comprehend complex info-texts has never been more critical. Every day on social media, skirmishes arise because a commenter reacts to a headline, not bothering to read the posted article, and subsequent commenters pile on with mounting outrage. We see the effects of weak info-text comprehension in every field—from public health to politics to education.

This book, *Making Deep Sense of Informational Texts: A Framework for Strengthening Comprehension in Grades 6–12*, and the strategic approach in which it guides readers, the Deep

Sense Approach, grew out of my concern for the young people with whom I have worked, and millions more like them—adolescent students whose comprehension skills are not yet developed enough for the world they must navigate. More specifically, I wrote this book for middle and high school teachers who (1) are worried about their students' ability to make sense of the articles, handouts, websites, and textbooks they need to read for class; (2) are frustrated by the shallow answers they hear during class discussions and read in assignments; and (3) have students who come to them with a distaste for, or downright resistance to, reading complex informational texts.

Whether you teach English language arts (ELA), reading intervention, English as a second language (ESL), social studies, science, or career and technical education (CTE) courses, this book provides a fresh perspective on the thorny problem of informational text comprehension and offers practical suggestions you can implement to help your students. This book will also be helpful to campus administrators, reading specialists, curriculum writers, instructional coaches, and professional developers who work with secondary teachers or directly with teenage students. Finally, I hope the book will be a useful resource for faculty in teacher preparation programs, especially those who work with prospective secondary teachers.

The Impetus for a Deep Sense Approach

My commitment to addressing adolescent students' difficulties with info-text developed over years of seeing my students struggle and trying to figure out how to help them. I taught state, American, and world history during my first nine years as a classroom teacher in middle and high schools in Seattle and Houston. At first, I focused on teaching social studies content and skills to my students. I prided myself on having highly interactive lectures and fun simulations of historical events.

Within a few years, I became increasingly worried that many students were struggling to understand our textbooks, articles, and handouts. I had a hard time getting them to read on their own. They lifted their written responses to my questions straight from the text. Many avoided participating in class discussions, leaving it to a few eager peers to carry the conversation. Group projects and presentations fizzled, mainly because students had never understood the background reading.

Over time, I came to believe that my students' need to understand the roles of, for example, John and Abigail Adams in the Early Republic was much less urgent than their needs to:

- Make deeper sense of info-texts
- Recognize how an author organizes ideas
- Prioritize and select the most useful information for a particular task
- Evaluate the quality of the ideas and information they read
- Accurately explain the ideas they encounter

So, I switched disciplines to ELA to focus more on my students' literacy needs.

By the time I retired from my district in June 2022, I had reached a personal milestone. In seventeen years as a classroom teacher in urban public schools, I had provided direct instruction to more than two thousand middle and high school students.

Every year, a few students entered my classroom with impressive skills in understanding, analyzing, and applying the ideas and information they read. These students' large vocabularies, broad background knowledge, and inference skills were evident from the first day of school. Some could read a passage once with little apparent effort and then answer all the accompanying comprehension questions correctly. Others would dig their highlighters out of their backpacks and begin marking up a text without prompting. In class discussions, these students made connections and inferences others missed (including me). When asked to respond in writing to open-ended questions, they composed well-organized, insightful responses, citing relevant evidence. They did not just cobble together piecemeal understandings of a text. They digested the text whole, understood it thoroughly, and could see the nuances of the author's meaning and style.

If most of my students had these skills when they came to me, I might not have felt compelled to learn and refine the practices that would come to make up the Deep Sense Approach. But that was not the case. Instead, many of my students:

- Struggled to focus and engage with complex info-texts they did not choose
- Had difficulty making sense of longer texts on unfamiliar topics
- Took shortcuts that caused them to miss essential information
- Rushed through assignments, demonstrating only a cursory understanding of the text

These issues did not just affect the students I taught. In addition to my classroom experience, I served as a middle and high school administrator for two years and spent nine years visiting schools in various district roles. While working as an instructional coach, trainer, and campus administrator, I saw and heard about the same issues in secondary classrooms throughout my district that I had witnessed in my own classroom. They were evident in classes across disciplines, including ELA, social studies, science, ESL, and CTE classes.

Where Secondary Students Are Stuck

Since 1992, the U.S. Department of Education's National Center for Education Statistics (NCES) has administered the National Assessment of Educational Progress (NAEP, n.d.a) to large nationwide samples of fourth, eighth, and twelfth graders. In the assessment framework created for NAEP, reading comprehension is described as a dynamic, active, and complex cognitive process that involves the following (American Institutes for Research, 2017).

- Understanding written text
- Developing and interpreting meaning
- Using meaning as appropriate to the type of text, purpose, and situation

Data suggest that most middle and high school students have adequate knowledge and skills to form a surface understanding of grade-level info-texts. However, many struggle with the deeper aspects of comprehension: interpreting, evaluating, synthesizing, and applying what they read. Data from state, national, and international assessments suggest this struggle touches students, teachers, and schools everywhere. An analysis of eighth and twelfth graders' NAEP performance sheds light on this phenomenon.

The NAEP grade 8 reading assessment was administered nationally seven times between 2009 and 2022. On those tests, between 70 and 78 percent of tested eighth graders met the *NAEP Basic* threshold. Similarly, between 70 and 75 percent of tested twelfth graders met the NAEP Basic threshold in six national administrations during the same time period (NAEP, n.d.b, n.d.c).

Much smaller percentages of eighth graders (figure I.1, page 4) and twelfth graders (figure I.2, page 4) crossed the more difficult *NAEP Proficient* threshold (NAEP, n.d.b, n.d.c).

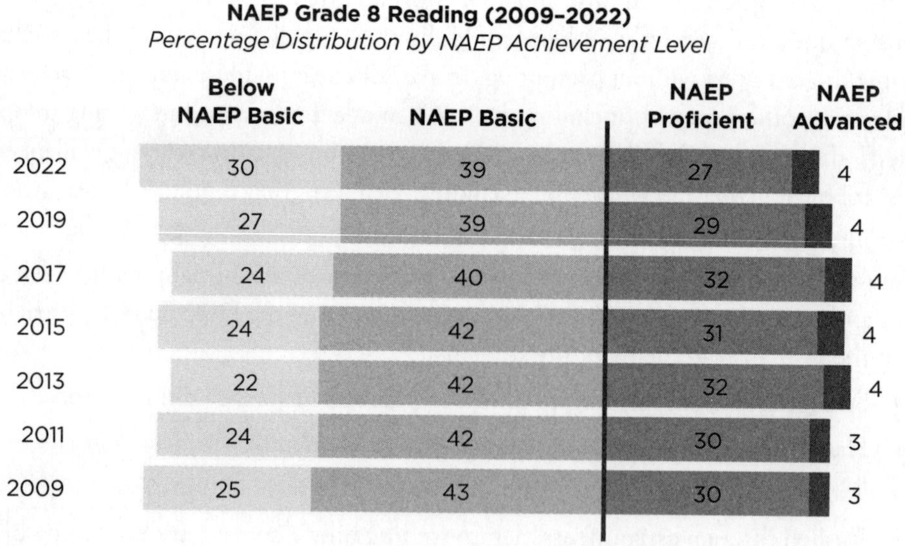

NAEP Grade 8 Reading (2009–2022)
Percentage Distribution by NAEP Achievement Level

Year	Below NAEP Basic	NAEP Basic	NAEP Proficient	NAEP Advanced
2022	30	39	27	4
2019	27	39	29	4
2017	24	40	32	4
2015	24	42	31	4
2013	22	42	32	4
2011	24	42	30	3
2009	25	43	30	3

Source: NAEP, n.d.b.

FIGURE I.1: *Percentage distribution by achievement level for NAEP grade 8 reading (2009–2022).*

NAEP Grade 12 Reading (2009–2019)
Percentage Distribution by NAEP Achievement Level

Year	Below NAEP Basic	NAEP Basic	NAEP Proficient	NAEP Advanced
2019	30	33	31	6
2015	28	35	31	6
2013	25	37	32	5
2009	26	36	33	5

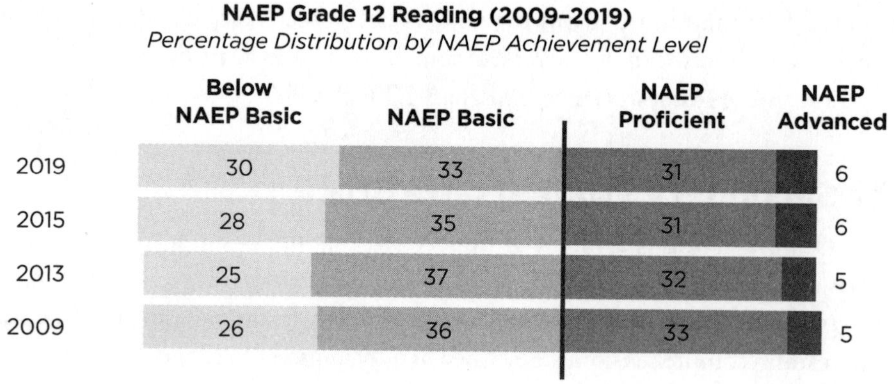

Source: NAEP, n.d.c.

FIGURE I.2: *Percentage distribution by achievement level for NAEP grade 12 reading (2009–2019).*

The same pattern holds among teenage students growing up in poverty. On the 2019 NAEP reading tests, about six in ten teenage students eligible for the National School Lunch Program (NSLP) met the NAEP Basic threshold (NAEP, n.d.b, n.d.c). This included 60 percent of eighth graders and 58 percent of twelfth graders eligible for NSLP. Less than one-quarter of NSLP-eligible secondary students scored at the NAEP Proficient level or above (19 percent of eighth graders and 23 percent of twelfth graders; NAEP, n.d.b, n.d.c).

These data suggest that most secondary students taking NAEP could make basic sense of the info-texts on the test. As a 2022 Congressional Research Service report explains, twelfth graders who achieved the NAEP Basic level on the 2019 test could "demonstrate an overall understanding and make some interpretations" of grade-level texts (Donovan, Stoll, Bradley, & Collins, 2022, p. 18).

This appears to be true for eighth graders as well. NCES prepares item maps to analyze students' performance on individual items. The maps list the literary and informational text skills assessed by various open-ended and selected-response items. Each skill is mapped to a scale score at which students had a high probability of correctly answering a question that assessed that skill (NCES, 2023a).

The item map for the 2022 NAEP reading assessment (NAEP, n.d.d) reveals that eighth graders scoring at the NAEP Basic level were likely to read an informational text and successfully:

- Describe an explicitly stated key idea
- Make a simple inference to recognize a problem discussed in the text
- Choose the best description of the main argument of the text
- Provide text evidence for a claim and explain how the evidence supports the claim

According to the item map (NAEP, n.d.d), only the 31 percent of eighth graders who met the more challenging NAEP Proficient threshold were likely to read an informational text and successfully:

- Recognize an implied reason for an action
- Propose an apt title for a set of texts and support with evidence
- Support an opinion about which photo best represents information from the text
- Describe similarities and differences by synthesizing information across two texts
- Select sentences from the passage that provide a specific explanation

Item maps for all grades 8 and 12 administrations of NAEP are available on the Nation's Report Card website in the Data Tools section (www.nationsreportcard.gov/data_tools.aspx).

I found a similar dichotomy in my analysis of the spring 2021 and 2022 Texas state reading assessments testing sixth through ninth graders (Texas Education Agency, 2023a, 2023b, 2023c). Most students had the skills needed to develop a surface-level understanding of an info-text, but most struggled to interpret, prioritize, summarize, and synthesize the ideas and information discussed in the text.

A CAVEAT ABOUT NAEP PROFICIENCY LEVELS

NCES clarifies that "the *NAEP Proficient* achievement level does not represent grade-level proficiency as determined by other assessment standards (e.g., state or district assessments)" (NCES, 2023c). A study conducted by NCES researchers finds that most "proficient" state standards in fourth- and eighth-grade reading and mathematics map to the NAEP Basic level (Bandeira de Mello, Rahman, & Park, 2018). Simply put, the NAEP Proficient achievement level is a high bar.

Over time, some students who struggle with info-text comprehension begin to avoid engaging with complex texts entirely. They accept failing grades on reading-dependent tasks. They steer clear of text-heavy courses. Unfortunately, the less experience students have with reading complex info-texts, the less opportunity they have to develop the skills they need to understand and use those texts.

When many students in a classroom (or a whole school) struggle to understand info-texts, teachers and administrators must make tough decisions about where to devote their energy. Teachers face a seemingly impossible dilemma when many of their students resist diving into complex texts.

Instead of asking students to read a difficult chapter in a textbook, teachers might prepare a slide presentation summarizing the most salient points (Greenleaf, Schoenbach, Friedrich,

Murphy, & Hogan, 2023). When faced with this dilemma as an eighth-grade U.S. history teacher accountable for the state test, I increasingly relied on paintings, photos, recordings, films, and homemade webpages to deliver content as substitutes or scaffolds for written text. Of course, these sources of information can engage students and enrich their understanding of a subject; text, in the broadest sense, can be anything conveying meaning. But when I knew I *must* find other sources of information because my students could not make deep sense of traditional texts, I knew something was terribly wrong.

If not adequately addressed, weak or incomplete info-text comprehension can wreak havoc in adolescents' academic lives. The consequences can multiply over time, eventually making it more difficult for graduating high school students to access higher education and professional careers. In particular, students in higher education have a rough go of it if they cannot fully comprehend and use the complex texts their professors assign. They might resort to paraphrasing in a way that does not show their own effort. They might skip challenging reading assignments and rely instead on watered-down internet content, their professors' slide presentations, or their peers' notes. Adults with weak comprehension might constantly find themselves in work dilemmas as well. They might skim a report or manual they were supposed to thoroughly digest. They may cover for their lack of understanding by dismissing the text as unimportant. They might withhold their comments and piggyback on peers' knowledge and work.

This is a much bigger problem than many realize. Data suggest that more than half of American adults struggle to understand info-texts deeply. On the 2023 Program for the International Assessment of Adult Competencies (PIACC) literacy test, nearly three in four adults aged sixteen to sixty-five (73 percent) could extract information from a short info-text to answer a question. However, only 44 percent of American adults could complete literacy tasks that required them to interpret or evaluate information, draw inferences, or connect ideas across larger chunks of text (NCES, 2024).

Based on my professional experience and research, I have come to believe the following.

- Nearly all secondary students can learn to comprehend, evaluate, and use complex info-texts.
- Many students have not developed all the strategies they need to do so.
- When students get the support they need to develop and apply these strategies, their comprehension and motivation increase.

Given the stakes for our students, we must help them overcome their difficulties with info-text comprehension. It cannot be our only literacy goal, but it is an important one that promises tangible benefits for our students and our schools. Enter the Deep Sense Approach, the focus of this book.

About the Deep Sense Approach

The Deep Sense Approach is a four-pronged, practitioner-informed, and research-backed method for deepening secondary students' info-text comprehension. It's designed to:

1. **Build students' confidence and motivation**
2. **Explicitly teach an updated set of info-text strategies**
3. **Provide meaningful context with text-centered discussions**
4. **Reinforce multiple strategies in shared info-text studies**

I developed this approach during my decades-long effort to help my students overcome their difficulties in making sense of info-text. My first teachers in comprehension instruction were expert practitioners like Cris Tovani, Stephanie Harvey, Anne Goudvis, Nancie Atwell, and Carol M. Santa. Their books and training offered practical advice I could immediately use and insight into the comprehension research available at the time (for example, Atwell, 1990; Harvey & Goudvis, 2017; Santa, Havens, Franciosi, & Valdes, 2012; Tovani, 2000). I continue to learn from these educators—their work has stood the test of time.

Since 2019, I have dug into a wide range of comprehension-related research, first to prepare for my doctoral studies and afterward to help me learn how to better support adolescent readers. I have slogged through books, dissertations, meta-analyses, expert-compiled reports, program evaluations, and journal articles. I have focused on research that examines the following.

- How the brain makes sense of text in general and info-text in particular
- How the various components of reading influence comprehension
- The strategies strong readers use to help them make sense of text
- The differences in how strong and struggling comprehenders use strategies
- Why, how, when, and to what extent specific strategies work for adolescent readers
- The instructional moves and learning conditions that promote comprehension and strategy uptake
- How well specific interventions have worked to improve students' comprehension
- The psychosocial aspects of reading (especially for adolescents)

You will find references to this research throughout the book. I have done my best to give credit for the ideas that have shaped my practice and provide enough references so you can verify my suggestions and pursue deeper study on the topics that most interest you.

About This Book

The book is organized into three parts. I have tried to distill each part and chapter to just what a busy secondary educator needs to implement the Deep Sense Approach. Throughout the book and online, you will find reproducible student-facing handouts and additional planning resources.

- **Part 1: The Case for the Deep Sense Approach**—In chapters 1 and 2, I continue to build the case for the Deep Sense Approach.
  - Chapter 1 explains how and why so many secondary students struggle with complex info-texts.
  - Chapter 2 explores the importance of teaching comprehension strategies and gives an overview of strategies that support the Deep Sense Approach.
- **Part 2: Teaching the Deep Sense Approach**—In chapters 3–6, I provide a practical overview of the Deep Sense Approach.
  - Chapter 3 focuses on building students' motivation and agency.
  - Chapter 4 gives guidance on explicit strategy instruction.
  - Chapter 5 homes in on text-centered discussion.
  - Chapter 6 lays out an approach to strategic shared info-text studies.

- **Part 3: The Deep Sense Approach Strategies**—In chapters 7–11, I introduce fourteen comprehension strategies, explaining why they are important, what they entail, and how to teach and assess them. These chapters are organized around the following topics.
  - Chapter 7 introduces two strategies that help students focus on making meaning.
  - Chapter 8 describes two strategies students can use to activate their minds and prepare to read.
  - Chapter 9 explains three strategies students can use to ensure they are actively making meaning throughout their reading process.
  - Chapter 10 introduces four strategies students can use when reading argumentative texts.
  - Chapter 11 describes three strategies students can use to consolidate their learning.

Learning guides and other student-facing materials are available to support explicit instruction of these strategies.

Where the Deep Sense Approach Fits In

The Deep Sense Approach is intended as a high-leverage component of a robust literacy program for secondary students. The strategies engage students in activating and building background knowledge and determining word meanings. Teachers can incorporate fluency practice, vocabulary study, writing-to-learn opportunities, and student-driven inquiry into their shared info-text study (SITS) plans.

The approach was designed primarily for core classroom instruction (what would be classified as Tier 1 in most intervention systems), though it can be adapted to dedicated intervention settings (Tier 2 and Tier 3). Research supports the effectiveness of direct instruction in a number of the Deep Sense Approach strategies in intervention settings, but the sustained application of these strategies with complex texts and diverse peers during core instruction helps solidify and deepen students' skills. Only in core instruction do we, as teachers, have the opportunity to give a wide range of students enough strategic information and scaffolded practice for them to fully comprehend complex info-texts on their own, for their own purposes.

The Deep Sense Approach is designed to be flexible. Of course, in an ideal world, students would receive explicit instruction in all the Deep Sense Approach strategies and have multiple opportunities to practice and apply them. In reality, teachers must balance many demands and constraints on their limited instructional time. Educators should feel free to use what they and their students need and have time for.

A grade-level teacher team can collaborate to introduce and reinforce Deep Sense Approach strategies across two or more classes. For example, the team can plan for the ELA teacher to introduce Deep Sense Approach strategies and provide initial practice. The science or social studies teacher can then lead shared studies of info-texts that communicate essential concepts and information aligned with their curriculum standards.

What's more, the Deep Sense Approach doesn't have to be tackled in one class in one year. For example, an ELA department can work together to design a vertical sequence of Deep Sense Approach strategies across two or more grade levels. Teachers at each grade level can provide explicit instruction on a subset of the strategies and practice them in SITS.

As Tenaha O'Reilly, Paul Deane, and John Sabatini (2015) of the Educational Testing Service explain, readers need a "constellation of knowledge, skills, and abilities . . . to understand, learn from texts, and communicate or represent that understanding to an audience" (p. 5). The Deep Sense Approach offers educators a tool kit to support secondary students as they develop the knowledge, skills, and abilities necessary to fully comprehend and use informational texts in and beyond school.

PART ONE

The Case for the Deep Sense Approach

The next two chapters continue to lay out the case for the Deep Sense Approach. In many secondary schools, teachers and administrators devote significant time, effort, and resources to improving their students' comprehension skills. In a sea of products and programs that promise to help improve comprehension, what makes the Deep Sense Approach stand out? What makes it worthwhile? I hope to answer these questions.

CHAPTER 1

Why and How Secondary Students Resist Reading Info-Texts

Since the beginning of my teaching career, I have puzzled over my students' aversion to reading info-texts. My conversations with fellow educators and my classroom observations have helped me understand that this is a widespread problem. Knowing that this psychosocial aspect of comprehension is a significant barrier for many adolescents, I have sought to understand the root causes.

In this chapter, I explain the challenges that secondary students face when reading info-texts.

- The info-texts we ask secondary students to read are often harder to comprehend than literary texts.
- Info-texts have gotten more complex since the students left elementary school.
- What we ask them to do with info-texts is often beyond their current skills.
- The school context can make it more difficult to get needed support.

In the face of these challenges, many students lose motivation and confidence (Troyer, 2017). The impact is even greater for students who already struggled with info-text comprehension in elementary school. As a result, they avoid reading complex info-texts whenever possible and do as little as necessary to get through the reading experience (Guthrie & Klauda, 2014). Later in this chapter, I describe some masks and coping strategies that make students' comprehension challenges hard to identify and address. When we understand how and why our students resist reading info-texts, we are better prepared to help them overcome that resistance.

Info-Texts Are Different

Literary and informational texts differ in terms of their purpose and structure. Unlike with literary texts, students must determine for each info-text they read how the author has structured the text and what the author's purpose is.

Writers of *literary texts* (such as short stories, novels, and plays) are storytellers. Their primary goal is to entertain readers. They follow ancient traditions to weave a narrative from universal story elements like plot, character, setting, and conflict. Literary texts typically use a universally

13

recognizable story structure (Hebert, Bohaty, Nelson, & Brown, 2016), making it easier for readers to make sense of the text.

In contrast, authors of *informational texts* write primarily to convey ideas and information to inform readers about some aspect of the natural or social world. Info-text authors vary how they organize the text depending on the specific ideas they want to convey (American Institutes for Research, 2017; Duke & Martin, 2019).

Informational text is a broad category that includes the genres, or types, shown in table 1.1. These genres vary in their purposes, structures, and techniques.

TABLE 1.1: *Types of Informational Texts*

Genre	Purpose	Examples
Literary nonfiction	The author seeks to relay a true story about a real person's experiences from a particular perspective.	Biography, autobiography, memoir, narrative essay, travel journal
Expository text	The author explains key ideas and factual information to help readers understand something better.	Textbook, science article, news report, informative website
Argumentative text	The author discusses an issue, considers different perspectives, and takes a position.	Essay, editorial (op-ed), formal speech, complaint letter, review
Persuasive text	The author seeks to convince the reader to believe or do something.	Blog post, speech, advertisement, letter
Procedural text	The author explains how to do something or how something works, step by step.	How-to guide, instruction manual, recipe, safety procedure
Visual representation with text elements	The author combines visual and text elements to communicate ideas and information effectively.	Infographic, diagram, chart, map, exhibit, social media post

These categories are not cut-and-dried. Many info-texts combine elements from two or more of the genres listed in table 1.1. For example, the author of a science article might explain an important issue to readers but also use some persuasive techniques, describing individuals' actions to address the problem and then adding a call to action in the concluding paragraph.

Literary nonfiction is a special case because it combines literary and informational text elements. Because memoirs, autobiographies, personal narrative essays, and travel accounts tend to have a narrative structure (such as telling the story of someone's life or the unfolding of an important event), this type of info-text is usually easier for adolescents to make sense of.

Texts, Tasks, and Context Get More Complex

As they move into middle school, students encounter more complex info-texts. Writers of info-texts designed for elementary-age students are often careful to use accessible language and simple sentence structures. They add text features (for example, headings and illustrations) and signal words (such as *first, second, in contrast,* and *for example*) to make it clear to young readers how the ideas in the text are organized.

Secondary students often encounter more challenging info-texts that contain unfamiliar topics, new terminology, and more complex syntax. The organization of ideas in these texts is also likely to be more complicated and less clear (Wharton-McDonald & Erickson, 2017). Even a short text with plenty of text features can use specialized vocabulary and complex syntax, making comprehension challenging.

Beyond the complexity of the texts, secondary school students often have to use the texts in more complex ways than they did in earlier grades. In middle and high school, we expect students to use what they learn in info-texts to help them complete challenging academic tasks. For example, middle and high school students might be expected to do the following.

- Compose paragraphs and essays that require them to understand and analyze an author's perspective, explain their interpretation, and select relevant text evidence.
- Summarize a complex text succinctly, capturing the most essential points and preserving the idea structure of the text.
- Select credible, relevant sources to independently learn more about a topic.
- Discuss key ideas and information presented in a text with peers.
- Prepare a presentation that synthesizes the most important ideas in several texts.

As a landmark RAND study puts it, "Any reader can be considered high-need depending on how challenging the text is . . . or depending on the way the reader is to demonstrate [their] understanding of the text" (Snow, 2002, p. 30).

Readers have to form a different mental map of the text depending on their purpose for reading. (You will learn more about mental maps in chapter 2, page 19.) Imagine that a tenth-grade student is assigned a science article for class. Consider the following three tasks the student might be assigned.

1. Read the article, along with two others, to get text evidence for an essay assigned in your English class.
2. Pass a multiple-choice quiz on the article in your biology class.
3. Prepare a synopsis of the article for a group research project.

In each case, a proficient reader would approach the reading differently, focus on different elements, make different connections, and, most likely, remember different information.

Compounding the complexity introduced by texts and tasks at the secondary level, the school context can add other challenges. When students transition to middle school, they often must quickly learn how to navigate six to eight different subjects, each taught by a different teacher. Their teachers don't have twenty-two students they see throughout the school day—they have one hundred or more spread across multiple classes. When the bell rings at the end of the period, students typically move on to the next room to learn with a different teacher, often a different constellation of peers, and a different set of info-texts.

Students suddenly have to juggle more texts and more assignments in multiple classes. Their teachers might not be able to help them as much as they did in elementary. Many secondary teachers barely have time to get through the planned lesson. They often have little time to support students struggling to understand assigned texts (unless the support is part of a deliberate intervention).

Secondary Students Lose Confidence and Motivation

By fourth grade or so, when the purpose of academic reading tasks shifts from enjoyment to productivity, students might come to associate reading info-texts with boredom or difficulty. They might blame the texts, the teachers, or school in general; but often, they blame themselves, assuming they are not competent (Sukovieff & Kruk, 2021). This happens especially for students who have endured years of required reading tutorials, intervention sessions, test-prep boot camps, and summer school.

As students experience a mismatch between texts, tasks, and skills year after year, they can easily lose their *self-efficacy*—the belief that they are competent enough to succeed in the task. Students can begin to give up on complex info-texts and on themselves as readers. To protect themselves, they might make pronouncements like, "I hate reading," "I don't care," or "This is boring" (Guthrie & Klauda, 2014).

The situation is even more challenging in classrooms where many students resist reading. When a teacher introduces a text and task and the class groans, the social pressure to disengage can affect individuals' motivation. As students enter adolescence, they become more concerned with what their peers think of them. Their fear of judgment can make the increasingly arduous task of reading info-texts feel like a high-risk, low-reward activity. Without knowing it, they rob themselves of opportunities to model positive reading behaviors for each other, support each other to push through moments of confusion and wandering focus, and encounter fresh perspectives.

Teachers are affected by this collective resistance, too. A well-planned lesson can fall flat. Efforts to engage students in meaningful conversation can be met with uncomfortable silence. With so many curricular demands pressing on them, secondary teachers can easily punt on collaborative text-centered discussion and assign more independent work. In schools under pressure to prepare students for high-stakes assessments, there can be a great temptation to lean on short passages, multiple-choice questions, practice packets, or isolated computer-based programs. For all these reasons, it is essential to address issues of motivation and self-efficacy.

Students Mask and Cope

Over time, many secondary students learn to mask their difficulties with info-text comprehension, making it harder for adults to recognize why they are struggling. In her book *Why Do I Have to Read This?*, Cris Tovani (2020) describes the masks her students have worn to cover their low self-efficacy as *anger, apathy, class clown, minimal effort*, and *invisibility*. In addition to adoption of these protective personas, I have noticed students use coping strategies—fake reading and sampling—that make their comprehension struggles harder to detect, as explained in the following sections.

Fake Reading

As a history teacher, I maintained a classroom library filled with historical fiction, biographies, and historical accounts written for middle-grade readers. Sustained silent reading was part of our daily routine. It is natural for readers to accidentally slip into fake reading occasionally, but I was amazed at how far some students would go to avoid reading. A few seemed to have made an art of it. Tovani (2000) beautifully describes the coping strategy of fake reading in her classic book *I Read It, but I Don't Get It*. Students sit still and keep their eyes in the general area of the text. They even turn the page once in a while, but their minds are far away.

When students do poorly on a reading assessment or cannot explain a passage, they might have never actually read it. Students might be so used to playing at reading that they are unaware they are doing it. When I frame fake reading to students as an unconscious habit that they must learn to monitor and address strategically, they usually get better at noticing when they have slipped into fake reading and work to overcome the habit. (Chapter 7 introduces the Focus Your Mind strategy, page 71, which provides guidance for monitoring and redirecting attention.)

Sampling

Another coping mechanism that students use to compensate for weak comprehension is what I call *sampling*. When the task requires only a surface-level understanding of a text, students can often find what they need by skimming the text and pulling out the most relevant nuggets. Given the many demands on older students' time, this habit is easy to justify.

Strategic readers scan and skim when they need only a surface-level understanding or a particular piece of information. Think of a pelican skimming the ocean's surface, suddenly diving beneath the water, and then emerging seconds later with a fish. In fact, skimming is sometimes recommended as a comprehension strategy, such as when determining the relevance of a section of text (see, for example, Wijekumar, Meyer, & Lei, 2017) or detecting bias in websites. Unfortunately, this practice is often not so strategic. Students might scan for a keyword mentioned in a question and stop when they find a passage with that word. Then, they cobble together a response using the question and text language. They might not stop to think about the question or whether their answer addresses it.

Another downside to the sampling habit is that when students encounter a patch of dense text within an assigned reading, they tend to skip or gloss over it. Of course, essential clues to the text's overall meaning lie in those dense patches, but students don't wonder about what they missed. It is an automatic, unconscious decision. They often do the same with unfamiliar vocabulary.

Students who skim the text rather than thoroughly read it struggle to make accurate inferences and connections (van der Schoot, Reijntjes, & van Lieshout, 2012). When strong comprehenders read complex info-texts, they often draw on information from multiple points in the text and call on their background knowledge to make valid inferences. If students are sampling, they skip over essential details. This can lead them to make inaccurate connections with background knowledge, fail to notice contradictions, or make inferences not supported by the text (Mateos, Martín, Villalón, & Luna, 2008; Wade, 1990). When I confer with students who have made an unsupported inference, we can often pinpoint where they tuned out. They might have:

- Skipped over a paragraph full of long sentences and obscure vocabulary
- Ignored a whole section that seemed irrelevant to their task
- Overlooked a sidebar or caption

It is not that they read carefully and made an inaccurate inference. Instead, they unconsciously skipped over the information needed to make an accurate inference. Other students learn to avoid making incorrect inferences; they play it safe, staying close to the literal surface meanings of the text.

By the time my students arrived in my classroom, they had spent years trying to read info-text, often with little guidance. Students' reliance on sampling is an understandable survival skill, but unfortunately, it can seriously impede comprehension. For many students, this habit is so deeply ingrained that it takes a great deal of strategic effort to counter it.

Concluding Thoughts

As I have explained in this chapter, many secondary students have lost confidence and interest in info-text reading—at least in school. Info-texts are inherently more challenging to fully comprehend than they may have been at earlier grade levels, and the challenges compound as students move through school. In the face of these challenges, many students come to believe they cannot improve their info-text comprehension, and they start to take shortcuts that undermine their comprehension. Unless we address the issues of motivation and self-efficacy described in this chapter, students are unlikely to take up the strategies and practices at the heart of the Deep Sense Approach. Chapter 3 (page 29) makes specific suggestions for creating conditions that help motivate and encourage secondary students to try again to make deep sense of info-texts.

CHAPTER 2
A Strategic Approach to Improving Comprehension

You may wonder why strong comprehenders can use, explain, and remember key ideas and information so effectively, while other readers struggle to do so. Strong readers tend to build accurate, detailed mental maps of the texts they read. Research suggests that in addition to mobilizing their relevant word and world knowledge, these readers employ dozens of strategies and skills to make sense of, evaluate, and use information from a complex text. They tend to activate the ones they need for the text and task, often with little apparent effort (Duke & Martin, 2019). Strong comprehenders use distinct strategies to make sense of info-texts.

In the previous chapter, I argued that we must bolster students' motivation and self-efficacy as we work with them to improve their info-text comprehension. In this chapter, I explain why it is also essential that we strengthen secondary students' info-text comprehension strategies.

As texts and tasks get more complex in secondary school, students must update their strategies. Later in this chapter, I introduce the Deep Sense Approach strategies, which are tailored to the needs of secondary readers who must make deep sense of complex info-texts and use what they learn to complete challenging academic tasks.

How Readers Make Sense of Text

Comprehension involves constructing what you might think of as a *mental map* of a text. This mental representation enables us to better understand the text and remember the most important ideas and information later. Though some readers may draw a diagram or write an outline to represent their mental map of the text, the brain seems to form these mental maps in the unconscious memory-encoding process.

According to Paul van den Broek and Anne Helder (2017), as we read, our mind forms a "mental representation in which individual elements from the text are combined with elements from the reader's background knowledge" (p. 361). As these researchers explain, "The resulting, interconnected representation goes beyond the meaning of individual words and sentences," forming "a network that provides structure to the reader's comprehension of the text (Goldman & Varma, 1995; Graesser & Clark, 1985; Kintsch, 1988; Trabasso & van den Broek, 1985)" (van den Broek & Helder, 2017, p. 361).

Research suggests that to make sense of a text as we read, our brain retrieves what it already has stored in memory about the words, the ways the sentences and paragraphs are structured, and the information and ideas the author is discussing. It makes connections between the information it already holds in memory and the new information it is receiving. If we already know a lot about the topic, the information in our memory bank will already be well organized and strongly encoded. We may have many neural pathways to that information (Kintsch, 2009; Kintsch & Welsch, 1991; McNamara, Kintsch, Songer, & Kintsch, 1996; van den Broek & Helder, 2017; van Dijk & Kintsch, 1983).

Numerous researchers and theorists have confirmed, refined, and built on our understanding of how a reader builds comprehension of a text (for example, Beach, 2019; Carlson, van den Broek, & McMaster, 2022; Cho & Afflerbach, 2017; Denton et al., 2017). The consensus seems to be that when proficient readers work to make sense of an info-text, they:

- Draw on their ability to recognize or decode words and access vocabulary knowledge
- Build meaning sentence by sentence, constructing a surface-level understanding of the ideas and content in the text
- Notice how the author has organized the ideas and information throughout the text to support the central claim or thesis
- Integrate what they learn with their existing knowledge
- Develop a mental map of the text

See figure 2.1 for paired depictions of a primitive map and a contemporary map (with a design based on more comprehensive information). The differences in the level of detail, accuracy, and applicability highlight, as a metaphor, the differences in mental maps of skilled readers versus mental maps of less skilled readers.

Readers with weak info-text comprehension often construct inaccurate, thin, or disorganized mental maps of complex texts. However, they can learn to build more accurate, detailed mental representations when they learn effective strategies.

How Strong Comprehenders Use Skills and Strategies

In the book's introduction (page 1), I describe reading comprehension as a dynamic, active, and complex cognitive process (American Institutes for Research,

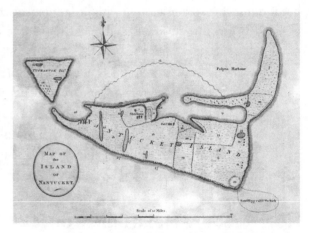

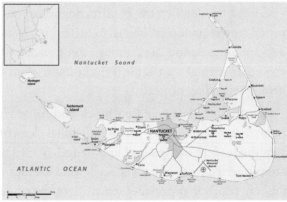

FIGURE 2.1: *Two maps as an analogy for the mental maps skilled and less skilled readers build.*

2017). This active process is familiar to students who are strong comprehenders. They draw on well-honed *skills*—automatic, largely unconscious processes developed over time—to make sense of and use an info-text (Afflerbach, Pearson, & Paris, 2008). They quickly evaluate the text and decide how they will approach reading it. They naturally manage their attention to maintain focus on meaning making. They draft a mental map before they even begin reading, then revise and build on it as they read.

Strong comprehenders slow down when meaning breaks down. Maybe their attention wanders, they run into a complicated sentence, or they come to a detail that contradicts an earlier statement in the text. When this happens, their reading becomes more deliberate as they draw on a suite of *strategies*—conscious, intentional, step-by-step procedures—to repair meaning (Cho & Afflerbach, 2017). Once they are back on solid ground, they move on, reading skillfully again.

The goal of teaching comprehension strategies is for our students to take them up and learn to use them quickly and effectively when faced with a complex new text or a challenging text-based task. With enough successful practice, the strategies become skills students automatically use when needed.

How Comprehension Strategies Evolve

You may wonder why secondary students have not already mastered such strategies. Actually, many elementary students learn to use a number of basic strategies to help them make sense of info-text. Their teachers help them activate and build background knowledge. They predict the topic by reading the title and scanning the pictures. They practice finding the main idea and locating text evidence. They fill out preprinted graphic organizers and summary paragraph frames. These are all developmentally appropriate strategies for younger students.

Often, strategies like these are presented as working for any age. I have encountered many cute strategy posters and exercises marketed online as suitable across K–12. These simple strategy explanations make it into secondary teachers' practice, sometimes directly and sometimes through curriculum prepared by rushed district specialists. I have also attended my share of training for reading programs designed for elementary students. In these trainings, secondary teachers are often casually told, "Oh, you can adapt this for your students." These reassurances do not reflect the reality that info-texts and tasks become more complex as students get older.

The simple strategies learned in earlier grades often fall short when students try to use them with more complex info-texts. In its 2012 position statement, the International Reading Association (now the International Literacy Association) explains that "as texts become increasingly complex, multimodal, and necessary for discipline-specific learning, middle and high school students must adapt by using more advanced, specific strategies for deeper understanding and composing (Moje, 2008; Shanahan & Shanahan, 2008)" (p. 4).

Even proficient readers can struggle with a complex text on an unfamiliar topic. Processes that are usually automatic can break down. In this moment, the reader must "slow down and become strategic," consciously choosing strategies that help them address whatever is getting in the way of their comprehension (Almasi & Fullerton, 2012, p. 2).

As an example of how strategies need to become more sophisticated over time, consider the commonly taught and assessed info-text strategy shown in table 2.1 (page 22). In elementary school, this strategy is often called "finding the main idea." The simple strategy taught to many

TABLE 2.1: *Finding the Main Idea Versus Determining the Central Idea*

Find the Main Idea	Determine the Central Idea
How a student might learn to find the main idea of a considerate text in elementary school:	How a skilled reader might determine the central idea of a complex text in high school:
1. Read the title and headings. Predict the topic of the text. 2. Read the first sentence or paragraph. Look for a sentence that identifies what the text is mainly about. 3. Write a main idea statement that paraphrases the sentence.	1. Skim the title, headings, and other text features. Connect with background knowledge. Determine the top-level text structure. 2. While reading, mark important ideas and details and jot notes. Pause briefly after each section to paraphrase the gist. 3. After reading, review text features and annotations, asking, "What is the central idea of the whole text?" 4. Draft a central idea statement aligned with the top-level text structure.

students in early grades works well with simple, clearly organized texts. However, when readers tackle more complex info-texts that demand inference and synthesis across the text, their strategy must evolve to determining, rather than just finding, the central idea among many important ideas without the help of an easily discernible text structure. When strategy instruction stops in elementary school, secondary students may apply simpler strategies like finding the main idea to complex info-texts, only to discover that their outdated approach leads them astray.

Why Info-Texts Require Unique Strategies

Readers use some strategies, such as previewing the text and checking for understanding, with a wide variety of literary and informational genres but might use them differently depending on the type of text. Other strategies are used almost exclusively with info-texts, such as evaluating the credibility of evidence and determining the idea structure of a text (Duke & Martin, 2019).

When I was preparing for my dissertation study, I was trying to settle on a workable list of info-text comprehension strategies I would introduce to my seventh graders over the course of the study. In the early 2000s, when I first started teaching comprehension strategies, the conventional wisdom was that there was a set of all-purpose strategies readers could apply with any kind of text.

As I began to learn more about the differences between literary and informational texts and how readers make sense of them, I had to throw out old assumptions and look for new models. Many of the professional books, curriculum materials, and research articles still treated comprehension strategies as genre neutral. Then I came across several papers by Educational Testing Service (ETS) researchers who challenged this notion. In the process of reconceptualizing how their organization designs and administers comprehension assessments to better capture how people make sense of and work with texts, they identified eleven key literacy practices that are essential for college and career readiness. These include fundamental practices like "Read Silently and Aloud," model-building practices like "Develop and Share Stories and Other Social Understandings," and application practices like "Analyze Craft and Literary Elements" (Deane et al., 2015). They devoted a paper to one of these literacy practices: "Build and Share Knowledge" (O'Reilly et al., 2015).

The paper offered a research-supported model of how readers mobilize an integrated set of strategies and skills to construct and communicate their understanding of informational text. That was earthshaking for me as a researcher and teacher. The ETS researchers' "Build and Share Knowledge" model is helpful because (1) it synthesizes a great deal of research on how strong comprehenders engage with informational texts, and (2) it shows how the strategies and skills work together when students read info-texts to learn and share their knowledge (O'Reilly et al., 2015).

This model informed the development of the Deep Sense Approach foundation strategies and two of the application strategies introduced in the next section and detailed in part 3 of the book. I also drew on ETS's "Discuss and Debate Ideas" literacy practice as I developed the "Evaluate Arguments and Evidence" strategies described in chapter 10, and I drew on ETS's categorization of skills in "Conduct Inquiry and Research" as I designed the "Consolidate Learning" strategies detailed in chapter 11 (Deane et al., 2015).

The Deep Sense Approach Strategies

The Deep Sense Approach strategies help secondary school students make deep sense of a complex info-text, evaluate the quality of ideas and information, effectively explain the text to others, and use the text to accomplish academic tasks. Each strategy meets the following four standards.

1. Strong comprehenders use the strategy to make sense of info-text.
2. The strategy can be taught through explicit instruction.
3. The strategy is versatile and valuable for adolescent students.
4. Middle and high school students will likely take up the strategy for their own use.

I have grouped the strategies into five info-text comprehension practices (see figure 2.2, page 24, for a visual representation) to help teachers and students work with them more easily. In reality, these five comprehension practices—(1) focus on meaning making, (2) prepare to read, (3) read actively, (4) evaluate arguments and evidence, and (5) consolidate learning—often overlap or are carried out in tandem. I have organized the strategies in a sequence that reflects how readers might naturally use them to understand, evaluate, explain, and use the ideas and information in a complex info-text. However, for any particular text and task, a reader might need to employ only a few strategies or use them in a different order.

The first seven Deep Sense Approach strategies grouped together in figure 2.2 are foundational for secondary readers. Without them, students will most likely struggle to make sense of complex info-texts. Some of our students are already skilled in these practices; others are already using the strategies to some degree. Many students have learned simpler versions that worked well enough with short, considerate texts, but now, they need to update the strategies to work for more complex texts and complicated tasks. Let's take a closer look at the foundational info-text comprehension practices.

- **Focus on meaning making:** Students need to regulate their attention so they can focus on making meaning of texts rather than just skimming them. They need to learn to talk about texts with their peers and teachers in learning conversations that allow them to express their own ideas about the text and consider the ideas of others.

- **Prepare to read:** Readers who jump right into complex info-texts need to relearn how to preview texts. As they examine and evaluate text features, they use what they learn

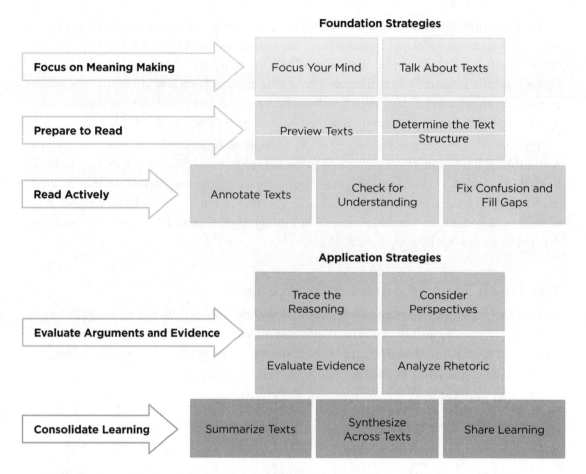

FIGURE 2.2: *Deep Sense Approach info-text strategies.*
*Visit **go.SolutionTree.com/literacy/MDSIT** for a free reproducible version of this figure.*

to access relevant background knowledge and decide how to approach reading the text. They also determine the text structure, which helps them build an accurate mental map as they read and retain more information later.

- **Read actively:** Secondary students must be able to stay engaged as they read, which can be challenging with assigned texts on unfamiliar topics. They understand and remember more when they annotate texts mindfully and purposefully. They need to check for understanding throughout the text and, when understanding falters, use strategies to fix confusion and fill gaps.

The next seven Deep Sense Approach strategies, those that are part of the application strategies group in figure 2.2, are more difficult for secondary students to master. However, they are at the heart of much of the academic work they must complete in many secondary and postsecondary classrooms. These strategies focus on helping students prioritize, evaluate, and use the ideas and information they read. Many students require support over time to develop these strategies into enduring skills. Let's take a closer look at the comprehension application practices.

- **Evaluate arguments and evidence:** Students benefit from learning how to trace the reasoning in an argumentative text. They need to learn to consider perspectives expressed in the text, formulate their own informed point of view, and seek to understand the perspectives of stakeholders affected by an issue. It is also critical that they learn to evaluate evidence to determine the relevance and credibility of the author's support for their claims. Finally, they need to be able to analyze the rhetoric an author uses in the service of their argument.

- **Consolidate learning:** Though students have been practicing summarization for years, many still struggle to accurately and adequately summarize texts. Students can consolidate their mental maps when they read additional sources and synthesize across texts. Finally, middle and high school teachers often expect students to share learning.

Chapter 4 (page 39) offers guidance for explicitly teaching the Deep Sense Approach strategies. Appendix A (page 169) contains a planning guide and sample lesson to help you plan strategy instruction. The five chapters in part 3 (page 69) each introduce one of the info-text comprehension practices and describe the Deep Sense Approach strategies designed to help strengthen that practice.

Concluding Thoughts

Secondary students continue to need support to build robust mental maps of informational texts, use the ideas and information they learned in those texts, and explain what they have learned to others. Though they may have had strategy instruction in elementary school, the more complex texts and tasks they encounter in middle and high school require more sophisticated strategies.

The Deep Sense Approach strategies are tailor-made for secondary readers, offering foundation strategies that help them make sense of complex info-texts and application strategies that help them evaluate texts and consolidate and share their learning.

PART TWO

Teaching the Deep Sense Approach

In the introduction, you learned that the Deep Sense Approach has four components.

1. Building students' confidence and motivation

2. Explicitly teaching an updated set of info-text strategies

3. Providing meaningful context with text-centered discussions

4. Reinforcing multiple strategies in shared info-text studies

In part 2, chapters are devoted to these components. In each chapter, I explain the rationale and research for its component and provide practical suggestions for implementation.

CHAPTER 3

Helping Adolescent Students Regain Their Reading Confidence

In explaining their groundbreaking self-determination theory, motivation researchers Edward L. Deci and Richard M. Ryan proposed that humans are motivated by three fundamental psychological needs (Ryan & Deci, 2000a, 2000b, 2017).

1. **Relatedness:** People have an inherent need to feel that they belong, that they are connected with others, and that they care about and are cared for by others in the learning community (Ryan & Deci, 2000a, 2002). In the classroom, students are more likely to accept instruction when they feel respected and cared for by their teacher (Ryan & Deci, 2000a).

2. **Autonomy:** This inherent human need is akin to self-regulation or self-governance (Ryan & Deci, 2017). As Ryan and Deci (2002) explain, people who are autonomous believe that they initiate their own behavior as an expression of themselves. Even when others influence their values and behaviors, they see themselves as having a choice in the matter.

3. **Competence:** Finally, people need to believe that they are good at, or can be good at, what they are being asked to do. This leads people to look for challenges that reinforce what they are good at.

Researchers have found that learning improves when teachers support students' sense of relatedness, competence, and autonomy (see, for example, Guthrie & Klauda, 2014; Mancini-Marshall, 2014; Niemiec & Ryan, 2009; Shkedy et al., 2021). In reading classrooms where these psychological needs are supported, students' comprehension improves. For their study of reading instruction involving over six hundred seventh graders, researchers Susan Lutz Klauda and John T. Guthrie (2014) designed an intervention that included "instructional support for choice, importance, collaboration, and competence, accompanied by cognitive scaffolding for informational text comprehension" (p. 387). The researchers found that this combination led to a significant improvement in students' info-text comprehension compared with traditional instruction. As they explain, "When students experienced relevance, personal meaning, competence in handling

29

complex text, and shared interpersonal relationships, they were energized to process the structures and connections in informational texts relatively deeply" (p. 405). This is a virtuous cycle: When students are motivated, they are more engaged in their reading; this engagement, in turn, increases how much they learn (Guthrie, 2014).

The good news is that motivation is "inherently social," and we can adapt the "social context" of our classrooms "to better support reading motivation" (Duke, Ward, & Pearson, 2021, p. 669). Research confirms that teachers who actively support students' sense of competence, autonomy, and relatedness can influence students' motivation to read (Troyer, 2017). As Guthrie (2014) explains:

> Because the context of a classroom is composed of its books, teachers, teacher actions, and student behaviors, we see that context does count for motivation. Although the drive to read is partly located in the learner, it is also significantly driven by the context, which is under our control. (p. 100)

When students feel connected, confident, and in control of their learning, they are more motivated. I have found that as students gain skill and confidence with a patient teacher and engaged peers in a supportive learning community, they become more willing to do the hard work needed to comprehend complex text.

In chapter 1 (page 13), I discussed why so many secondary students have lost their confidence and motivation when it comes to reading informational texts. In this chapter, I offer six motivating practices that teachers can enact to help their students rediscover or build their reading confidence. For some students, the most important comprehension work we can do is help restore or build their belief that they are capable of deeply understanding info-texts and have a good reason to do so. Research confirms what teachers know from experience: Motivation matters (Guthrie, 2014).

Motivational Practices to Help Students Build Their Confidence

The Deep Sense Approach includes powerful comprehension strategies and teaching methods proven to strengthen students' comprehension, but there's a catch. Students must feel motivated to take up those strategies and learn from those methods. Six practices can help build students' sense of relatedness, autonomy, and competence so they are able to benefit from instruction.

1. **Shift the perspective.**
2. **Normalize growth and struggle.**
3. **Respect students' experience.**
4. **Share your own reading experience, warts and all.**
5. **Treat students as competent contributors.**
6. **Quietly insist on inclusion.**

In the following sections, we look more closely at each of these motivational practices.

Shift the Perspective

When a student refuses to engage in reading or responding to a text, it can affect the spirit of others around them. If the student's resistance is public and assertive, it can derail a whole lesson.

Maintaining your compassion in those moments can be a genuine struggle, but shifting your perspective on these challenging behaviors helps.

If students have low self-efficacy in reading, they may have become accustomed to adopting the face-saving masks that Cris Tovani (2000) describes (see chapter 1, page 13). It can feel risky to be seen trying hard when they are fairly certain they will fail. Instead of treating students' masking and coping behaviors as willful defiance or incompetence, I find it helpful to think that if a student *won't* embrace a task, they might feel like they *can't* do it.

Instead of a willful teen, you can envision a child who is afraid (of embarrassment, of failure, and so on) and is desperate for self-protection. Students who skip assignments might feel overwhelmed. Students who used to easily juggle their homework in earlier grades can suddenly find themselves underwater, unable to catch up. Students who act bored might be exhausted. Students who act angry might have just had a blowup with a parent or friend. Over time, giving students the benefit of the doubt that they are doing their best given current circumstances can build trust. They often repay the gift with willingness.

Normalize Growth and Struggle

Many secondary students with whom I have worked believed that reading skills are relatively stable. They were under the misconception that one is either a "good" reader, for whom reading is "easy," or a "bad" reader, for whom reading is "hard" (Guthrie, 2014; Tovani, 2000). Educators and parents often make this assumption as well.

If students believe they are bad readers, their low sense of self-efficacy can affect their ability and willingness to grow. Why work hard at something when the evidence suggests it is a waste of time? As C. Patrick Proctor, Samantha Daley, Rebecca Louick, Christine M. Leider, and Graham L. Gardner (2014) explain, for students who struggle with comprehension, their beliefs about themselves as readers and their "willingness to commit mental resources to what will be an uphill effort with challenging texts" are of critical importance (p. 81). Many students do not know that info-texts are uniquely difficult to understand and that texts and tasks get harder as they move through school, so they may assume that there is something inherently wrong with them as readers.

Research suggests that these readers will be much more receptive to comprehension instruction if we can help them change their thinking from "I'm a bad reader" to "I have some room for improvement, and I can improve with support and hard work" (Tipton et al., 2023).

Even students with strong comprehension skills can be negatively affected by the belief that reading ability is fixed. They might skim a challenging text, believing they should not have to read slowly to make meaning. They may resist the work of annotation and rereading, thinking that these are strategies for "weak" readers. They become more receptive when they learn that all readers can struggle with a particular text or task, regardless of their reading strengths, and that all of us understand texts more deeply when we take more time and care with them.

The belief that readers are either good or bad is so deeply ingrained in many students that we must counter it explicitly, giving them information to counter the belief.

First, we can let them know that they will continue to build their comprehension skills and vocabulary knowledge throughout their lives if they keep working at it. Professor of psychology and education Scott G. Paris (2005) posits that unlike skills mastered in the early stages of reading (such as knowledge of the alphabet and phonemic awareness), comprehension skills and vocabulary knowledge are *unconstrained*—they continue to expand and deepen over time. Students regain hope and confidence when they learn that the skills of vocabulary development and comprehension can continue to improve into adulthood with hard work and enough support.

Second, we can share the information discussed in chapter 1, explaining that informational texts are uniquely difficult to comprehend, and that info-text reading gets a lot harder in fourth grade and beyond. I have been surprised by how students lean in and listen when I share this news. This knowledge is empowering because students realize they are not alone in struggling with informational texts. At the end of this chapter, you will find a reproducible student handout you can use to introduce this information to your students (page 36).

Though it is important to help them understand why info-text comprehension is so challenging, it is equally important to communicate your firm belief they can get better with support and practice. When we help students think of growth and struggle as normal, healthy aspects of reading, they are better able to persist through challenging reading tasks. In my experience, students will borrow your confidence as they develop their own.

Respect Students' Experience

Another teaching move that helps build reading motivation is honoring students' previous literacy experiences. At the beginning of the school year, you can work with students to delve into their reading histories and unearth positive reading memories. In particular, you can help students tap into positive associations with info-text reading ("Remember those fun *Guinness World Records* books?"). This practice is adapted from literacy development expert Alfred W. Tatum's (2009) work on textual lineages.

Of course, many students remember negative reading experiences as well. As we are apt to say in Texas, "This ain't their first rodeo." Some have been experiencing remedial strategy instruction for years. A student might think, "Yeah, I tried that three years ago in Ms. Ellis's class. It didn't work. I still failed the test." Respectful private conversations with readers can validate their frustrations and negative experiences and help you understand how those experiences have shaped their beliefs about reading and themselves as readers. Students who grew up without a great deal of reading support at home or in school can often connect with the pleasure of being read to or even hearing stories told by relatives.

Researchers Donna E. Alvermann and Elizabeth B. Moje (2013) define *adolescent literacies* as "the vast array of literate practices that young people bring to, [and take from], schooled learning" (p. 1073). Students may be unused to having their out-of-school reading experiences validated. Some students with little enthusiasm for school reading are interested and engaged in reading about current events on social media. Many students read to learn more about a hobby or personal interest. In those spheres, they can often share deep knowledge and insight. When we acknowledge the ways they read (such as dialogues they have with gamers across the world or how-to videos they consume about a favorite hobby), it signals that they belong to the world of readers. This boosts their sense of competence. I have found that when students feel respected in their literacies, they become more open to the texts and literacy practices that are privileged in academic settings (Alvermann, 2009).

It is important to honor students' prior knowledge of strategies, vocabulary, and literary concepts as well, understanding that they may not be conscious of or able to articulate all they know. You can affirm that they already have knowledge and skills they can build on. When a student shrugs and says, "I don't know," or does not demonstrate competence in a comprehension strategy, it helps to assume they might be unable to articulate the idea or don't want to risk speaking up, rather than to assume they never learned.

Some students have had little autonomy in their past experiences with strategy instruction. They were given worksheets and told to complete them, or they were assigned to an intervention class and told to log into an online reading program. They may have become conditioned to passivity in their school reading experiences. Helping them see their literacy assets can help them to take greater risks and responsibility.

Share Your Own Reading Experience, Warts and All

This motivational move may seem counterintuitive. It is well known that teacher modeling of exemplary literacy practices is an important part of reading instruction. This scaffolding contributes to students' sense of competence, as it provides a road map for how they can approach a text (Guthrie, 2014).

Students need to see their teachers modeling fluent, purposeful reading, but we should also model how we motivate ourselves to engage in the difficult work of comprehension with various texts and tasks. In chapter 7 (page 71), you will learn how to help students develop their own motivation by finding what is important and interesting about the text. However, acknowledging that this is sometimes a struggle can put students at ease.

You can also support students' sense of competence and relatedness by confessing your own imperfection when it comes to info-text comprehension. You can tell them about times you have slipped into sampling (chapter 1, page 13) and misinterpreted a text or missed an important detail. You might share your experiences with fake reading: Describe the book or article, where you got lost, when you realized you had tuned out, and how you backtracked to find the last place you had made sense of the text.

Treat Students as Competent Contributors

Students comprehend more when they are able to discuss the texts they read, as I delve into in chapter 5 (page 49), but they also are motivated by this scaffolded, collaborative meaning making. Text-centered discussion supports their need for relatedness and provides real-time modeling that supports their sense of competence.

As I discuss in chapter 5, many students hesitate to share during text-centered discussions, not always because they are unprepared or shy. They can get the impression that the teacher already knows all that is to be known about the text, so it makes sense for them to just wait to hear it from the expert rather than venture their inexpert opinion.

Students gain confidence in sharing their ideas when their teacher uses *tentative language*, such as "I wonder if . . . ," "Could it be that . . . ?," "Maybe it means . . . ," and "I think maybe the author . . ." These phrases signal that multiple perspectives are welcome and that the teacher's view isn't the final word. I first learned this move in a cognitive coaching seminar (an example of which you can find in Costa & Garmston, 2002), and I have used tentative language with students ever since. Tentative language signals that you are feeling your way through the text, too, making sense of it *with* your students.

The more space you create for students' expertise, as well as your own, the more comfortable students will be in telling you they found something different. In each text study I conduct, students see something I missed or ask a question that causes me to rethink my understanding. Over time, even reluctant readers come to see themselves as contributing members of our community of readers.

Students can learn to use tentative language too. When they talk about texts with their peers, this language helps keep their conversations collaborative rather than argumentative. In chapter 7, you will learn the Talk About Texts strategy (page 76), which teaches students conversation moves, including tentative language.

Encouraging students to participate more actively in class discussions requires taking a step back. The more familiar you are with a text, the harder this is, but try to remember that every class is coming to the text anew. If you hold back your interpretation for a while and stay open-minded and curious, your students will have more room to make their own meaning.

This doesn't mean leaving students with misconceptions. If the class is misinterpreting a point in the text, they might have missed a detail in a different part of the text. But instead of just giving them the answer, you might say something like this.

> *"Hmm . . . OK, I think I read something that contradicted that. Let's see . . . Oh, here it is, way back on page 2. Can you all look back and see what you think? Yeah, right there at the top of the second column."*

This framing builds their sense of relatedness and competence. If students are missing essential background knowledge, you might prompt the class to join you in a quick informal internet search to see what you can learn about a specific term, person, or idea. This "What do you think?" approach builds students' agency as they learn how strong comprehenders deal with breakdowns in meaning. Over time, they grow more confident that they can figure out what they don't understand. (Chapter 9, page 105, introduces the Fix Confusion and Fill Gaps strategy.)

Quietly Insist on Inclusion

Students come to our classrooms with a wide (sometimes shocking) range of academic preparedness and reading comprehension skills. I have had classes in which the students' assessed reading levels spanned nine or more grades, an experience that I know is not unique.

As we work to build agency and confidence through our interactions with individual students, we must also counteract patterns of exclusion and judgment that can arise during peer interactions. I have often been moved by how carefully many students treat each other when it comes to reading skills. But students can sometimes become impatient or even unkind when their peers struggle with reading.

From the beginning of the year, work with each class to establish, uphold, and model community agreements. Explicitly teach students how to work productively with peers in text-centered discussions and collaborative tasks. When you consistently model and monitor respectful, patient, nonjudgmental interactions, students usually adjust to using language and behavior that protect the dignity of their peers. In a classroom that supports competence, relatedness, and autonomy, students become more motivated to take up the teacher's positive values (Guthrie, 2014). You can gently call on them to tap into what President Abraham Lincoln called "the better angels of our nature" (Tucker, 2021).

Sometimes, you must have a private conversation with a student who is teasing a peer or expressing impatience or judgment. Though it is important to set clear boundaries about how you expect students to treat each other (and you), you can also acknowledge their skills and listen to their concerns. Sometimes, the student needs coaching in empathy, but other times, they have a legitimate concern. I have seen instances where a strong reader had been paired with the same struggling peer in several classes over the years and frequently ended up doing the lion's share of the work.

Though peer interaction is an essential scaffold for comprehension instruction, you must avoid overburdening your strong comprehenders. When the chemistry between two students is not right, I find it helpful to change the seating arrangement as discreetly as possible, making other changes at the same time. Always, always try to help all students involved save face.

When middle and high school students know they are in a classroom environment where their emotional safety is a priority, they are more likely to take the risks necessary to become stronger readers.

Concluding Thoughts

If students' previous experiences with info-texts and comprehension instruction have left them feeling defeated, they need hope in order to risk trying again and sticking with their efforts long enough to see improvement. By adopting motivational practices to support students' sense of competence, autonomy, and relatedness, we can help restore their hope in themselves, in us, and in reading.

Following, you will find a reproducible student resource, "Overview: Making Deep Sense of Info-Texts" (page 36), that you can use with your students to introduce the concepts discussed in the previous chapters in student-friendly language.

Overview: Making Deep Sense of Info-Texts

We read *informational texts*, or *info-texts*, every day. We encounter a variety of info-texts in school and our personal lives, such as articles, books, webpages, and how-to videos.

Info-texts communicate factual ideas and information, allowing us to better understand the world, ourselves, and others. These texts can be challenging to understand, especially as the texts we read become more complex. Though sometimes we just need to find an answer or get the gist of an info-text, we often need to truly understand the text. This may take active thinking and work before, during, and after reading. In this overview, you will learn about info-texts, why they can be so challenging, and how we can make deeper sense of them.

Types of Informational Texts

Since childhood, we have heard and read *narratives*, or stories. We know what to expect when encountering a narrative, whether it's a fairy tale, short story, novel, or movie. In contrast, info-text authors write to communicate specific ideas and information to their readers. They organize their ideas and information differently depending on their topic, purpose, and audience.

Info-texts can be long or short, on paper (print) or online (digital). Some contain only words, while others mix in pictures, audio, or video. The following table shows six basic informational text *genres* (or types): (1) literary nonfiction, (2) expository text, (3) argumentative text, (4) persuasive text, (5) procedural text, and (6) visual representation with text elements. Each has a different purpose. Authors might combine types in long, complex texts.

Genre	Purpose	Examples
Literary nonfiction	The author seeks to relay a true story about a real person's experiences from a particular perspective.	Biography, autobiography, memoir, narrative essay, travel journal
Expository text	The author explains key ideas and factual information to help readers understand something better.	Textbook, science article, news report, informative website
Argumentative text	The author discusses an issue, considers different perspectives, and takes a position.	Essay, editorial (op-ed), formal speech, complaint letter, review
Persuasive text	The author seeks to convince the reader to believe or do something.	Blog post, speech, advertisement, letter
Procedural text	The author explains how to do something or how something works, step by step.	How-to guide, instruction manual, recipe, safety procedure
Visual representation with text elements	The author combines visual and text elements to communicate ideas and information effectively.	Infographic, diagram, chart, map, exhibit, social media post

Construction of a Mental Map

To make meaning of an info-text as you read, your mind retrieves relevant memories (what you already know and think about the words, ideas, and information in the text). It connects those memories with the new information and ideas from the text. In the process, the mind organizes a kind of *mental map* that captures the most important ideas from the text and how they are connected to each other and to what you already know.

page 1 of 2

Making Deep Sense of Informational Texts © 2025 Solution Tree Press • SolutionTree.com
Visit **go.SolutionTree.com/literacy/MDSIT** and enter the unique access code found on this book's inside front cover to access this reproducible.

You may not be aware of how hard your mind is working to encode this mental map in your memory, but you can see the evidence. When your mental map of a text is well formed, you can remember key ideas and details and accurately explain how they are connected. If you are unable to do this, it's a sign that you need to help your mind make a better mental map.

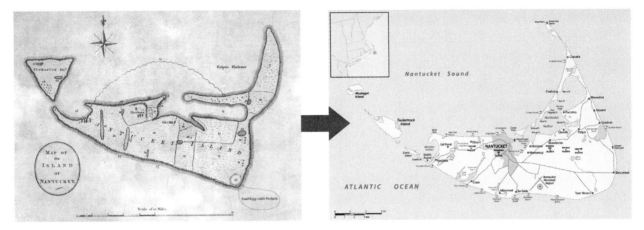

Info-Texts' Increasing Complexity

In elementary school, you probably read short info-texts with mostly familiar words and simple sentences. They were often about topics you already knew something about. They used text features like headings, bold print, and pictures to help the reader see how the ideas were organized. These made it easier for your mind to make an accurate, detailed mental map.

In middle school and beyond, the info-texts your teachers assign are more complex than in elementary school. The sentences are longer and more complicated, containing many words that aren't often used in conversations. There are fewer images and text features to help you. The author is less likely to tell you upfront what the text will be about. When you read these complex info-texts, you have to work harder to identify the key ideas and see how those ideas are connected to each other and to what you already know.

To make things more difficult, you are often asked to complete more challenging tasks with the info-texts you read, such as writing reports and making presentations. Your teachers might expect you to complete these tasks without much help.

Strategies to Help Us Make Deep Sense

It takes attention and effort to comprehend a complex info-text well enough to accurately recall, explain, and use the key ideas and information. Effective readers use *strategies*—step-by-step procedures—to help them make sense of what they read. Even the strongest comprehenders use strategies to make sense of challenging info-texts. They choose the strategies they need to make sense of a particular text for a specific purpose. Though you learned strategies in elementary school, you will need to update them to work with more complex info-texts. No matter how challenging the text and task, these strategies will help you make deep sense.

CHAPTER 4
Integrating Strategy Instruction That Works

Some secondary students have picked up sufficient strategic knowledge at home, in school, or in other settings to tackle the info-texts that come their way, no matter how challenging. However, many still need their teachers to explicitly teach comprehension strategies and provide scaffolded practice opportunities (Almasi & Fullerton, 2012).

In their practice guide focused on improving adolescent literacy, Michael Kamil and colleagues (2008) report strong evidence for direct and explicit comprehension strategy instruction that includes the following components.

- Teacher modeling and specific explanations
- Guided practice and feedback on the use of the strategies
- Promotion of independent practice to apply the strategies
- Active student participation
- Sufficient scaffolding, or support, to ensure success

Explicit instruction is essential for students struggling with comprehension (Snow, 2002). When students who previously avoided or struggled with complex info-texts begin to feel competent in using a set of strategies that can work for them in class and on their own, they are likely to become more active, diligent, and even confident readers. However, explicit instruction also benefits strong readers whose strategies need updating to work with more complex texts.

The explicit instruction described in this chapter helps students build and update their strategic knowledge. To truly take up the strategies and make them their own, students also need the meaningful context provided by text-centered discussions and the embedded practice provided by shared info-text studies. I take up these topics in chapters 5 and 6 (pages 49 and 57).

In the next section, I offer general recommendations for introducing the Deep Sense Approach strategies to your students. These suggestions are adaptable to your content area and your students' needs. As you plan your lesson, you can refer to the "Strategy Instruction Planning Guide" (see appendix A, page 169), which is aligned with the suggestions and considerations discussed throughout this chapter. The chapter ends with an example of how a middle school social studies teacher might instruct students in a Deep Sense Approach strategy. You will find the

39

accompanying sample lesson plan in appendix A. In part 3 (page 69), I provide specific guidance for teaching and assessing each of the fourteen strategies aligned with the step-by-step process discussed in the next section.

Recommendations for Explicit Strategy Instruction

In this section, I lay out a flexible step-by-step approach to strategy instruction. As with other kinds of explicit instruction, students learning new comprehension strategies benefit from a gradual release of responsibility approach (Fisher & Frey, 2021). P. David Pearson and Margaret C. Gallagher (1983) developed the gradual release of responsibility model specifically to guide explicit instruction of comprehension strategies. Pearson has continued to evolve his perspective on the model he envisioned decades ago, and other researchers and practitioners have adapted it over time.

The gradual release of responsibility model is not intended to be applied rigidly or to proceed in only one direction. The model also does not neatly coincide with a class period or tight lesson cycle. It might take days, weeks, or months for students to be able to use a strategy without prompting or guidance (Fisher, 2008). Further, Sandra Webb, Dixie Massey, Melinda Goggans, and Kelly Flajole (2019) point out that it is a mistake to reduce the gradual release of responsibility approach to a simplistic "I do, we do, you do" sequence. Instead, it "offers a model for helping teachers make comprehension accessible to students through ongoing scaffolds" (pp. 78–79).

As you will learn in chapters 5 and 6, explicit strategy instruction is just the beginning. Too often, students are given strategy lessons in isolation. Unless teachers reinforce this explicit instruction by providing meaningful experiences with complex texts and tasks, the new learning is likely to be short-lived.

Effective strategy lessons incorporate the following six components.

1. **Assess and activate background knowledge.**
2. **Explain and model.**
3. **Lead guided practice.**
4. **Facilitate independent practice.**
5. **Assess strategy knowledge and application.**
6. **Provide feedback and reteaching.**

Following, I provide suggestions for each of the strategy lesson components.

Assessing and Activating Background Knowledge

The first step in teaching students a comprehension strategy is to assess what they already know and think about the strategy. Because secondary students often come to us with prior experiences with a strategy, this step is critical. It helps to build a bridge between the known and the new that makes students more receptive to the strategy and more likely to learn and retain it. This step also enables you to tailor your instruction to meet their needs.

Following are some suggestions for assessing and activating students' background knowledge.

- **Ask low-stakes questions:** Ask students to discuss or write their responses to open-ended questions related to the strategy. For example, before teaching the Focus Your Mind strategy (chapter 7, page 71), you might ask students to discuss in pairs what they do when they are struggling to concentrate on a chapter or article in class. This also serves to activate and build background knowledge.

- **Observe practice:** Ask students to engage in a task that allows you to see how they currently approach the strategy. For example, before teaching the Talk About Texts strategy (chapter 7, page 71), you might have students engage in team and pair discussions on nonacademic topics and circulate to observe their current habits. Before instructing them in the Annotate Texts strategy (chapter 9, page 105), you can ask them to annotate a short text and observe how they approach the task. Even if students do not know the language or steps of a strategy, they might have experience enacting it.

- **Honor background knowledge:** Acknowledge what students already know and can do. Invite them to try the updated strategy, which might work better with challenging texts. Adolescents have years of reading experience under their belts, and many have developed methods that work well for them. On the other hand, some teenage students have had few encounters with strategy instruction, and some have had frustrating experiences that soured them on the very idea of strategy instruction.

Explaining and Modeling

When I started working with comprehension strategies in the classroom, I focused on planning instructional experiences that incorporated the strategies. In time, I learned that I needed to help my students build specific strategic knowledge, rather than just having them "do" the strategy. Literacy education experts Janice F. Almasi and Susan King Fullerton (2012) recommend giving students a description of the strategy and explaining the declarative (what), conditional (when and why), and procedural (how) knowledge associated with the strategy.

The Deep Sense Approach learning guides introduced throughout part 3 are designed to give teachers a text from which to work as they explain a strategy. You will find these learning guides and other instructional materials at the end of the chapter in which they are discussed. (Visit **go.SolutionTree.com/literacy/MDSIT** and enter the unique access code inside this book's front cover to access reproducible versions of these guides.) Though strategic knowledge is necessary, it is insufficient. Students must also see accomplished models of the strategy in action.

Following are some suggestions for explaining and modeling this book's strategies to students.

- **Introduce strategic information:** Refer to each strategy's learning guide as you discuss the rationale for the strategy, engaging students in discussion as you go. (It helps if each student has a paper or digital copy to keep as a reference.) Give examples as you introduce students to the terms and concepts associated with each step. Use personal stories, metaphors, and common experiences to help them connect with abstract content.

- **Model each step:** Depending on your students' needs, you might model each step or wait until you have introduced all the steps for a strategy. You might model by—

    - Thinking aloud as you write or mark up a text while students observe your process on the screen

    - Leading the class in analyzing a teacher- or student-created model

    - Demonstrating with a willing student or team (after pulling them aside to ask for their consent)

You can model with a text students have already read (in your class or a colleague's) or a text the class will study soon. If the strategy's learning guide includes questions, you can use those to guide your think-aloud. Pause your modeling to involve students, asking them for their insights or help. (They might need a quick turn-and-talk to consult with their shoulder partners and learning guides.)

- **Provide processing time:** Students need time to process and engage with the new information. You can have them annotate their learning guides or make notes separately. You might ask them to review the steps in the learning guide and think about what they saw you do. They can talk with a peer about what they currently understand and what questions they still have.

If most of your students are already proficient in a strategy, you might conduct small-group instruction for students who need additional support. Also, you can quickly introduce the strategy to all your students and then provide additional modeling for a small group.

Leading Guided Practice

After the teacher has explained and modeled the new strategy, students need structured practice and scaffolded support as they apply it with different types of texts and tasks. Scaffolding is intended as a temporary instructional support calibrated to a student's current understanding or skill level (Bruner, 1985; van de Pol, Volman, & Beishuizen, 2010; Wood et al., 1976). Though the goal of strategy instruction is for students to be able to use the strategies independently, they often need several scaffolded experiences with a strategy before they can successfully use it on their own.

If left on their own too soon, students can become frustrated. When they do not have enough understanding of the strategy to succeed on their own, they may practice in a way that reinforces unhelpful habits and old beliefs or give up on the strategy before they know what it can do.

Teachers are usually thought of as the ones to provide scaffolding, but peers can also scaffold the effective use of a new strategy, individually or as a group (Maybin, Mercer, & Stierer, 1992; van de Pol, Mercer, & Volman, 2019; van Lier, 2004). As researchers P. Karen Murphy, Ian A. G. Wilkinson, Anna O. Soter, Maeghan N. Hennessey, and John F. Alexander (2009) explain, "Children develop reading skills and abilities through authentic participation in a literacy-rich environment and are apprenticed into the literate community by more knowledgeable others (for example, parents, teachers, or more capable peers)" (p. 741). For any particular text, strategy, or task, a student might take their turn as a knowledgeable other.

Following are some suggestions for implementing guided practice.

- **Lead whole-class practice:** After introducing and modeling a step or the whole strategy, ask students to work along with you as they practice with a familiar text, a new section of the text you modeled, or a short new text on a familiar topic that lends itself to the strategy. Continue to use the key terms introduced in the learning guide.

- **Scaffold with discussion:** The questions embedded in many of the learning guides can frame whole-class, team, and peer discussions. Discussions in different constellations allow students to observe and practice the strategy and get feedback in real time. Chapter 5 (page 49) is devoted to suggestions for leading text-centered discussions.

- **Release students to guided pair or team practice:** Have students continue reading, thinking, writing, and discussing in pairs or teams as you circulate and coach. Encourage them to refer to the learning guide as they work. You might also post an anchor chart with key information from the learning guide to keep the information accessible while they practice applying the strategy steps. For writing tasks (like annotating, generating questions, or composing a central idea statement), you might ask students to draft independently, discuss and compare their work with a partner, and then revise as needed.

- **Clarify as needed:** If you notice students struggling to apply some aspect of the strategy, you can pull the class back together, give clarification or model some more, and then release the students to work again with their peers in teams or pairs. Circulate as they continue working, coaching on just that issue. If individuals are struggling with a particular step, privately check in with them, asking them what they think the issue might be.

Facilitating Independent Practice

As they become familiar with the strategy, students need time to wrestle with texts and apply the strategy independently.

Following are some suggestions for implementing independent practice.

- **Move from external to internal dialogue:** The questions in many of the learning guides can be used for independent practice once you have modeled thinking through the questions aloud and had students discuss the questions with peers. You might have students practice first with a short mentor text the class has previewed, read, and annotated before having them try their hand at a new and more complex text.

- **Structure and scaffold written tasks:** The tasks should give clear instructions and provide a rubric or checklist to set a standard for successful practice. Graphic organizers, paragraph frames, and sentence stems help students practice correctly. You can provide an example of the written product (created by you or a student), either including it in the assignment or providing it to students needing extra support. To avoid overscaffolding, you can provide an example completed for a different text or topic.

Assessing Strategy Knowledge and Application

Low-stakes formative assessment informs the teacher and the students. Teachers learn what concepts or steps they need to reinforce through explanation, modeling, practice, or coaching. Students learn where they are becoming proficient and where they need more support and practice. Even when evaluating students' final product for a shared info-text study or a unit, you can provide helpful feedback and plan for later opportunities to engage with the strategy.

Throughout part 3, you will find specific assessment suggestions for each Deep Sense Approach strategy, including key terms, strategic knowledge questions, and evidence of mastery, but the following are some big-picture suggestions for assessing how well students have learned the strategy.

- **Assess students' strategic knowledge:** Students are unlikely to independently use a strategy if they do not remember its key components. Formative assessments of strategic knowledge serve to reinforce students' learning of the following.

  - *Key terms*—Assess whether individual students can recognize or produce accurate definitions of the key terms. To assess whether they can use the terms accurately, you might ask them to work with a peer or independently to combine the key terms in a sentence or two that explain the gist of the strategy. Students who have taken up the key terms will use them as they practice the strategy with their peers or in whole-class discussions.

- *Strategy questions*—Ask questions about key concepts and practices. Helpful question stems include the following.
  - "Why is it important to . . . ?" or "How does it help to . . . ?"
  - "Which _____ do you think is most important?" or "Which _____ do you use the most?"
  - "What can you do when . . . ?"
  - "When should you . . . ?"
  - "What do you need to keep in mind when you . . . ?"

  You might ask students these questions verbally during initial strategy instruction. Then, you can post the questions for students to discuss in pairs or teams during guided practice. After they have worked with the strategy for a while, you might ask students to independently write their answers.

- **Assess students' strategy application:** How a teacher assesses the successful practice of a strategy depends on its nature. Strategy assessment might involve observing students as they work or listening in as they discuss. Their strategy use might be revealed in their annotations or other written work, or how they carry out a task.

- **Make time for self-assessment:** After students have practiced applying the strategy steps with varied texts, ask them to reflect on how the strategy has changed their thinking and behavior. They might use the frame, "I used to _____, but now I _____, which helps _____," to discuss and then write about changes in their perspective or practices. They can also review the learning guide and reflect on which elements (such as steps, tips, guidelines, or criteria) they have adopted and which ones they still need practice with.

Providing Feedback and Reteaching

What you see as you assess students' work will inform your next steps. If you repeatedly see the same issue as you observe or read students' work, you might need to provide precise feedback, coaching, and perhaps targeted reteaching. If the problem is more isolated, you might work with a small group or individual who needs more support.

Following are some feedback and reteaching suggestions.

- **Provide precise feedback quickly:** Students cannot improve if they do not know what they did well or poorly or what they need to do differently. A number—whether a rubric score or a traditional grade—does not reveal much to students. Ideally, a teacher can provide individual written feedback or confer with students one-on-one to show them where they are missing the mark. However, teachers can be hard-pressed to find the time for these practices in secondary settings. Instead, you can observe the class or review students' work and then compile a list of observations to share in a whole-class discussion.

- **Compare and revise:** Students improve more quickly when they understand the criteria used to evaluate their work. You might walk them through a checklist or rubric, then have them work with peers to assess a model response. I use a student model if possible but typically keep the model anonymous and ask the student for permission. I might polish a student example or combine excerpts from several students' work. After discussing the model in light of the criteria, students can work with a peer to compare their work to the model to identify areas for improvement. Afterward, they should have an opportunity to revise.

- **Reteach:** Reteaching might entail explaining a particular step differently, modeling the step again with a different text, or analyzing a new teacher- or student-prepared exemplar together. You might need to reteach the whole class, a small group, or an individual.

An Example of a Strategy Lesson

This section provides a glimpse of how a hypothetical teacher we'll call Anthony Abara might introduce the Annotate Texts strategy detailed in chapter 9. You can find a sample lesson plan mirroring this lesson in appendix A (page 169).

Mr. Abara teaches seventh-grade social studies in a Los Angeles middle school. The class has read in the textbook about the Spanish and Portuguese colonization of South America, including Hernán Cortés's fateful meeting with the Aztec emperor Moctezuma. Mr. Abara has found a lesson that asks students to consider various accounts of this encounter—a perfect opportunity to help them read like historians. He wants them to annotate each excerpt to help them make better sense of the texts, but he knows they have scant experience with annotation. He decides to integrate strategy instruction into the Cortés–Moctezuma lesson. Following, you will see how the teacher leads students through the steps outlined throughout this chapter: assessment and activation of background knowledge, explanation and modeling, guided practice, independent practice, assessment of strategy knowledge and application, and feedback and reteaching.

Assessment and Activation of Background Knowledge

Mr. Abara leads students through a think-write-pair-share in response to this prompt.

"What does it mean to 'annotate' a text? What do you do when you annotate?"

As students share their discussions, Mr. Abara notes some misconceptions he will need to address. He also notices that several students do not seem familiar with the term *annotate*. He assures students that they already have some experience with annotating, but they will update the strategy to ensure it is useful for them as they read more complex texts in middle school, high school, and college.

Explanation and Modeling

Mr. Abara distributes the "Learning Guide: Annotate Texts" reproducible handout (page 115) and introduces the strategy. He points out that college students and professionals annotate to help them think about the text and lay a breadcrumb trail they can follow later when looking for text evidence or summarizing. He walks students through the strategy steps, having them turn and talk after each step and then asking for their insights and questions. Afterward, he debriefs and clarifies points of confusion.

Using his document camera, Mr. Abara projects an annotated copy of the textbook passage the class has recently read. He asks students what they notice about his annotation. One student blurts out, "It's kinda messy!" Some students laugh, as does Mr. Abara. He builds on this observation, saying, "Yes! That's because I quickly annotate as I read. That's what I want you to do, too." He asks what evidence students can see that he was following the strategy steps. Several students make observations.

Mr. Abara projects a new text on the screen: an excerpt from a letter Cortés wrote about his encounter with the Aztec emperor. He explains that he will be modeling the strategy steps and students only need to pay close attention. He reads aloud the first two paragraphs, pausing to mark and jot quick notes, incorporating some of the step 2 stems from the learning guide. He narrates his thinking as he goes. Afterward, he asks, "What did you notice during my modeling?" and has students turn and talk with a partner.

Guided Practice

Mr. Abara passes out copies of the Cortés account, asking students to imitate his model for the first two paragraphs and then finish annotating the short passage. He circulates to make sure students are on the right track and coaches a few who are struggling.

He asks pairs to compare their annotations and discuss the following questions.

- What words and phrases did you mark? Why did you decide they were important?
- What did you write—questions, connections, ahas, paraphrases?

He circulates as students discuss the questions, checking their work and pausing to coach several times.

He projects his completed annotations for the passage and briefly explains what he marked and wrote. He invites students to add marks and notes from his model that they think would improve their annotations.

Next, Mr. Abara distributes a handout with two more versions of the encounter, one created by Aztec scholars in the 1500s and another excerpted from a recent book by a leading scholar of colonial Latin American history. He asks students to use the strategy steps to annotate both passages. He silently annotates along with them on the document projector. After most are finished, he asks students to compare and discuss their annotations with their shoulder partners. He circulates and again checks their work and coaches.

Independent Practice

In their next class meeting, Mr. Abara has students listen to a radio story marking the five-hundred-year anniversary of the conquest. Students recognize the historian who wrote the excerpt they read previously. Afterward, he asks them to discuss with their teams what surprised them, what they knew already, and what questions they had. The class agrees that the most interesting question was what really happened to Moctezuma—whether he surrendered as the Spanish claimed or if that was just a cover story.

Mr. Abara distributes copies of the story transcript and instructs students to annotate it. He reminds them they can refer to their learning guide and use the learning guide's step 2 stems if they get stuck. He circulates as they work. After most have finished, he collects their annotated handouts.

Assessment of Strategy Knowledge and Application

Mr. Abara instructs students to write a one-paragraph summary of the radio story without referencing the text. He reminds them that a strong summary includes a central idea, key ideas, key details, and key terms. He quietly huddles with several students who need extra support, providing them with a paragraph frame.

At the beginning of the next class, he asks students to grab an index card and pen. He posts the terms *annotate*, *selective*, and *margin note* and instructs students to use them in a one- or two-sentence description of the Annotate Texts strategy. He then asks them to write their responses to the following questions on the back of the card.

- Why is it important to annotate as you read a complex info-text?
- What do you need to keep in mind as you annotate?
- What surprised you about the strategy?

Feedback and Reteaching

When Mr. Abara reviews the summaries after class, he is impressed with how much his students have retained compared with their previous attempts. As he scans students' index cards, he sees that most could recall and synthesize the strategy information, but a few would need more time with the strategy. He makes a note to front-load a review for those students before their next annotation practice.

Mr. Abara reviews students' annotated transcripts and notices that several students who are English learners left large gaps unmarked and made few margin notes. Their summaries confirm they did not make much sense of the text. He pulls those students together to discuss their annotation decisions and challenges during the next period. He reviews the learning guide with them, and then they practice annotating a short text. He coaches them to hold their pens as they read, mark only important words and phrases, and use the learning guide's step 2 stems. They lean over to help each other, and he shares his work.

Over the weeks and months, the class annotates print and digital texts for different purposes. Depending on the text and task, they underline or highlight key ideas, unfamiliar terms, or interesting quotes. They jot down questions, connections, or definitions. They refer to their annotations as they have discussions and as they write short-answer responses, prepare summaries, and create presentations.

Concluding Thoughts

The interactive, supportive strategy lessons described and modeled in this chapter are an essential first step in helping students deepen their info-text comprehension. You might have noticed that pair, team, and whole-class discussions are woven throughout the lesson cycle. In the next chapter, you will learn more about implementing text-centered discussions that enable students to practice newly learned strategies in a collaborative, meaningful context.

CHAPTER 5
Leading Text-Centered Discussions

In previous chapters, I have referred to text-centered discussion as a key component of the Deep Sense Approach. Teachers across the world and across the decades have asked questions about texts and sought responses from their students. When done well, discussions anchored in a text not only deepen students' comprehension of that text but also improve their general comprehension skills.

A solid body of research shows the positive impact of text-centered discussion on comprehension and validates its importance in comprehension strategy instruction (Boardman et al., 2008; Croninger, Li, Cameron, & Murphy, 2018; Kamil et al., 2008; Langer, 2009; Murphy et al., 2009).

Text-centered discussions can help students:

- Engage more fully in reading
- Clarify what they already know, have learned, and do not understand
- Consider and integrate multiple perspectives
- Access others' background knowledge
- Practice new strategies
- Improve comprehension of the text at hand and new texts they read on their own
- Build confidence in their own scholarly voices

When students engage with their teacher and peers to make sense of a text, they gain insight into how others approach and learn from it. They see strategies in motion. They hear others using essential vocabulary and wrestling with ideas. They see evidence of others' mental maps (Garas-York & Almasi, 2017). Getting a window into their peers' thinking can cause students to set a higher bar for their own.

But not all discussions are created equal. Researchers and expert practitioners have promoted effective classroom discussion for decades (Garas-York & Almasi, 2017; Nussbaum, 2002; Wei & Murphy, 2018; Zhang, Niu, Munawar, & Anderson, 2016). They have documented the characteristics of comprehension-building discussions. However, teachers face daunting challenges as they try to engage secondary students in meaningful conversations that improve engagement, comprehension, and learning.

In this chapter, I discuss how text-centered discussions can fall short and explain the hallmarks of effective discussions. Then, I share specific recommendations to help teachers ensure their students get the most out of the discussions they lead. As with the other Deep Sense Approach components, you are encouraged to adapt these suggestions to fit within your context and meet the needs of your students.

What Gets in the Way

Secondary teachers often express the concern that their students do not talk much in class, at least not about the topic of the day's lesson. Many factors can contribute to adolescents' reluctance to engage in academic conversations. They might simply not be interested in the topic or have not prepared for class. They might hesitate to jump into face-to-face discussions if they habitually communicate with their phones or other devices. For some students, social-emotional and mental health issues—including stress, social anxiety, and negative self-concept—can make classroom conversations difficult (Brown & Knowles, 2014; Hall, 2016; Medaille & Usinger, 2020).

However, some of students' reluctance to participate can stem from a lack of positive experience with focused, in-person classroom discussions. The COVID-19 pandemic seems to have made this situation worse. Since the pandemic began, NCES (n.d.b) has surveyed public schools regarding these issues. Some of NCES's findings are as follows.

- Four out of five public schools agreed or strongly agreed that the pandemic and its lingering effects continued to negatively impact students' behavioral development (83 percent in May 2022; 80 percent in May 2024) and social-emotional development (87 percent in May 2022; 83 percent in May 2024).

- Three-fourths of public schools (75 percent) reported that students' lack of focus or inattention had a "moderate" or "severe" negative impact on learning, while 45 percent of schools reported that their students were having trouble working with partners or in small groups (May 2024).

The ninth-grade class that came to me in the fall of 2021 started out as the quietest group of students I had ever worked with. (They did get better, though!) Many had spent the previous year and a half learning from home. They were used to sitting quietly with their cameras off, listening (or not) to the teacher or a recording, and completing work alone on their computers.

Of course, the reluctance to engage in class discussions did not begin with the pandemic. When I worked in the district professional development department, I learned about research that documents a long-running and pervasive pattern in whole-class discussions sometimes called *recitation* (Mehan, 1979). These assessment-focused discussions follow a predictable sequence.

1. The teacher initiates a yes-or-no or short-answer question to test recall.
2. The teacher quickly calls on an individual student.
3. The student responds with a brief answer or hesitates.
4. The teacher follows up with evaluative feedback.

The teacher controls the exchange during recitation, often throwing out dozens of questions. Most questions aim to evaluate whether students understand and remember previously introduced material. If students answer a question incorrectly, the teacher may correct them, call on another student, or answer the question. The recitation pattern is so widespread that researchers rarely see a different kind of whole-class discussion.

In their book *Quality Questioning*, Jackie Acree Walsh and Beth Dankert Sattes (2016) describe the role of *target students*—those who regularly volunteer to answer the teacher's evaluative questions during recitation while the rest of the class sits back. Over time, many students learn to fly under the radar during traditional whole-class discussions, leaving their eager peers to take the lead.

Despite many hours of training, planning, and coaching other teachers, I have found the recitation habit hard to break. When I recorded and transcribed whole-class discussions for my dissertation study, I was surprised to see how often I slipped into the recitation pattern.

The first recording I transcribed showed me struggling to sustain my seventh-grade students' attention as I peppered them with evaluative questions. As we moved to more authentic open-ended questions, students seemed more willing to answer, but they had difficulty taking up each other's ideas. As I probed, I realized many students had no idea what the previous speaker had said. Despite my best intentions, I fell back into the habit of calling on a few target students who could give me what I was looking for. At times, I answered my own questions. In some team discussions, students tuned out their peers just as they had during whole-class discussions. They took turns speaking because I had instructed them to do so, not because they were curious what their peers thought. They did not see themselves as responsible for taking up others' ideas, only for expressing their own.

It took a lot of explicit instruction and intentional practice to change my students' old habits. It helped that I knew what comprehension-building discussions could look like. In the next section, I share what I have learned.

The Qualities of Meaning-Making Discussions

Since the late 1990s, researchers have investigated classroom discussion, seeking to identify the attributes that support comprehension (Applebee, Langer, Nystrand, & Gamoran, 2003; Mercer, Wegerif, & Dawes, 1999; Nystrand, 1997; Soter et al., 2008; Wilkinson, 2020). Multiple studies have found that comprehension-building discussions are not primarily focused on evaluating whether students already understand the text or get the "right" answer. Instead, the main goal is to collaboratively build the meaning of the text.

As part of a large multi-pronged study, Anna O. Soter and colleagues (2008) set out to identify the discussion features that indicate high-level learning and comprehension, according to existing research, and then code transcripts collected across nine discussion approaches to confirm their understanding of what constitutes quality discussion. A clear picture emerged of what happens during comprehension-building discussions.

- The teacher and students ask authentic open-ended questions that signal a genuine curiosity in others' perspectives (versus test questions soliciting a particular answer). These questions invite diverse responses rather than one right answer.

- Questions and responses build on each other, with each speaker taking up what others have said.

- Responses are more extensive than during recitation, with speakers elaborating their reasoning and evidence, sometimes prompted by others' follow-up questions.

- Questions and responses move beyond basic comprehension, with participants engaging in analysis, generalization, or speculation. The conversation draws out connections with personal experience, world knowledge, and other texts.

As an example of one teacher's attempt to incorporate these components, here's how a meaning-making discussion unfolded in my eighth-grade class in February 2022. In our thematic unit on the power of influence, we investigated the bystander effect—witnesses' impulse to remain uninvolved in the presence of bullying directed at someone else. After we read and annotated an advice column on the subject, I asked students to respond individually to the following questions in their journals.

- According to the author, what is the bystander effect? In your experience, how valid is the concept?
- What piece of advice in the column most resonates with you? Why?

This private writing activity gave students time to privately reflect on a sensitive topic and integrate their background knowledge with new information. We then moved directly into a team discussion anchored in the following prompts.

- What does the writer mean in saying that bullying is "everyone's problem"? What evidence does she use to support this statement?
- In paragraph four, what does the author mean by "the abuse cycle"? What could happen if an abuse cycle is allowed to continue? Explain.
- What balance does the author recommend between standing up for others and protecting oneself? Explain, citing specific details to support your thinking.
- How does the columnist's advice square with your own experience?

These questions engaged students as they collaboratively grappled with the author's meaning, new concepts, and their personal responses. My students were well versed in meaning-making discussions after several months of practice, and all our practice clearly paid off. As I circulated, listening in on conversations and coaching as needed, I was impressed with how well the teams stayed focused. They thoughtfully shared and built on their peers' and the author's ideas. They consulted the article regularly, working to integrate the ideas in the text with their own experiences and thoughts.

Text-Centered Discussion Planning

Meaning-making discussions may spontaneously happen in the classroom, but they are much more likely to succeed with careful preparation (Hall, 2016; Wei, Murphy, & Firetto, 2018). I have found it useful to plan open-ended questions in advance and intentionally structure a variety of discussion configurations. I explore these practices in more detail and make suggestions for enacting these practices in the following sections.

Planning Open-Ended Questions

Some literal and low-inference questions have one answer explicitly stated in the text. When you are leading text-centered discussions, it is often appropriate to pose a few of these questions to ensure that students have built an accurate mental map and to unearth any misconceptions or gaps in understanding. However, most discussion questions should leave room for interpretation.

As the class works together to answer challenging questions, dozens of brains—not just a few—actively engage in making meaning. When teenage students understand that even the strongest readers must wrestle to make meaning of a complex text, they realize it is OK not to immediately know the answer.

In addition to purely text-centered questions, it is often helpful to weave in some questions that evoke students' personal experience, knowledge, or perspective. These questions tend to draw students into conversation. They also help students integrate their mental map of the text with their background knowledge, which is essential for deep comprehension.

I recommend planning key open-ended questions that you will pose throughout a text-centered discussion. To make sure students understand the questions and can refer to them throughout the discussion, it is helpful to post the questions in written form.

The learning guides introduced throughout part 3 can help you design strategy-aligned discussion questions. Beyond the Deep Sense Approach resources, you will also find open-ended questions accompanying texts published in textbooks or online platforms. With some tweaking, multiple-choice or narrow open-ended questions can be transformed into authentic open-ended questions that invite meaningful discussion. For example, consider the difference between these two questions.

1. What did the author mean when she said, "_____"?
2. What might the author have meant when she said, "_____"?

The simple addition of tentative language changes the spirit of the question, signaling that multiple perspectives are welcome.

Planning for Varied Structured Discussions

In 1992, writing expert and English professor Lois Matz Rosen described a discussion-rich classroom in an almost poetic way:

> A classroom that is afloat on a sea of talk is full of language interactions—*talk* between students in pairs and small groups; *talk* between teacher and students one-to-one, in small groups, or in whole class discussions; *talk* between the classroom texts and the readers of those texts. Language-centered classrooms are also full of writing—*talk written down*—adding another dimension to the rich interactions of classroom discourse. (p. 10)

To capture the web of meaning-making interactions that Rosen describes, I developed the model shown in figure 5.1 during a 2018 pilot action research study that informed my dissertation (Pauloski, 2020).

As the model depicts, the text anchors a variety of conversations: between the teacher and students, between peers, and between the student and the author. It is in the context of these varied and frequent discussions that students co-construct their understanding of the text and take up new strategies.

I recommend weaving in pair, team, and whole-class discussions throughout your lessons. These discussions can be brief or more extensive, depending on your students'

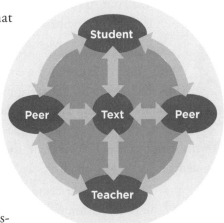

Source: Pauloski, G. J., 2020.

FIGURE 5.1: *Interactions in a text-centered discussion.*

readiness and your purpose. You can see an example of how a teacher might incorporate these varied discussions in the sample lesson described in chapter 4 (page 39), which is also available as a lesson plan in appendix A (page 169). You will also find varied discussions in the two sample text studies included in appendix B (page 177).

Sometimes, it makes sense for class discussion to unfold organically. However, many students benefit from more structure to help them focus on academic content and ensure equity of voice. When you introduce a new discussion structure, you can use the fishbowl method to model the structure with one or more students while the rest of the class observes. After the class debriefs, the students are better prepared for their own discussions.

In the following sections, I give specific recommendations for each configuration. This book's Digital Resources guide (available online at **go.SolutionTree.com/literacy/MDSIT**) provides links for the organizations, structures, and applications mentioned here.

Team Discussions

Team discussions are useful for several purposes. For example, teams of three or four can brainstorm, crowdsource background knowledge, identify multiple perspectives, and review text evidence. *Kagan Cooperative Learning* offers dozens of learning structures, including the following, that can work well for team discussions (Kagan & Kagan, 2009).

- The Numbered Heads Together structure creates individual accountability because the team doesn't know which member will be called on to report to the whole class.
- The All Write Round Robin structure helps students tune in to their peers. Each team member takes a turn responding to a teacher-posed question, and all team members write down the response.

The National School Reform Faculty (NSRF, n.d.) has developed text-centered protocols that can be adapted for student discussion. Following are a few of my favorites.

- In the Text Rendering Experience protocol, participants each share a sentence they think is significant in the first round, then a phrase in the next round, and then a word in the third round as the facilitator scribes. The team reads the collected sentences, phrases, and words aloud and then discusses insights from the experience. (I have also successfully used this protocol to structure whole-class discussions.)
- The Four As protocol works well for high school students discussing an argumentative text. Team members all take turns sharing what assumptions they think the author holds, as well as what they agree with, argue with, and aspire to in the text.

When teams are assigned a common task, they might divide the work if left to their own devices. I find that this default approach often leaves individual team members with only pieces of the knowledge they need. On the other hand, traditional team assignments can devolve into several members killing time while one or two peers do the lion's share of the thinking work. In my own practice, I recommend the following flexible, talk-based collaborative tasks to help students focus on learning from the text and each other.

- Comparing text-centered process writing (such as notes, annotations, graphic organizers, summaries, and outlines)
- Co-composing short statements (such as gist statements and definitions)

- Choosing among options and generating a rationale for the choice (such as selecting the best text evidence, examples, summary statements, or inquiry sources)
- Reporting out key points or questions from pair or team discussions

These tasks are useful scaffolds for writing and can be woven into a wide range of lessons.

Pair Discussions

Students can work with shoulder partners to generate options, compare notes, discuss their approaches to a task, give and receive feedback, or identify points of confusion. Coauthoring usually works best in pairs. Two pairs of students can meet to share the gist of their discussion. Pair discussion structures abound, the simplest of which are turn-and-talk and think-pair-share.

- Spencer Kagan and Miguel Kagan (2009) offer several pair discussion structures, including Mix-Pair-Share, in which students wander around as music plays, pair up, discuss a teacher-posed question, and then move on to the next partner.
- Seidlitz Education's QSSSA structure builds on the traditional think-pair-share with a posted *question*, a *sentence starter*, a *signal* that pairs are ready, and the *accountability* of calling on multiple pairs to share (Gonzalez, 2019).
- NSRF's (n.d.) Block Party protocol is an excellent pre-reading pair activity; students choose a strip with a quote from the text and then roam and share with several peers in turn.

Whole-Class Discussions

A whole-class discussion can serve as a model before students write or break into pairs or teams; it can also help the class synthesize what students have discussed in smaller configurations. Whole-class discussions can be scaffolded with posted questions, suggested conversation stems, and think time.

- The teacher can set up a Socratic seminar for longer, more formal discussions.
- The class can also engage in written conversation using the NSRF (n.d.) Chalk Talk protocol, in which the students and teacher respond to an initial question, writing silently on a large sheet of butcher paper, and then responding to each other's comments.

Engaging text-centered discussions can also be structured in digital spaces. Students can post text or video responses to a Padlet (https://padlet.com) or contribute text or video responses to a discussion board in your learning management system. The class can then engage with and respond to peers' posts. Teachers can modify settings for posts, responses, and moderation depending on their students' needs. You can also post questions in a Pear Deck (https://peardeck.com) and then build on students' written responses in a class discussion.

Concluding Thoughts

Leading text-centered discussions is difficult work for the teacher. You must simultaneously pay attention to how students make sense of the text, work with each other, and use the strategies they have learned. Along the way, you must calmly respond to personality conflicts and student resistance, working to draw students into the discussion and address their learning needs. Regardless of how you structure the discussion, clear instructions, time limits, and individual accountability help keep students on track.

Many students are unused to the engaged meaning-making discussions I described in this chapter. If they are accustomed to letting a few target students do the heavy cognitive lifting, they may resist working so hard. If they are afraid of making a poor impression on you or their peers, they may hesitate to participate. In chapter 7 (page 71), I introduce the Talk About Texts strategy, which teaches students how to successfully engage in meaning-making discussions. This is the second strategy in the Deep Sense Approach tool kit, with good reason. I begin working with students on this strategy during the first week of school because engaging in meaning-making discussion is essential for building their comprehension skills.

No matter how carefully you plan your discussions, you will also need to respond in the moment. As is often the case in my classroom, you might find that a particular discussion is not going as planned. If a planned prompt is leaving students with little to say, you might need to elaborate further on the question or provide more background knowledge. It may also help to shift to another configuration. For example, when a whole-class discussion becomes listless, you might pivot to pair discussions and then bring the class back together to share what was discussed. If the same issue arises in several groups during team discussions, you might need to pull the class together for a quick discussion to address the issue, and then release students back to their team discussions as you circulate.

Facilitating these discussions can sometimes feel like a high-wire act, but the payoff in terms of improved comprehension, strategy uptake, and student motivation makes all the effort worth it. In the next chapter, you will learn about the last component of the Deep Sense Approach: the shared info-text study (SITS). These in-depth studies are perfect vehicles for the discussions featured in this chapter.

CHAPTER 6
Reinforcing Strategies With Shared Info-Text Studies

The final component of the Deep Sense Approach is the shared info-text study (SITS). Though multiday, close readings of literary texts are found in many secondary English classrooms, this kind of deep dive focused on making meaning of informational texts is less common. In other disciplines, secondary students may engage with complex info-texts, but usually without the support of text-centered discussion, shared reading, and strategy application.

However, the benefits of the SITS are clear. These studies engage the whole class in strategically exploring an interesting, complex text across several class periods. The alchemy of shared text studies sometimes seems like magic. The class can come alive with sustained, collective attention to a text. Once too shy to comment on a text, students begin to lean in, take risks, venture theories, consider their peers' ideas, and talk about the author as a living, breathing person. Together, the class gains insights that the teacher had not considered.

In this chapter, I share my own experience with implementing SITS and introduce the key components of effective text studies. Then, I detail a flexible process for planning a SITS that integrates those components. In appendix B, I provide a planning guide that distills the suggestions and considerations from this chapter and two sample SITS plans showing how two hypothetical teachers—a middle school science teacher and a freshman English teacher—design their SITS plans. I encourage you to look at the guide and samples to help you envision how to make SITS a reality in your classroom context.

My Experience With Shared Info-Text Studies

Though I have led students in info-text studies for decades, I have been trying, since 2019, to integrate what I have learned from research—my own and others'. At times along the way, I have stumbled and struggled. Even if some instructional programs call for "fidelity of implementation," I have found that when it comes to leading shared studies of complex info-texts, perfection is impossible. I encourage you to take up the SITS practice, or refine what you are already doing, knowing your efforts do not have to be perfect. The great news is that students will still benefit greatly if my experience is a guide.

My dissertation study focused on a series of three shared info-text studies. My seventh graders and I had already started a unit on intergenerational learning; we had just finished reading Amy Tan's (1989) story "Two Kinds" (from *The Joy Luck Club*), and each shared text built on our unit theme.

Our first SITS focused on a feature article explaining the threats to endangered languages worldwide and describing efforts to save them. Before we began reading, I worked to update students' understanding of text features, and we used what we saw to activate their background knowledge. During a team discussion after the first reading round, I coached students on taking up each other's ideas. My strategy instruction was rudimentary, and they struggled mightily. During our second reading round, we focused on determining and articulating the article's central idea. As students worked on composing central idea statements with partners, I realized they were so used to looking at the title and skimming the first paragraph for the main idea that they were missing the bigger picture. I stopped to teach them how to determine a central idea in a complex text, and we all worked to co-construct a more complete central idea statement. Because I was not prepared for how hard this would be for students, I had to punt on other activities I had planned. In the third reading round, students learned about different types of evidence and then worked together to identify and evaluate the evidence the author had included. Again, this work was slow going, requiring more scaffolding than I had initially planned.

In the following weeks, I felt my way through the next two text studies, learning as I went. Though I was still new to integrating explicit strategy instruction into a multiday info-text study, my students' growth was undeniable. They began making deeper sense of the texts we studied. They annotated, summarized, and discussed texts more effectively. Their confidence and agency improved. Most also demonstrated general comprehension improvement in standardized tests administered soon after the third SITS and then six weeks later. My students taught me that my imperfect efforts would pay off.

In the next two and a half years, I designed shared info-text studies on topics ranging from civil rights to disaster survival and implemented them in my seventh-, eighth-, and ninth-grade ELA classes. During the pandemic, learning remotely, and then in a hybrid setup, my students still benefited from engaging in a SITS as a class, even when they resisted turning on their cameras in front of all their peers. I have continued to refine my approach as I model the SITS method for prospective teachers in university classes.

These experiences have enabled me to winnow the must-have from the nice-to-have components of shared text studies. They have also helped me develop a more pragmatic approach than one might find in research journals and other professional books. In the rest of this chapter, I do my best to translate what I have learned into practical advice on how to implement your own SITS.

SITS Components

Several SITS components are essential for deep comprehension and strategy uptake.

- **Shared study of a complex text:** In 2012, reading specialists Douglas Fisher, Nancy Frey, and Timothy Shanahan likened reading complex text to lifting weights, pointing out that without weight or resistance, it is impossible to build muscle. In a SITS, students read one version of the central text, though they might get varying levels of support. Where possible, students read the text as it was published.

- **Integrated strategy instruction:** Research suggests that strategy instruction is most effective when students learn how to orchestrate a repertoire of strategies rather than focusing on only one (Kamil et al., 2008; Snow, 2002). Students need help seeing how related strategies can work together, and they need supported practice applying multiple strategies before, during, and after reading. Something beautiful about the SITS approach is that the teacher can use one text to introduce and practice multiple strategies and concepts.

- **A spiraled reading sequence:** In her seminal research on comprehension, Linda K. Crafton (1982) finds that building comprehension of a text is an extended process that begins before reading and continues long after the last word is read. Repeated text readings for different purposes allow students to refine their mental maps and accumulate background knowledge. Often, familiarity breeds not boredom but engagement. As students gain expertise in the topic of the text, their interest tends to grow.

- **Text-centered discussion:** In a SITS, the teacher facilitates pair, team, and whole-class discussions before, during, and after reading. These discussions enliven the SITS and enrich learning. In chapter 5 (page 49), I made recommendations for structuring and facilitating text-centered discussions. In chapter 7 (page 71), which introduces the Talk About Texts strategy, you will find an approach to teaching teenage students to productively engage in these meaning-making conversations.

- **Formative assessment, scaffolding, and stretching:** Students must wrestle with complex texts to develop deeper comprehension skills, but many need scaffolding for their reading efforts to bear much fruit. Scaffolding is built into the SITS design process. Strong comprehenders who are under-challenged by the text and task need ways to engage more deeply so they can grow as well. Multiple reading rounds allow students to become more and more familiar with a complex text. Supporting texts fill in knowledge gaps or provide additional challenge. Discussion enables peers to serve as knowledgeable others for each other. In addition to planned scaffolds and stretch opportunities, the teacher also listens in on conversations, observes students at work, and reads through written responses. Based on what they learn, they adjust the course, adding or removing support as needed.

- **Emphasis on student agency:** As I discussed in chapter 3 (page 29), middle and high school students need to feel they are competent members of a classroom community. When the teacher frames the SITS as a community endeavor and asks for students' input along the way, their investment increases. Students also feel autonomous, not that they always work alone, but that they feel in control of their learning. Students can weigh in on numerous decisions typically made by the teacher. When students are invited to participate in low-stakes meaning-making discussions and reflective writing, they start to trust that their insights and perspectives are valued.

In addition to these components, you can weave in other literacy experiences over the course of the SITS as needed: fluency practice, vocabulary study, writing to learn, formal composition, research, visual representation, and creative expression.

SITS Planning

In this section, I offer practical guidance for each step of the SITS planning process. You will find two sample SITS plans and a SITS planning guide in appendix B (page 177). The planning guide condenses the suggestions and considerations in this chapter, taking you through these four steps.

1. Selecting and evaluating texts
2. Planning the reading sequence
3. Planning strategy instruction
4. Planning assessment

Although I explore each of these in more detail in the following sections, there is no need to re-create the wheel. If you already have a curriculum that incorporates the study of complex info-texts, please use what you have and build in additional SITS components. You can follow the SITS format modeled in appendix B's two sample SITS plans or your campus or district planning format.

A fully developed SITS can take about four or five hours of instructional time, though it will vary depending on several factors, including the following.

- The length of the text
- How much background knowledge students need to build
- How many strategies you introduce
- Whether you include all reading rounds
- Which text-based tasks you incorporate

Teachers can tailor a SITS to meet their students' unique needs, address specific learning standards, and fit within their available instructional time. I recommend starting small and adding more components as you get comfortable with the process.

Selecting and Evaluating Texts

The first step in SITS design is to select a central text and evaluate its complexity, structure, style, and knowledge demands. If you or your team members have a textbook with interesting, complex info-texts, you can take advantage of the planning suggestions provided in the teacher's edition. Beyond textbooks, though, there is a world of possibilities.

Texts can be found in curriculum units, nonfiction trade books, newspapers, magazines, journals, blogs, websites, and student-facing text platforms. They can be printed or digital; primarily text based; or a combination of text, visual, audio, and numeric content. The Digital Resources guide available online at **go.SolutionTree.com/literacy/MDSIT** provides links to some of my go-to info-text sources.

It is important to ensure that all students in the class can read the text with sufficient scaffolding. Info-texts can be complex in numerous ways, such as the following.

- The topic requires specialized background knowledge.
- The author assumes the reader is familiar with the topic.
- The text includes many low-frequency words or specialized vocabulary.
- The sentences are long and complicated.
- There are too few text features, or they are misleading.
- The ideas are poorly or unclearly organized.
- The layout is cluttered and cramped or presents long blocks of text.

Because students' lack of familiarity with a topic exacerbates text complexity, it helps to choose texts that discuss topics they might connect with and perspectives they might find interesting.

If students need to learn an unfamiliar topic or an abstract, difficult concept, they might need a more considerate text.

On the other hand, the central text should be challenging enough to engage students who are already strong comprehenders and complex enough to sustain several days of study. I recommend avoiding carefully controlled texts with prominent text features, simple sentences, and well-marked key ideas (though these can be great supporting texts).

Read through the text to understand the author's purpose, central idea, and top-level text structure. (See chapter 8, page 85, for information about previewing the text.) Also, keep an eye on how the author uses language to achieve their purpose. Look for writing that is lively but scholarly enough to serve as a mentor text.

You can weave in supporting texts before, while, or after studying a central text. You can use supporting texts to help set the stage for reading, fill gaps in background knowledge, and provide different perspectives. Your selection of supporting texts will depend on the central text, the tasks students need to complete, and the strategies they will learn.

For example, the class might read a short article or chapter excerpt that defines or describes people, places, objects, situations, phenomena, or issues important for understanding the central text. (I like to compile several images and webpage links in a Wakelet [https://wakelet.com] collection for students to explore.) The class might read a poem that addresses the same topic as the central text or examine an infographic from a government website that depicts key information discussed in the text. I love to grab students' attention with a relevant but somewhat mysterious photograph as a way into the text.

Research suggests that when students choose their texts, their motivation increases, which increases the volume of text they read and, in turn, helps them practice comprehension skills (Guthrie & Klauda, 2014). You can involve students in finding relevant supporting texts. You might ask them to conduct a quick guided internet search to find an apt definition or illustration. You can offer a set of texts for inquiry or knowledge building from which students can choose. You can even ask students to help compile a list of relevant reference or inquiry texts.

Planning the Reading Sequence

The next step is to plan how you will lead students deeper and deeper into the central text. They need to wrestle with the text and examine it from different angles. They also need to practice orchestrating multiple strategies along the way.

In a typical SITS, the class first engages in a strategic pre-reading routine and then works together through multiple rounds of reading, moving from surface comprehension to analysis to evaluation. After reading, the class consolidates learning through post-reading activities. Students might also read additional texts (going "beyond the text") for comparison or inquiry and synthesize what they have learned. You'll learn more about these in the following sections.

The Talk About Texts and Focus Your Mind strategies introduced in chapter 7 (page 71) are important throughout the reading sequence. The rest of the Deep Sense strategies can help focus and guide the work in each phase. In table 6.1 (page 62), I suggest when to emphasize each strategy during the reading sequence. Even before students are formally introduced to a strategy, you can begin to engage them in thinking, discussion, and tasks that cause them to experience the strategy in action.

TABLE 6.1: *Strategy Integration in the Reading Sequence*

Chapters	Strategies	Pre-Reading	Round 1	Round 2	Round 3	Post-Reading	Beyond the Text
Chapter 7: **Focus on Meaning Making**	Focus Your Mind	●	●	●	●	●	●
	Talk About Texts	●	●	●	●	●	●
Chapter 8: **Prepare to Read**	Preview Texts	●					
	Determine the Text Structure	●					
Chapter 9: **Read Actively**	Annotate Texts			●			
	Check for Understanding		●	●			
	Fix Confusion and Fill Gaps		●	●			
Chapter 10: **Evaluate Arguments and Evidence**	Trace the Reasoning			●	●		
	Consider Perspectives				●		
	Evaluate Evidence				●		
	Analyze Rhetoric				●		
Chapter 11: **Consolidate Learning**	Summarize Texts					●	
	Synthesize Across Texts						●
	Share Learning					●	●

Pre-Reading

Key strategies: Preview Texts, Determine the Text Structure (see chapter 8, page 85)

Key features: Engaging in collaborative discussion, evaluating text features, determining text structure, activating and building background knowledge, making a reading plan

You can introduce the SITS by asking students to think about, write about, and discuss a guiding question. You might ask them to investigate a quote or an image they will encounter later in the text study. The goal is to pique their interest and help them activate relevant background knowledge. Afterward, you can explain the purpose and learning objectives of the text study.

Once students are introduced to the Preview Texts and Determine the Text Structure strategies, you can lead them through these strategies, releasing more of the responsibility to them as they are ready.

If students need to understand terms, details, or concepts that are not clearly explained in the text, you might plan a quick knowledge-building activity during this phase. In addition to mini-lectures and explicit vocabulary instruction, I find the following activities useful for building background knowledge.

- Reading supporting texts
- Exploring images, music, quotes, or objects
- Crowdsourcing student knowledge
- Looking up information as a class
- Conducting polls or surveys

Reading Round 1

Key strategies: Check for Understanding (see chapter 9, page 105)

Key features: Fluent reading model; chunk-and-chew for long texts; questions and coding focused on the gist, connections, and points of confusion; text-centered discussion

In the first reading round, the class might read the whole text or, if the text is long, read enough of the text to get the gist of it. Depending on students' needs and the complexity of the text, you might read the text aloud or play an audio version.

Students need to hear a fluent reading of the text and be able to focus on meaning making. This is especially important for students who have learning challenges and those who are still acquiring academic English. Traditionally, a teacher might have used "popcorn" or "round-robin" reading (calling on students at random to read the next section) to get through a read-aloud of a text. I caution against this practice. It can generate such anxiety for some students that they cannot listen at all. Others tune out while their peers read, quietly waiting and rehearsing their turn.

Students need something to focus on as they read the text. Typically, I encourage them to keep a few questions in mind, such as the following, that align with this round's primary focuses: the gist, connections, and checking for understanding.

- **Gist:** "What seems to be the author's central message? What is this section (or text) mainly about? What does the author want me to know? Why did the author write this text? What ideas seem most important?"
- **Connections:** "What is most interesting to me? What do I already know about this? How can I connect with this?"
- **Checking for understanding:** "What confused me? What do I wonder? What do I need to know? Is this what I expected to learn?"

If students can mark up the text, you might ask them to code it with symbols during or after the read-aloud using language such as, "This is important or interesting," "I know something about this," and "This is unclear or unfamiliar."

After you read the whole text or a section of a long text, ask students to reflect on the focus questions and then discuss in pairs or teams. You might have them capture quick notes before or after their peer discussions on a simple foldable or index card or in the margins of the text.

As you debrief with them in a quick whole-class discussion, focus on their insights and questions. You may point out something they might have missed or clarify something that is confusing to many. Finally, ask them to reflect on how the first reading round changed their thinking about the text compared with their preview.

Reading Round 2

Key strategies: Annotate Texts, Check for Understanding, Fix Confusion and Fill Gaps (see chapter 9, page 105)

Key features: Annotating the text, checking for understanding, addressing confusion and knowledge gaps

Once students have previewed the text and read it along with the class, they will be prepared to read more carefully to build an accurate mental map. I usually have students read and annotate independently during round 2, but I have found the Say Something method (Short & Harste, 1996) to be useful for my sixth- and seventh-grade students and in small-group instruction.

To use this strategy, in pairs, have students take turns reading a paragraph or two aloud (quietly). When the reader stops, the partner responds with a comment or question. As needed, you can provide stems such as the following.

- "I think this is saying . . ."
- "I thought it was interesting/important that . . ."
- "I'm not sure I understand . . ."
- "I wonder if/why/whether . . ."
- "This reminds me of . . ."

After students read and comment, they can pause to annotate their copies of the text. If students cannot mark up the text, it is still important for them to pause to make notes as they read. They might make notes on a simple foldable, an index card, or a sticky note. You might also prepare a guided notes page for them to complete as they read.

To support students in checking their understanding, you might pause for them to discuss their insights and questions with peers. For helpful questions, refer to the Check for Understanding strategy in chapter 9 (page 105).

After students have discussed with peers what they are still unclear about, you can make a list of their questions. If there is a context clue the whole class is missing, you can suggest they reread a particular paragraph or section. If a question cannot be answered by information in the text, you can pause to have students access additional resources such as a dictionary or website to fill gaps in their background knowledge. As students gain mastery of the Fix Confusion and Fill Gaps strategy (chapter 9, page 105), they can take up this work themselves with less and less scaffolding.

If you have students who are still developing their reading speed and prosody, this is a good time to build in fluency practice for the whole class or a small group. You can also include a word study focused on key terms.

Reading Round 3 (Optional)

Key strategies: Trace the Reasoning, Consider Perspectives, Evaluate Evidence, Analyze Rhetoric (see chapter 10, page 121)

Key features: Rereading in a focused way, annotating and discussing text evidence, evaluating and analyzing, doing independent strategy practice

Depending on your goals for the SITS, you might want to have students return to the text one more time for a specific purpose and with a specific focus. This is especially important for texts that have elements of argumentation, since meanings are not always explicit, and the author's true purpose and perspective can be tricky to discern. For example, students might add to their annotations, commenting on the strength of the evidence presented to support a key claim.

Depending on your students, the text, and the task, it can be helpful to have students engage with a partner or team for some or all of their work in this round. Or you can have them work independently and then check their work with a peer.

Text-centered discussions might explore the author's purpose, the quality of evidence, or a consideration of multiple perspectives on the validity of the claim. Students should refer to their annotated texts throughout these discussions and make additional notes.

After students have engaged with the text, it is useful to bring them back together for a whole-class discussion to reinforce key ideas, address misconceptions, and allow them to hear a variety of perspectives.

Post-Reading

Key strategies: Summarize Texts, Share Learning (see chapter 11, page 143)

Key features: Summarizing, presenting, discussing, evaluating

In the post-reading phase, students consolidate their learning. Depending on the text and strategy focus, students might do the following.

- Compose a summary of the central text
- Respond to an open-ended prompt in writing or orally
- Prepare an informal presentation independently or with peers
- Prepare for a whole-class discussion focused on several open-ended questions

Post-reading tasks allow students to practice strategies independently, and these tasks serve as assessments of text comprehension and strategy uptake. I often have students work with peers at the beginning of a text-based task, especially if the task is complex or they have little experience with it. However, they must have an opportunity to demonstrate their own understanding and skills.

It is easy to underestimate how long students need to complete a text-based task. I have found it helpful to work through the task myself, following my prepared instructions. Usually, I find I need to further clarify my instructions or prepare an exemplar.

> ## Beyond the Text (Optional)
>
> **Key strategies:** Synthesize Across Texts, Share Learning (see chapter 11, page 143)
>
> **Key features:** Inquiring, synthesizing, presenting

When students explore other texts about an aspect of the topic they just studied, they can deepen their understanding of key ideas, add detail to their mental maps, and practice synthesizing ideas and information. Think about what the central text leaves unexplored. The class might further investigate the author or the topic or seek different perspectives on the same issue.

Inquiry can be as simple as a ten-minute exploration of a digital resource list followed by a quick team discussion to identify information that added to, confirmed, or contradicted information in the central text. Inquiry can also be more extensive, having students work together or independently to generate questions, find and read resources, and share their findings. Note that students reading complex texts during this phase should be supported in applying the relevant strategies.

Planning Strategy Instruction

The Deep Sense strategies you will introduce before or during a SITS will depend on your students, your learning standards, and the text itself. A strategy can be introduced before a SITS begins or when the strategy will be used. You might want to collaborate with colleagues, with one teacher providing explicit strategy instruction and another leading a SITS to practice the strategies.

You might introduce a strategy using a short text or one that students are familiar with and then practice the strategy during the text study. Or, you can pause at the appropriate moment in the SITS reading sequence to introduce the strategy with a minilesson and then immediately practice with the central text.

As you plan the reading sequence, note other opportunities to apply multiple Deep Sense strategies. When you reach the point in the text study when a strategy is most useful, you can quickly refresh your students' recollection of the strategy steps and then support them as they practice. As students become more proficient in the strategy, you can release responsibility to them.

Planning Assessment

When planning assessment, first, decide which aspects of student learning you need to assess. You might evaluate students' mastery of target standards, comprehension of the central text, or strategy application. Consider the following as you do so.

- **Target standards:** Your target standards might focus on content, process, or literacy. How you assess students' mastery depends on the nature and specifics of the strategy.

- **Comprehension:** Decide which specific ideas, details, and terms introduced in the central text you want to make sure students understand. Though multiple-choice assessment questions can be helpful, you might get a clearer sense of students' understanding of a text by reading their summaries or responses to open-ended questions or listening to their contributions during discussions.

- **Strategy application:** You can assess how successful students are in applying a strategy or group of strategies. Depending on the strategy, you might observe students engaging with the text and their peers or look for evidence of strategy application in students' independent work products. You can look for their strategic knowledge and awareness through reflections, discussions, or exit tickets. (You will find strategy-specific assessment suggestions throughout part 3.)

Consider building in scaffolds to ensure that all your students can accomplish the task. Clear instructions, assessment criteria, and models are essential scaffolds. In addition, paragraph frames, sentence stems, and word banks can be built into the assignment or offered to individual students. Discussion can also serve as a scaffold to ensure students understand the assignment and, if appropriate, generate ideas. Finally, decide when you will formatively assess students' progress toward mastery during the SITS.

Appendix B contains two sample SITS plans (pages 183 and 188) demonstrating how teachers can integrate content instruction and strategy practice to deepen students' learning.

Concluding Thoughts

In Part 2, we explored the four practices that make up the Deep Sense approach: using motivating practices to build students' confidence, explicitly teaching comprehension strategies, facilitating text-centered discussions, and engaging in shared info-text studies (SITS). SITS provide scaffolded opportunities for students to practice new strategies in the company of their teacher and peers. Students grow in confidence and skill as they learn to apply the strategies strong comprehenders use to make deep sense of informational texts.

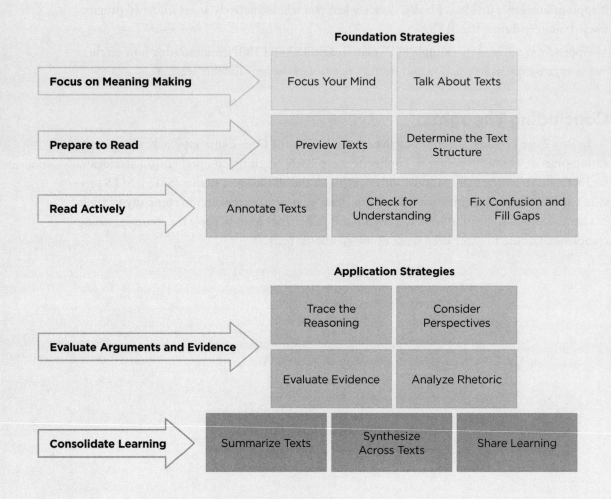

FIGURE P3.1: Deep Sense Approach info-text strategies.

PART THREE

The Deep Sense Approach Strategies

In chapter 2 (page 19), you got an overview of the fourteen Deep Sense Approach strategies. You learned that the strategies are organized into five info-text comprehension practices: (1) focus on meaning making, (2) prepare to read, (3) read actively, (4) evaluate arguments and evidence, and (5) consolidate learning (see figure P3.1).

In part 3, chapters are devoted to each of the five info-text comprehension practices. In each chapter, I explain the research related to its aspect of comprehension and detail the strategies aligned with that practice. At the end of each chapter, you will find student-facing learning guides and other instructional materials to take the guesswork out of Deep Sense Approach strategy instruction.

CHAPTER 7
Focus on Meaning Making

Strategies in This Chapter

- Focus Your Mind

- Talk About Texts

Many teens who struggle to understand complex info-texts in school can read difficult material when they want to learn more about a hobby or other personal interest. The problem arises when they must read texts they did not choose on unfamiliar topics for other people's purposes. This is especially true if they and their peers are used to engaging in the masking, fake reading, and sampling I discussed in chapter 1 (page 13).

The strategies introduced in this chapter help students concentrate on meaning making when reading challenging texts. The Focus Your Mind strategy offers students information about how the reading mind works and suggestions for better managing their attention as they read. The Talk About Texts strategy gives them the discourse, or discussion, tools they need to build meaning with others. Both strategies' learning guides and instructional materials are available at the end of this chapter and online. (Visit **go.SolutionTree.com/literacy/MDSIT** and enter the unique code found on the inside front cover of this book to access these materials.)

Once these strategies become embedded in classroom culture and individual practice, they serve as scaffolds that help students take up the rest of the Deep Sense Approach strategies. As you plan strategy instruction, you can reference the general recommendations in chapter 4 (page 39) and the planning resources in appendix A (page 169).

The Focus Your Mind Strategy

As a classroom teacher, you have likely observed teenage students sitting back or slumping forward when they read articles, essays, webpages, and chapters. They stare motionlessly at the paper or screen, except to flip the page or scroll down, their focus rapidly diminishing. Soon, they stop making sense of the text but might not notice at first. When they regain focus, they start reading at that point rather than rereading what they missed.

What might appear to be a lack of concern, motivation, or ability often turns out to be a genuine struggle to maintain attentional control. This challenge predated the internet and personal electronic devices, but in modern classrooms, the impact of technology on students' attention can seem overwhelming.

Adolescents are frequently tempted to turn to their cell phones, open up multiple tabs on their laptops, or slip in their earbuds. They have become conditioned by the relentless barrage of information, the urgency of notifications and clickbait, and the constant shifting and division of focus demanded by gaming and social media (Carr, 2020; Wolf, 2018).

When I talk to teenage students about their struggle to focus when reading challenging texts, they are often unaware of what is happening. Often, students who know why they are struggling lack a sense of agency and perceive themselves as powerless to change the situation. Students need to know why their minds wander as they read and how they can keep their focus on meaning making. In the next section, you will get important background information about various aspects of managing focus while reading. Subsequent sections outline the steps of the Focus Your Mind strategy and provide guidance for teaching and assessing the strategy.

Helpful Context for Managing Reading Focus

The Focus Your Mind strategy helps teenage students become more *metacognitive*, meaning they pay attention to where their minds are focused, what they think, and which strategies they use. It introduces students to four metacognitive tools: (1) managing motivation, (2) filtering out distractions, (3) tuning in to your inner voice, and (4) adjusting your reading approach. These tools strengthen students' *executive skills*—the complex processes that enable people to regulate their thoughts and behaviors to achieve their goals (Cartwright, 2015).

Executive skills develop throughout childhood and adolescence, and all our students are in the process of refining their executive skills, consciously or unconsciously. According to the Center on the Developing Child at Harvard University (n.d.), adults play a pivotal role in helping children improve their executive skills by providing them with the scaffolding they need to practice the skills on their way to independence. The Center on the Developing Child (n.d.) researchers go on to explain that "some children need more support than others to develop these skills." Executive skills can be a particular challenge for students with added attentional challenges, including attention deficit hyperactivity disorder (ADHD; Miller, Nevado-Montenegro, & Hinshaw, 2012). Though more research needs to be done with secondary students in school settings, there is evidence that executive skills training can make a significant difference in children with ADHD (Shuai et al., 2017).

Managing Motivation

Students' capacity for regulating their attention is affected by their motivation. Even struggling readers can monitor their thoughts and filter out distractions when interested in a topic or invested in a task. Unfortunately, many adolescent students have difficulty mustering interest in their school reading assignments.

Those of us who work with teenage students have heard, "This is boring!" (often much louder than we want). Though I used to get defensive about this, I realized that students often perceive text in a binary way: Either it is interesting, or it is not. Many do not see themselves as having control over their level of interest.

As a teacher, you can mitigate this effect by framing reading tasks in a way that is more likely to engage your students. For example, you might begin a text study with a universal question that piques their interest and use videos and other supplementary texts to help them access background knowledge. However, students also need to be able to generate their own motivation without these supports, and this strategy supports them in doing this.

Filtering Out Distractions

Though some readers seem able to read regardless of the noise and chaos around them, many are not so lucky. (I'm certainly not.) Whenever students read in your classroom, it is important to keep the environment as quiet and distraction-free as possible. However, even in a quiet room, there is much to distract their attention from the text. Feet tap, papers shuffle, and the air-conditioning unit rattles as it kicks on. Maybe you walk over to a student to talk about a recent absence, a friend giggles, or a student's phone vibrates in their pocket. And these are just the external distractions. A student's stomach might growl or cramp. They might be mulling over an encounter with their crush in the cafeteria or an argument at home.

Students often assert that listening to music through earbuds helps them focus, and it certainly helps filter out some outside noise. But the lyrics of their favorite song can compete for their attention, too.

In the Focus Your Mind strategy, students learn about the mind's distractibility and how being constantly pulled away from the text affects their comprehension. They seem to appreciate hearing they are not alone in their struggles.

Tuning In to Your Inner Voice

One way students can monitor whether they are making sense of a text is to tune in to their inner voices. Though students in the early elementary grades (kindergarten through third grade, generally) typically learn to read aloud first, they soon take their reading voices inside their minds. Research suggests that most people experience their inner reader's voice as if being read to (Perrone-Bertolotti et al., 2012; Stephane, Dzemidzic, & Yoon, 2021).

When readers are lost in a novel, their inner chatter might fall silent as the story sweeps them away. They might hear and see the story unfold almost as if they were watching a film. However, with difficult informational reading, even proficient comprehenders can struggle to stay focused on hearing the text. Their inner reading voice stops, and distracting thoughts take over. When this happens, readers can learn to rely more on their inner thinking voice in dialogue with the text as they ask questions, clarify, and summarize.

Adjusting Your Reading Approach

When strong comprehenders notice they are not making much meaning of a text, they shift their reading approach. For example, they might adjust their reading speed, begin annotating, or pause to switch their playlist to a chill instrumental.

Students can learn to assess and adjust their reading approach. This is especially important when students work to make sense of a long, dense text. They can experience mental fatigue when learning about a new topic while deciphering unfamiliar words. Their working memory can overflow. When this happens, they can experience cognitive overload, and their reading mind can shut down. Students can learn to look for signs of mental fatigue and take action to mitigate it.

The Strategy Steps

The Focus Your Mind strategy consists of the following steps.

1. **Build your own motivation:** In this step, students learn that the mind pays attention to what it thinks is interesting and important. When they notice their minds wandering as they read, you can encourage them to refocus on what is interesting about the text and why reading it is important to them. The Preview Texts (chapter 8, page 85) and Check for Understanding (chapter 9, page 105) strategies build on this practice.

2. **Filter out distractions:** This step introduces the idea that the mind is easily distracted. Students practice monitoring their attention and checking for distractions when their attention wanders. They also get tips on how to avoid and manage those distractions.

3. **Tune in to your inner voice:** In this step, students learn to monitor whether their inner voice is reading, trying to make sense of the text, or talking about something else. Students practice reading "louder" in their minds to quiet other thoughts. They also pause to silently think about their reading, ask themselves questions, or "talk" with the author. You will find more about this in the Check for Understanding strategy.

4. **Adjust your reading approach:** This step helps students reflect on and adjust their reading speed and strategy when they notice their attention wandering or mental fatigue settling in.

How to Teach the Strategy

Consider the following suggestions for introducing the Focus Your Mind strategy. You are encouraged to adapt them as needed for your students and your classroom context.

- If you have not introduced students to the "Overview: Making Deep Sense of Info-Texts" handout in chapter 3 (page 29), I recommend doing that first before teaching this strategy.

- As you introduce the Focus Your Mind strategy using the "Learning Guide: Focus Your Mind" (page 80) reproducible, relate your personal experiences and connections with wandering attention. You might share with your students that we *all* lose focus and stop making meaning at times, especially when a text is dense or the topic is unfamiliar. I often describe a time when my brain seems to just shut off as I read a challenging book or article. This confession serves as an invitation for students to share their own struggles with attention. It can be a pivotal moment for some students.

- For this strategy, it makes sense to introduce each step separately in one class period or spread them out across several days. Explain step 1 (build your own motivation), and then introduce an unfamiliar text, modeling how you might think about what is interesting and important in light of the reading purpose. For steps 2–4, explain the step and engage with students as you introduce the tips for that step. Then, have the class read silently for five to ten minutes, focusing on that step. After the reading session, share what you noticed as you read and any tips you found useful. Then, ask students to discuss with a partner what they noticed and which tips they used. Debrief their conversations in a quick whole-class discussion.

Focus on Meaning Making 75

- Whenever students read silently in your class, continue to gently remind them to pay attention to their thinking and reading behavior. Acknowledge when you struggle to focus during silent reading (or even while reading aloud!). Briefly interrupt when students seem to be getting restless or sleepy. Invite them to notice where their minds are and refocus if needed.

- When students struggle with a text, ask them to review the four strategy steps in this strategy's learning guide. Some students new to metacognitive reading might need reminders long after their peers, but in my experience, many students eventually have a breakthrough.

- If a student struggles with focus, carefully observe them during independent reading. Check in with them privately. You might be able to pinpoint a particular strategy step. You might discuss suggestions and help the student select one or two to focus on. It can be helpful for the student to have this strategy's learning guide or an index card with a few selected tips on hand as they read.

- Students face various issues that affect their ability to focus on complex info-texts in class. They might have an identified or unidentified attentional issue. They might have a language or learning challenge that leads them to cognitive fatigue more quickly than their peers. They might have a motivational issue with a particular text, assignment, or class. They might have emotional concerns that crowd out thoughts of the text. The more you observe and listen to them, the more you can tailor your coaching and support to the student's needs.

Assessment Suggestions

The Deep Sense strategies take time for students to internalize and use independently. In this section, I make suggestions for assessing before, during, and after instruction. You can better tailor your strategy instruction when you assess what your students already know, believe, and do before you begin. Assessing at key points during instruction informs your next instructional steps. And once students have learned about and practiced the strategy for a while, you can assess whether they have retained the new learning and provide additional support if they have not.

Following, you will find definitions of key terms and strategic knowledge questions to help you assess how well students understand the strategy. Then, I provide guidance to help students build metacognitive awareness of their strategy use. Finally, I offer evidence you can look for as you assess how well students apply the strategy.

- **Key terms:**
  - *Metacognition*—Thinking about one's thinking
  - *Motivation*—The desire or willingness to do something
  - *Reading purpose*—The reason why one is reading a text
  - *Distraction*—Something that keeps a person from their intended focus
  - *Inner voice*—The voice one hears inside one's mind without speaking aloud
  - *Reading approach*—How a reader tackles a particular text, including the speed with which they read, how carefully they attend to the details, and the strategies they use

- **Strategic knowledge questions:**
  - How does being metacognitive help your reading comprehension?
  - How can you build your motivation when reading a text for school?
  - How can you filter out distractions as you read?
  - What do you need to keep in mind when listening to music as you read?
  - How can you use your inner voice when you read something difficult?
  - When might you need to adjust your reading approach? What are some options?
- **Self-assessment:** After practicing the strategy for a while, ask students to reflect on how it has helped them focus as they read in your class and other classes. You can also ask them to review the learning guide and reflect on which step or tip they were already using, which one has made the most difference to their reading experience, and which one they still need to work on.
- **Evidence of mastery:** When students have mastered the Focus Your Mind strategy, you can observe them taking active steps to reduce distractions and manage their attention. They might ask if they can move seats or take a quick break. They might cover their ears or start sweeping their finger under the words. You will not hear complaints that a text is "boring." Further, if you check in with students during a quiet reading period, they will be able to tell you what they just read. When you ask them to check in on their inner voice, they will be able to tell you whether it is reading aloud, talking about the text, or narrating other thoughts.

The Talk About Texts Strategy

In cubicles, homes, and online chats, strategic readers talk about info-texts and the ideas they gleaned from them in order to clarify their thinking, share their insights, and gain the perspectives of others. These text-centered discussions are a primary way in which many adults engage with texts in their everyday lives (Duke & Martin, 2019). Chapter 5 (page 49) offered guidance for planning and leading text-centered discussions. The Talk About Texts strategy empowers students with information, guidelines, and conversation stems they can use to successfully engage in these meaning-making discussions. The following sections detail steps for this strategy, guidance for teaching the strategy, and several suggestions to support assessment.

The Strategy Steps

The Talk About Texts strategy consists of the following steps.

1. **Contribute to the conversation:** This step emphasizes that each voice in a text-centered discussion is important and that all participants are responsible for keeping the discussion flowing. Students use conversation stems to elaborate on their ideas and share background knowledge and connections.
2. **Listen actively:** This step reduces the stigma of tuning out during text-centered discussions. Students learn that it is common for our minds to wander during discussions but that we lose out on vital information when this happens. They use conversation stems to help them engage with their peers and ask for clarification.

Focus on Meaning Making   77

3. **Respect others' ideas:** This step introduces the practice of taking up and building on others' ideas. Conversation stems model how students can expand on or disagree with the previous speaker's ideas. Students learn to avoid verbal arm wrestling and focus on meaning making. They learn a practical definition of *tentative language* and learn to use tentative words and phrases like *maybe, could, perhaps, I wonder*, and *I'm not sure* to signal their openness to other perspectives.

4. **Refer to text evidence:** The text has an important role in discussions, as it represents the author's voice. When students implement this step, a team might fall silent as all the participants return to the text to reread a statement or look for evidence of a particular point.

5. **Capture important ideas:** When students discuss texts, it often helps to capture in writing the important ideas, information, and questions that arise. To keep the conversation going, students can jot down quick, informal notes, which they can add to or amend later. Like annotation, informal note making is a way to clear their working memory to make room for new information.

How to Teach the Strategy

Consider the following suggestions for teaching the Talk About Texts strategy.

- As you introduce this strategy, ask about and acknowledge students' previous experiences with classroom discussion. They might have had years of frustrating discussions that have left them hesitant to take risks.

- At the end of this chapter, the "Learning Guide: Talk About Texts" (page 82) reproducible briefly explains each step and then offers discussion guidelines and conversation stems to support that step. Depending on your students' age and experience, you might explain, model, and practice one or two steps at a time.

- Demonstrate what each step sounds and looks like in practice. Your students might enjoy seeing you model a nonexample. For example, after explaining step 3 (respect others' ideas), you can model dismissing and talking over others as they attempt to answer a question. Then, enlist an individual or group to help you show how to follow the guidelines and use the stems for a step. (Make sure to pull aside students in advance to let them know what to expect.)

- Once students understand the essence of each step, they need to practice it with peers as you circulate, monitor, and coach. You can weave this practice into the study of a traditional text, but you can also have students discuss a photograph (historical or current), an infographic, or a video clip.

- Post the discussion guidelines and conversation stems on an anchor chart as a visual reminder, or provide a copy of the reproducible, "Learning Guide: Talk About Texts" for each team to keep handy. Students are more likely to take up these new practices if you regularly refer to the guidelines and stems, consciously model their use, and coach students when their discussions get off track.

- If the whole class struggles with a particular step, it can help to reteach just that step and then have the students focus on following the learning guide and using the stems associated with that step. If individual students or teams struggle, you might privately check in with them to better gauge the issue. Based on what you discover, you can coach as needed.

Assessment Suggestions

In this section, I make suggestions for assessing before, during, and after instruction. You can better tailor your strategy instruction by assessing what your students already know, believe, and do before you begin. Assessing at key points during instruction informs your next instructional steps. And once students have learned about and practiced the strategy for a while, check to make sure they have retained the new learning and provide additional support if they have not.

Following, you will find definitions of key terms and strategic knowledge questions to help you assess how well students understand the strategy. Then, I provide guidance to help students build metacognitive awareness of their strategy use. Finally, I offer evidence you can look for as you assess how well students apply the strategy.

- **Key terms:**
    - *Discussion guidelines*—Behaviors a group is expected to demonstrate during a discussion
    - *Conversation stems*—Words and phrases a speaker can use to start and frame their comments to help keep a conversation productive
    - *Tentative language*—Words and phrases that show the speaker has an open mind and considers other points of view, such as *maybe, could, perhaps, I wonder*, and *I'm not sure*
    - *Airtime*—How often and how long a person speaks during a discussion
    - *Turn taking*—Quietly waiting for one's turn to speak without really listening to others
    - *Building on ideas*—Referring to other speakers' ideas and integrating their points into one's own
    - *Arm wrestling*—Debating to win the argument without trying to understand other perspectives
- **Strategic knowledge questions:**
    - How does it help your comprehension to discuss a text with others?
    - Why is it important to use tentative language in discussions? What are some examples of tentative language?
    - What can you do when you realize you tuned out during a discussion?
    - What should you do when you disagree with a peer during a discussion?
    - When is it important to refer to the text during a discussion?
    - Why is it important to take notes during or after a discussion?
- **Self-assessment:** After practicing the strategy for a while with different texts, have students reflect on how using the conversation stems and following the guidelines have changed their experience of text-centered discussions. You can ask them which discussion guidelines are most important, which are most difficult for them, and which conversation stems they use most often.
- **Evidence of mastery:** When students have mastered the Talk About Texts strategy, you can observe them doing the following during peer, team, and whole-class discussions.
    - Sharing airtime
    - Using tentative language

- Sticking to the topic
- Building on peers' comments
- Pausing to look at the text
- Referring to the text as they speak
- Using the conversation stems

Concluding Thoughts

As you continue to help your students focus as they read and coach them on productively discussing what they read, you can expect to see a marked improvement in their comprehension over time. But this is just the beginning. The Focus Your Mind and Talk About Texts strategies lay the groundwork for the rest of the Deep Sense Approach strategies. In the next chapter, you will learn about two strategies that help students update their pre-reading routine to work with complex info-texts.

Learning Guide: Focus Your Mind

Some readers can easily focus on reading, but many of us are not so lucky. In this technological age, it is harder than ever to slow down and focus on an info-text, especially if it is long or difficult. With the simple tools outlined in this guide, you can improve your ability to make sense of the text. Begin by understanding why this strategy is helpful and when you can use it.

1. Build your own motivation.
2. Filter out distractions.
3. Tune in to your inner voice.
4. Adjust your reading approach.

- **Why:** The Focus Your Mind strategy helps you become more *metacognitive*, thinking about your thinking (*meta* meaning "beyond or above" and *cognitive* meaning "related to thinking"). When readers are metacognitive, they pay attention to where their minds are focused, what they are thinking, and which strategies they are using. When they lose focus, they adjust their approach. This strategy helps you understand the text better and remember more of it later.

- **When:** Practice the Focus Your Mind strategy throughout your reading process. You might need to repeatedly refocus as you work to understand a text.

Strategy Steps

Though it can be challenging to stay focused as you read a difficult info-text, four tools can help improve your focus: (1) building your own motivation, (2) filtering out distractions, (3) tuning in to your inner voice, and (4) adjusting your reading approach.

1. Build Your Own Motivation

When you have a genuine interest in a topic, you can more easily focus as you read about it. The mind pays attention to what it thinks is interesting and important.

When your attention wanders, you can remind yourself of your *reading purpose*—why you are reading the text. It is tempting to say, "This is boring!" when you are reading a difficult text, especially one you did not choose. But every text has *something* interesting about it! When you consider a text's interest and importance, you can convince your brain to pay attention.

2. Filter Out Distractions

The mind is easily distracted. The hum of the air conditioner, people's voices, your stomach growling, thoughts of a conversation you had earlier—all these things can distract your mind as you read. You might find your eyes moving across the page or screen while you are thinking about something else. With practice, you can notice what is distracting you and decide what to do about it.

To reduce distractions, try the following.

- Close extra tabs on your laptop, or close the laptop altogether. Put your phone on Do Not Disturb and move it out of sight.

- Block your sight line to the distraction, turning in your chair or shielding your eyes.

- Move away from the distraction, if possible— to a quiet corner or another location.

- Ask others to talk more quietly or turn down the TV or music a little.

- Put on headphones or earbuds with quiet instrumental music or white noise.

page 1 of 2

Making Deep Sense of Informational Texts © 2025 Solution Tree Press • SolutionTree.com
Visit **go.SolutionTree.com/literacy/MDSIT** and enter the unique access code found on this book's inside front cover to access this reproducible.

Here's a tip about listening to music as you read: Though music can block outside noise, it can also compete with the text for attention. The mind can make meaning of only one thing at a time. It will happily focus on the lyrics of a favorite song rather than a difficult text. Experiment to find music that allows you to stay focused on the text, like classical music, lo-fi music, chill instrumental music, or music designed for meditation.

3. Tune In to Your Inner Voice

Children often hear others reading aloud, including family members, teachers, librarians, and recorded authors. They learn to take the storyteller's voice inside themselves. They might whisper-read for a while, but they eventually hear their reading voices inside their minds. You might not even notice your inner reading voice now that you are older. When you have difficulty focusing on a text, try to tune in to your *inner voice* and use it to help you make sense of the text.

To tune in to your inner voice, try the following.

- Check in to listen to your inner voice. Is it "reading aloud" in your mind? Is it trying to make sense of the text? Or is it "talking" about something else?

- If it is hard to hear your inner reading voice, practice with individual phrases and then sentences. Read them aloud, whisper them, and then speak them in your mind.

- Practice reading louder in your mind to quiet your other thoughts.

- Pause to silently talk with yourself about the text.

- Give yourself a quick pep talk, telling yourself, "Come on, you've got this. Let's focus."

4. Adjust Your Reading Approach

When you find it difficult to focus on the text, you can change *how* you are reading.

To adjust your reading approach, try the following.

- If you sit back, slump forward, or lie down as you read, your body and brain might think it is time to rest. Try to sit up as you read.

- If you find yourself skimming the text, slow down your reading pace.

- If you sit very still and your mind wanders, try to interact with the text. Run your finger under the words or use your mouse to point to one paragraph at a time. Better yet, read more actively using the Annotate Texts and Check for Understanding strategies.

- When you read a long, difficult text, your thinking brain can easily get tired. Give yourself a short brain break. Drink some water and take a few deep breaths. If you can, stand up and stretch or walk around.

- If your mind wanders while reading a long info-text, try making notes after each section. This will help you offload the information in your working memory.

Making Deep Sense of Informational Texts © 2025 Solution Tree Press • SolutionTree.com
Visit **go.SolutionTree.com/literacy/MDSIT** and enter the unique access code found on this book's inside front cover to access this reproducible.

Learning Guide: Talk About Texts

Teachers often ask students to discuss texts as a whole class, in a team, or with a partner. Two heads or more are often better than one when making sense of a complex text. If you follow a few simple guidelines, text-based conversations can help you deepen your understanding.

| 1. **Contribute to the conversation.** |
| 2. **Listen actively.** |
| 3. **Respect others' ideas.** |
| 4. **Refer to text evidence.** |
| 5. **Capture important ideas.** |

- **Why:** People often work together to make sense of info-texts. Professionals analyze reports with colleagues. College students study textbook chapters together. Friends share and discuss articles about their common interests. When you talk with others about a complex info-text, you can clarify your own thoughts and get other perspectives and information. Together, you can build a better understanding.

- **When:** You can have a text-centered discussion before, as, or after you read a complex text.

Strategy Steps

It can be challenging to discuss complex info-texts. You must form and express ideas, find evidence, check your information, consider others' views, find common ground, and record the most important ideas. You also have to monitor your participation and help ensure everyone can contribute. Each of the following steps includes helpful discussion guidelines as well as conversation stems you can use to help you follow the guidelines.

1. Contribute to the Conversation

Each voice in a text-centered discussion is important. *All* participants are responsible for keeping the conversation flowing. When appropriate, share what you already know about the ideas discussed in the text. Make connections between the ideas in the text and your experiences, other texts, and what you know about the world. But make room for peers to share, too, watching your *airtime*.

To contribute to the conversation, do the following.
- Share what you know and make connections.
- Watch your airtime and share the floor.

Conversation Stems to *Connect*

- "This reminds me of . . ."
- "I can connect with . . ."
- "That's like . . . (self, text, world)."

Conversation Stems to *Contribute*

- "It seems to me that . . ."
- "I wonder if/why/whether . . ."
- "I think this is saying . . ."

2. Listen Actively

Our minds can easily wander when someone else talks, but we risk missing vital information. Watch out for *turn taking*. It can be tempting to quietly wait your turn without really listening to others. You can avoid this by working hard to hear and understand each person's ideas.

To listen actively, do the following.
- Keep an open mind and show interest.
- Make sure you understand others' ideas.

Conversation Stems to *Invite*

- "What do you think, _____?"
- "Who has a different idea?"
- "Do you have a different perspective?"

Conversation Stems to *Clarify*

- "Are you saying that . . . ?"
- "I'm not sure I understand . . ."
- "Can you tell me more about . . . ?"
- "Can you give an example?"

Making Deep Sense of Informational Texts © 2025 Solution Tree Press • SolutionTree.com
Visit **go.SolutionTree.com/MDSIT** and enter the unique access code found on this book's inside front cover to access this reproducible.

3. Respect Others' Ideas

The goal of text-centered discussions is to deepen our understanding. Build on others' ideas to show you have considered their points of view. Use *tentative language*—words and phrases like *maybe, could, perhaps, I wonder,* or *I'm not sure*. This signals you are open to other perspectives. Watch out for *arm wrestling*. When discussions turn into debates focused on winning, we stop trying to understand other perspectives. When you disagree, remind yourself that everyone is entitled to their point of view.

To show respect for others' ideas, do the following.
- Build on others' ideas using tentative language.
- Express differences thoughtfully.

Conversation Stems to *Build on Ideas*
- "I agree that . . . because . . ."
- "I'd like to add . . ."
- "To build on that . . ."
- "This also makes me think . . ."

Conversation Stems to *Express Differences*
- "I agree that . . . , but . . ."
- "I see it differently."
- "Could it also be that . . . ?"

4. Refer to Text Evidence

When we discuss a complex text, it is important to understand what the author meant. Return to the text often during a discussion, looking for evidence to support your ideas. If a question arises, reread to ensure you understand what the author meant.

To refer to text evidence, do the following.
- Return to the text for supporting evidence.
- Reread when you are unsure.

Conversation Stems to *Support*
- "I think this is supported by . . ."
- "Where is that in the text?"
- "What makes you think that?"
- "What is your evidence?"

5. Capture Important Ideas

When you make notes to capture the most important ideas, it is easier to remember those ideas later. Add annotations to the text during or after the discussion, or jot down ideas on a sticky note or in your notebook. Or take more formal notes, such as Cornell Notes, or use a graphic organizer.

To capture important ideas, do the following.
- Jot down key points during the discussion.
- Add to your notes after the discussion.

Conversation Stems to *Sum Up*
- "What were the most important ideas we discussed?"
- "What conclusions did we draw?"
- "What do we want to report out?"

CHAPTER 8
Prepare to Read

Strategies in This Chapter
- Preview Texts
- Determine the Text Structure

The next step in helping students make deeper sense of info-texts is to update their pre-reading routine. Think about how you prepare to read a long professional article or informational chapter. You might flip or scroll through it to assess how long the text is. As a strong comprehender, you probably skim the title, note the visuals, and immediately begin making connections. Chances are, you already know why you are reading the text and what you want to get out of it. With your reading purpose in mind, you might skim the headings to see how the text is organized. Finally, you decide how to tackle reading the text: what you will read carefully, what you will skim, and what you will ignore altogether. You probably do all of this in less than a minute—the routine is natural and automatic (Almasi, Garas-York, & Shanahan, 2006; Filderman, Austin, Boucher, O'Donnell, & Swanson, 2022; Hall, 2015; Kelley & Clausen-Grace, n.d.; O'Reilly et al., 2015; Ritchey, Palombo, Silverman, & Speece, 2017).

You do this because previewing info-texts helps readers:

- Select a text that meets their reading purposes
- Draft a mental map of the text
- Use what they know to help them understand new information
- Get the information they need
- Remember key ideas later

Unfortunately, students often skip pre-reading when they read info-texts independently. If they remember to pre-read, they may struggle to adapt their approach to longer, more complicated texts. Some secondary students have already developed effective pre-reading strategies, but many need an updated routine they can independently use with a wide range of texts.

This chapter introduces two strategies that combine to form a powerful pre-reading routine: (1) Preview Texts and (2) Determine the Text Structure. Both strategies' learning guides and instructional materials are available at the end of this chapter and online. (Visit **go.SolutionTree. com/literacy/MDSIT** and enter the unique code found on the inside front cover of this book to access these materials.)

85

The Preview Texts Strategy

With the Preview Texts strategy, students quickly assess text features, looking for those that highlight key ideas, communicate the author's purpose, or add relevant information. Based on their preview, they reflect on what they already know about the topic, tapping into and assessing their background knowledge. Then, they make a reading plan, deciding how to approach the text to meet their reading purpose.

In the Deep Sense Approach context, a *text feature* is a visual or text element added to the main text by the author or publisher, such as a title, table of contents, chart, or caption. Text features have been added to info-texts for centuries to emphasize and illustrate important concepts (see figure 8.1).

In the next section, you will learn important information about text features. In subsequent sections, I outline the steps of the Preview Texts strategy and provide guidance for teaching and assessing the strategy.

Helpful Context for Text Features

Authors and publishers use text features to do the following.

- Grab and keep readers' attention.
- Signal the importance or organization of ideas.
- Illustrate or elaborate on key concepts.
- Provide needed context.
- Include additional information that would interrupt the flow of the main text.

Source: British Library.
FIGURE 8.1: Text features in an antique text.

Many students learn about text features in elementary school. During read-alouds of picture books, their teachers linger over the title and illustrations to help them predict key plot elements and make inferences about characters. The first chapter books children read often contain illustrations as well.

As students progress in school, the stories and novels they read include fewer text features. When I ask my middle and high school students to describe their process for choosing a novel, most go no further than looking at the cover art and skimming the blurb on the back cover. They do not expect to find text features within the novel that might help them decide whether it interests them.

In contrast, the info-texts secondary students must read for school are often rife with text features. The captions get longer, the diagrams are more complicated, and inset text boxes and graphics pepper the text. However, instead of seeing these as important clues to meaning, teenage students might ignore them.

When I taught eighth-grade U.S. history, my students and I worked through many sample test questions together in preparation for the spring state assessment. I realized my students often overlooked the test items' sidebars, text boxes, charts, maps, and captions, though they were packed with relevant information. When they missed the correct response, it was often because they had skipped over these text features. They did not do this intentionally; it was as if they did not even see these features!

Three Types of Text Features

Though there are many ways to group and label text features, I find it useful to focus on the following three categories, which you'll find examples of in figure 8.2. This chart is also included in the "Learning Guide: Preview Texts" reproducible (page 99).

1. **Key idea signal:** Key idea signals, such as titles, headings, and font changes, provide clues to help readers determine the most important ideas and see how the author organized those ideas. Strong comprehenders might be able to figure this out just by reading carefully, but many readers struggle to infer the importance and organization of ideas based on the text alone (García, García-Serrano, & Rosales, 2022; McNamara et al., 1996).

2. **Important context:** Important context, like a note from or about the author, can help the reader understand the author's intentions and evaluate the credibility of the source.

3. **Added information:** Added information, such as inset boxes, sidebars, and visuals, can help readers better understand the concepts in the text and point them toward the next steps in building their knowledge about a topic.

Purpose	Examples
Key Idea Signal (KIS)	
• Highlights the most important ideas • Shows how ideas and information are organized	• Titles, subtitles, headings, and subheadings • Numbered lists, summaries, and content outlines • Font changes, such as **bold** or *italicized* words, highlighting, or changes to font size or color • Layout, color scheme, section breaks, and dividers
Important Context (IC)	
• Helps readers determine the author's purpose • Helps readers evaluate credibility and point of view	• Publication information • Notes from or about the author or publisher • Tables of contents and navigation bars
Added Information (AI)	
• Illustrates and elaborates on key ideas • Points to additional resources	• Photos, illustrations, diagrams, and videos • Maps, infographics, captions, labels, and legends • Sidebars, insets, and footnotes • Hyperlinks, citations, and related articles

FIGURE 8.2: *Three types of text features.*

Each type of text feature contributes to our understanding of a text (Hanson & Padua, 2011). Authors and publishers might add many or just a few of these features depending on their purpose. The text sample (an abbreviated version of the article available at https://theconversation.com/the-heroic-effort-to-save-floridas-coral-reef-from-extreme-ocean-heat-as-corals-bleach-across-the-caribbean-210974) in figure 8.3 includes the three types of text features. In the sample, the title signals the central idea of the article. The author information provides important context. The photo, caption, and hyperlinks illustrate and elaborate on key ideas and information. (The text sample is from the beginning of a scientific article written by Michael Childress [2023], an associate professor of biological sciences and environmental conservation at Clemson University. Appendix B, page 177, includes a sample SITS plan that uses the article as the central text.)

Source: Childress, 2023. Used with permission.
FIGURE 8.3: Text sample with three types of text features.

Evaluation of Text Features

Even texts written for elementary students can be overrun with illustrations and insets, making it hard to sustain focus on the main text. When I examined the info-texts used to assess fourth graders' comprehension in the 2017 NAEP, I was surprised to find a scientific article with many distracting text features. For example, an inset map demanded my attention until I realized the added information was irrelevant to the central idea. One question referred to "the last paragraph," though a half-page inset to the right of the main text made it unclear which paragraph the test makers were referring to.

By asking themselves why an author or publisher included certain text features, students can learn to challenge their assumptions. Titles and headings in considerate texts communicate key ideas. However, in an online environment, the publisher might introduce each section with a mysterious phrase that tantalizes the reader but gives little understanding of what's to come. With practice, students can become savvy in discerning the meaning of a text feature and why and how it was used within a text.

Activation of Background Knowledge

Strong comprehenders use their text feature preview to mobilize relevant *background knowledge*, which is what the reader already knows, believes, and feels about the concepts and information discussed in a text. These strategic readers evaluate the text in light of their background knowledge, integrating the new with the known (Denton et al., 2015). Numerous studies confirm the connection between background knowledge and comprehension (Smith, Snow, Serry, & Hammond, 2021).

Some secondary students do not have much academic and topic-specific background knowledge to draw from when trying to make sense of texts on unfamiliar topics. Even so, it is helpful for them to think through what they know, believe, or feel might be relevant.

Teachers often help students activate and build background knowledge before reading. They might show a video or conduct a minilesson to ensure students can grasp the main points of a text. Students need to engage in this metacognitive process on their own as well. Eventually, with scaffolded practice, they can learn to assess their background knowledge, activate what they know or think, and seek the information they need to make sense of the text.

Chapter 9 (page 105) introduces students to the Check for Understanding and Fix Confusion and Fill Gaps strategies, which can help them continue assessing, building, and updating their background knowledge as they read.

Planning

Strategic readers approach info-texts intentionally to meet specific goals. They assess the text's difficulty and structure and then mobilize specific strategies to help them make sense of the text (Botsas, 2017). Students usually take up their teacher's reading purpose and plan without thinking much about it. They might not be accustomed to thinking through their own reading purpose or making their own reading plan. When students have to read texts independently, they might decide quickly (and unconsciously) how to approach the text. Unfortunately, their default plan often is to skim the text, hunting for information. Though this approach is helpful for some purposes, students often skim when they need to understand the text more deeply than a quick, cursory read will allow.

When students make a mental *reading plan*, they decide how they will read a text or texts in print or digital environments to meet their learning needs (Cho, 2013; Cho & Afflerbach, 2017). The text preview informs this quick planning process. Making a conscious decision about their reading approach, especially in school settings, can also help students feel they have agency over their reading.

The Strategy Steps

With practice, the Preview Texts strategy evolves into a flexible pre-reading routine that students can independently and quickly use with a variety of texts. The strategy includes these steps.

1. **Evaluate text features:** In this step, students learn to identify the three types of text features commonly found in info-texts as described in the "Learning Guide: Preview Texts" (page 99) reproducible. They learn to avoid getting lost in the small details by focusing on features that communicate something about the key ideas and the author's

purpose. They evaluate features that provide added information to determine which ones are relevant to their purpose and which are just there to grab readers' attention.

2. **Activate background knowledge:** Based on their text preview, students consider questions to help them assess and activate relevant background knowledge.

3. **Make a reading plan:** This step helps students make a conscious plan that meets their reading purpose. They learn to ask themselves questions to identify what they need to learn from and do with the text. They then decide how to approach reading the text to meet their purpose.

How to Teach the Strategy

The following recommendations can help you successfully teach the Preview Texts strategy to your students.

- Select an info-text (such as a magazine article or textbook chapter) that includes the three types of text features. This will be the text you work with throughout the explanation and modeling of the strategy. You might project a digital version or use a document projector to display a printed copy. Explain to students that they will be reading the text soon. Ask them to reflect on what they would typically do before they begin reading. After they discuss with a shoulder partner, call on several students to describe their approach. Students might be stumped by the question, or they might say that they read the title and look at the illustrations.

- Distribute digital or paper copies of the "Learning Guide: Preview Texts" reproducible, and walk students through the introductory paragraph, why and when to use the strategy, and the definition of *text feature*. Then walk them through the three types of text features, referring to the Three Types of Text Features chart in the learning guide.

- Work with students to identify examples of the three types of text features in the article you introduced earlier. You can code the features with the abbreviations *KIS*, *IC*, and *AI* (as modeled in figure 8.2, page 87) or use different colors, symbols, or underline styles. Have students refer to the Three Types of Text Features chart in their learning guide to help you decide. If students have their own copy of the text, you can ask them to code their text as you do.

- Continuing to refer to the learning guide, introduce this strategy's first step (evaluate text features). Explain the different uses of text features and then use the questions to think aloud as you model evaluating the various features of the text you previously introduced.

- Explain step 2 (activate background knowledge) and step 3 (make a reading plan). Then model the two steps with the same text, thinking aloud as you ask the questions provided in the learning guide. Describe how your reading plan might change depending on your task, such as summarizing the key ideas, preparing to take a test over the content, or getting the gist of an unfamiliar topic before reading other texts.

- After checking to make sure students are comfortable with these steps, you can have them work with a partner or team to apply the three strategy steps with a new info-text that contains the three types of text features.

- When students are ready to formulate a reading plan, they will need to know the text-based task they must complete. If the class will not be studying the text soon, give them a hypothetical task.
- Revisit the strategy steps as needed as the class reads new info-texts, having students quickly review their learning guides before pre-reading.
- Talk about your own pre-reading practices and experiences, including your assumptions, revelations, and frustrations. For example, you might share a news article you encountered that had mysterious or misleading headings. Invite students to reflect on and share their own experiences. During an informal online inquiry, you might ask them to find examples of texts with unhelpful headings or no headings at all. Discuss how to adapt the pre-reading routine as needed.
- As they learn more Deep Sense Approach strategies, ensure students revisit text features throughout the reading process for various purposes.

Assessment Suggestions

In this section, I make suggestions for assessing students' understanding of and ability to apply the Preview Texts strategy. First, you will find definitions of key terms and strategic knowledge questions to help you assess how well students understand key concepts. Then, I provide guidance to help students build metacognitive awareness of their strategy use. Finally, I offer evidence you can look for as you assess students' application of the strategy.

- **Key terms:**
  - *Pre-reading routine*—A set of strategies a reader uses before they read an info-text
  - *Preview*—A look ahead to assess a text
  - *Text feature*—A visual or text element added to the main text by the author or publisher, such as a title, table of contents, chart, or caption
  - *Key idea signal*—A text feature that highlights an important idea in a text or shows how key ideas and information are organized
  - *Important context*—A text feature that helps readers determine the author's purpose or evaluate the author's credibility and point of view
  - *Added information*—A text feature that illustrates and elaborates on key ideas or points the reader to additional resources
  - *Background knowledge*—What the reader already knows, believes, and feels about concepts and information discussed in a text
  - *Reading plan*—How the reader decides to read a text or texts in print or digital environments to meet their learning needs
- **Strategic knowledge questions:**
  - Why is it important to preview a complex info-text before you read it?
  - What are the three types of text features? How can each type help you prepare to read?
  - Why is it important to activate your background knowledge before you read? How can text features help you do this?
  - What do you need to decide when making your reading plan?

- **Self-assessment:** After students have practiced the strategy for a while with different texts, have them reflect on how their pre-reading routine has changed and whether it differs depending on the content, format, and purpose (for example, a familiar topic versus an unfamiliar topic, print text versus digital text, or assigned reading versus independent reading). Ask them to review the learning guide and assess how closely their pre-reading routine aligns with the suggestions, either discussing with a peer or writing independently. Ask them what aspects of the strategy they want to improve.

- **Evidence of mastery:** When students have mastered the strategy, you will see them flipping or scrolling through the text before beginning to read in earnest. When you check in with students during their pre-reading, they will be able to answer questions like the following.

  - What text features do you feel are most important in this text?
  - Based on your preview, what does the text seem to be about? What do you expect to learn? Which text features helped you decide?
  - What can you tell about the author?
  - Which added information features do you plan to skip? How did you decide?
  - What is your reading plan? How did you decide?

The Determine the Text Structure Strategy

In addition to activating background knowledge and making a reading plan, students also benefit from determining the text structure as part of their pre-reading routine. Readers who don't notice text structure might read inefficiently, giving every detail and word equal attention. This can quickly lead to cognitive overload. They will also have more trouble forming a mental map of the text that mirrors the author's organization of ideas.

Research has confirmed that students' comprehension improves when they learn to identify the various idea structures of expository texts (Hebert et al., 2016; Meyer & Ray, 2011). In their study of explicit text structure instruction, Kausalai Wijekumar, Bonnie J. F. Meyer, and Puiwa Lei (2017) find that most seventh graders benefit from this instruction. Bonnie J. F. Meyer, David M. Brandt, and George J. Bluth (1980) identify five text structures commonly used by authors of informational texts.

1. **Description:** Authors use the description structure to provide definitions, facts, details, or examples or to describe characteristics or components of something.

2. **Sequence:** Authors use the sequence structure to present things in order, such as a sequence of events, the steps in a process, the stages of a cycle, or an ordered list.

3. **Problem-solution:** Authors use the problem-solution structure to explain a problem and discuss potential, attempted, or enacted solutions.

4. **Cause-effect:** Authors use the cause-effect structure to explain the causes and effects of something, including describing a chain reaction of events.

5. **Compare-contrast:** Authors use the compare-contrast structure to describe similarities and differences, compare different points of view on a topic, consider benefits and drawbacks, or evaluate two or more things by comparing their features.

If students learned about text structure in elementary school or in middle school intervention sessions, they might have been introduced to these five text structures with short definitions, simple diagrams, and common signal words. They might have practiced identifying the structure of short passages with helpful text features, perhaps filling in preprinted graphic organizers. Though this approach is a perfect starting point for young readers, students might get the following incorrect impressions.

- Authors intentionally choose just one of these structures to organize their text.
- These are the only ways authors organize their ideas.
- Authors always emphasize their idea organization.
- The text structure is always simple and easy to recognize.

Students need help updating their knowledge of common info-text structures so they can better recognize them in more complex texts. Figure 8.4 (page 94) presents diagrams that represent some variations of these text structures.

Students need to understand the following caveats when working to determine the text structure in complex texts.

- **Writers might nest multiple structures in one text:** Authors of informational chapters and long articles often employ one top-level text structure but then organize some paragraphs and sections using other structures.
- **Writers do not always signal their idea organization:** Authors writing for a general audience can be less intentional about using text features and signal words than those writing for children. They might assume the reader can follow their idea trail because they are writing in a logical sequence.
- **Not all writers carefully organize their ideas:** I have noticed feature articles, opinion columns, and other published texts that are loosely organized in a cumulative, conversational manner.
- **Some writers use text structures unique to their genre:** For example, biographers and other authors of literary nonfiction might organize their texts as a sequence of events, but they might also use a narrative arc like that found in a novel to structure their writing.

The following are two examples of the compare-contrast structure in real-world texts.

- **Example 1:** A university website has devoted a full page to the red-tailed hawk to help enthusiasts identify the bird. The page includes photos and briefly describes the species, compares it with similar birds, and then describes its appearance, behavior, and habitat. The page then provides links to articles that mention red-tailed hawks and even a link to a bird cam showing a live feed of a red-tailed hawk nest. The top-level structure of the text is description, but the author uses a compare-contrast structure to organize one section.
- **Example 2:** On its website, a nonprofit civil liberties organization has posted an article on seven types of democracy. In the introduction, the author states she will discuss the seven types' similarities and differences. After an overview that discusses democracy in general, she presents seven sections, each devoted to one type of democracy. Each section discusses the relative benefits and drawbacks of the type and compares and contrasts it with the other types. Though the author uses a compare-contrast structure to organize the article, a simple Venn diagram cannot accurately represent the structure.

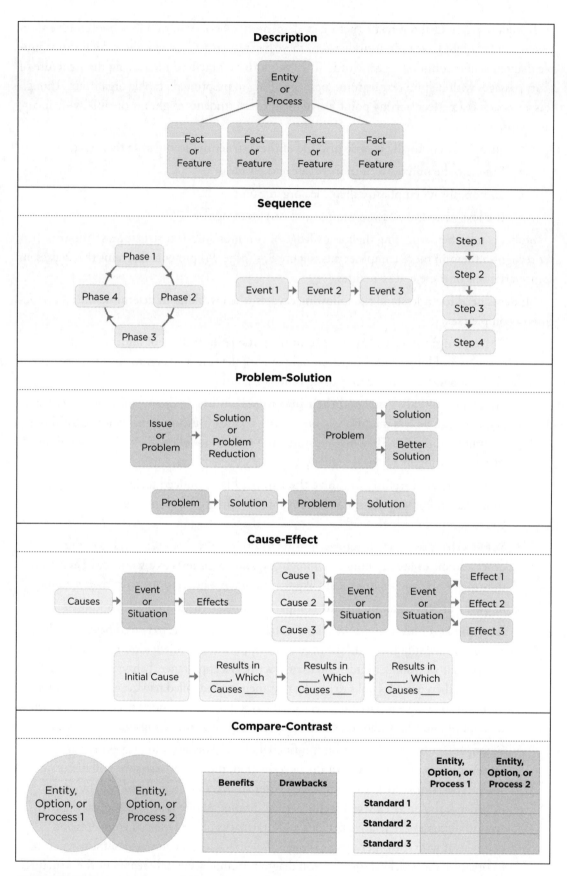

FIGURE 8.4: Text structure variations in complex texts.

Visit **go.SolutionTree.com/literacy/MDSIT** for a free reproducible version of this figure.

The following sections detail steps for this strategy, guidance for teaching the strategy, and several suggestions to support assessment.

The Strategy Steps

In this strategy, students get updated information about common informational text structures and learn some methods they can use to determine the top-level text structure. It consists of the following steps.

1. **Consider the author's purpose:** This step begins with a review of the important context features, like the author's note and introduction. (Refer to figure 8.2, page 87, for a list of text features.) Students consult the "Learning Guide: Determine the Text Structure" reproducible (page 101) to read through possible purposes associated with the five common text structures and decide which structure best aligns with the author's purpose.

2. **Review the key idea signals:** In this step, students review the key idea signals throughout the text while referring to a chart that lists terms often used to signal the five most common text structures.

3. **Assess organization issues:** This step emphasizes that there are no hard-and-fast rules about how info-text authors use and communicate text structure, only helpful guidelines. Authors of texts written for general audiences do not always explicitly signal their idea organization.

4. **Determine the top-level text structure:** In this step, students learn that authors of complex texts tend to use one top-level text structure as their main organizing scheme. After working through the first three steps, they consider questions to help them decide which text structure they think the author used to communicate their central idea.

How to Teach the Strategy

Consider the following suggestions as you plan to teach the Determine the Text Structure strategy, adapting them as needed for your context.

- Provide students with copies of the "Learning Guide: Determine the Text Structure" reproducible.

- As you walk students through the reproducible's introductory paragraph and why and when statements, probe to determine whether they have previously learned about text structure and, if so, what they remember. Explain that they need some updated information about text structure because they are now reading much more complex texts. To refresh students' memory of the common text structures, you can ask them to discuss scenarios like the following in teams or pairs (adapted from Roehling, Hebert, Nelson, & Bohaty, 2017).

  a. *Description*—Describe your favorite room to somebody who has never seen it.

  b. *Sequence*—Explain what you did after school yesterday, step by step.

  c. *Cause-effect*—What might happen if our school was visited by the most famous person you can think of?

d. *Problem-solution*—What is an important problem that occurs in our school? What are some possible solutions?

e. *Compare-contrast*—Describe the similarities and differences between your favorite show and another one you have watched.

Explain step 1 (consider the author's purpose), and demonstrate it with a think-aloud. Use a text for which students have already evaluated text features with the Preview Texts strategy described earlier in this chapter. Return to the important context features (see figure 8.2) and point out clues that reveal the author's purpose. Have students refer to the Possible Purposes chart in the "Learning Guide: Determine the Text Structure" reproducible and work with a partner to determine which purpose most closely aligns with what they have learned so far about the text. If they cannot decide, ask them to make note of the options they are considering. Debrief to come to a consensus on the author's purpose.

- Explain step 2 (review the key idea signals) and then model the step with the same text. Revisit the title, headings, and other key idea signals and point out any signal words or other clues to text structure. For example, you might say, "Let's see . . . OK, the title isn't much help, I don't think, but the first heading mentions a crisis. I wonder if the author will mention some sort of solution to that crisis later on."

- Refer to the learning guide as you explain step 3 (assess organization issues). Emphasize the idea that info-text authors might not always clearly signal their text structure. If you notice issues of this kind in the model text, draw students' attention to them. Otherwise, ask for students' help in identifying ways the author signals their text organization.

- Use the learning guide to introduce step 4 (determine the top-level text structure). Point out that in many texts, authors use one top-level structure to communicate their central idea, but they might organize particular sections or paragraphs using secondary structures. Have students return their attention to the model text. Pose the two questions in the learning guide and field students' responses.

- Once you have introduced students to the strategy steps, give them a digital or paper copy of the "Deep Sense Approach Resource: Determine the Text Structure" reproducible (available at the end of the chapter [page 103] and online at **go.SolutionTree.com/literacy/MDSIT** with use of the unique access code inside the book's front cover). This chart presents diagrams, purposes, signal words, and question stems for the five common text structures. Continue to engage students in this strategy after they have worked through the Preview Texts strategy with new texts, gradually releasing them to work with peers and then independently. Ask them to talk through the steps in pairs or teams and discuss their evidence for a particular top-level structure.

- Continue to show students how to identify the structure of new texts, including poorly organized ones. Talk with students about the author's organizational decisions. Encourage students to consult the two pre-reading strategy learning guides when previewing a new text.

Assessment Suggestions

In this section, I provide key terms and strategic knowledge questions related to the Determine the Text Structure strategy, which you can use to assess students' understanding of key strategy knowledge before, during, and after instruction. It is also important to assess whether they can distinguish among the five common text structures introduced in this chapter. Most importantly, they need to demonstrate that they can successfully apply their knowledge of text structure to identify the author's purpose, recognize key idea signals, and identify the top-level text structure. This challenging strategy will take time for many students to internalize completely. As they face complex texts with unclear text structures, they may continue to struggle to apply their strategy knowledge. Formative assessment lets you know how much support students will need as they apply this strategy with new texts.

- **Key terms:**
  - *Central idea*—The big idea that the author discusses throughout a text
  - *Text structure*—How an author organizes the key ideas and details in the text
  - *Mental map*—A representation of the text in the reader's mind that allows the reader to remember the text's key ideas and how they are organized
  - *Signal words*—Words and phrases in the text that hint at the author's text structure
  - *Top-level text structure*—The main organizing scheme of the text that communicates the central idea
- **Strategic knowledge questions:**
  - Why is it important to identify the top-level text structure of a complex info-text?
  - How can you use text features to help you identify the text structure?
  - What do you need to keep in mind when you are identifying the text structure?
- **Self-assessment:** After practicing this strategy for a while, in combination with the Preview Texts strategy, ask students to reflect on how applying the strategy steps during pre-reading has increased their awareness of text structure as they read. Post a list of the five common text structures, and ask students to reflect on which they find easiest to recognize and which are still difficult to identify. You might ask them to complete a journal entry responding to an open-ended prompt such as, "What do you notice about text structure now that you did not notice before?"
- **Evidence of mastery:** When students have mastered the Determine the Text Structure strategy, you will hear them discussing with peers the clues to text structure they have identified in the key idea signal and important context features. They will be able to successfully identify the author's top-level text structure and explain how they did so. When the top-level structure is unclear, they will be able to narrow down the possibilities and discuss why the structure might be one of these. Their annotations and summaries will reflect the author's top-level structure (this will be discussed more in chapters 9 and 11).

Concluding Thoughts

When students adopt the pre-reading routine outlined in this chapter, their brains will be primed to make deeper sense of the text they read. The three strategies introduced in the next chapter will help them stay focused on understanding as they move into reading the text.

Learning Guide: Preview Texts

Strong readers use a quick *pre-reading routine* before they read info-texts. When you were younger, your teachers might have taught you to *preview* text features like titles and pictures to help you predict what you would learn. Now, it is time to update your pre-reading routine to work with more complex texts.

| 1. **Evaluate text features.** |
| 2. **Activate background knowledge.** |
| 3. **Make a reading plan.** |

- **Why:** It is tempting to skip over text features when we read. However, they are often full of important information. When you preview the text, you can—
  - Tap into what you already know to help you understand new information
  - Get what you need out of what you read
- **When:** Preview the text before reading chapters, articles, and other complex info-texts. You can repeat the steps for each section of a long text. Combine this with the Determine the Text Structure strategy.

Three Types of Text Features

Purpose	Examples
Key Idea Signal (KIS)	
• Highlights the most important ideas • Shows how ideas and information are organized	• Titles, subtitles, headings, and subheadings • Numbered lists, summaries, and content outlines • Font changes, such as **bold** or *italicized* words, highlighting, or changes to font size or color • Layout, color scheme, section breaks, and dividers
Important Context (IC)	
• Helps readers determine the author's purpose • Helps readers evaluate credibility and point of view	• Publication information • Notes from or about the author or publisher • Tables of contents and navigation bars
Added Information (AI)	
• Illustrates and elaborates on key ideas • Points to additional resources	• Photos, illustrations, diagrams, and videos • Maps, infographics, captions, labels, and legends • Sidebars, insets, and footnotes • Hyperlinks, citations, and related articles

Strategy Steps

To make previewing texts part of your pre-reading routine, you can take three steps before reading a new complex info-text such as a scientific article or textbook chapter.

1. Evaluate Text Features

A *text feature* is a visual or text element added to the main text by the author or publisher, such as a title, chart, or caption. A complex info-text might have many text features. Authors and publishers add text features to accomplish the following.

Making Deep Sense of Informational Texts © 2025 Solution Tree Press • SolutionTree.com
Visit **go.SolutionTree.com/literacy/MDSIT** and enter the unique access code found on this book's inside front cover to access this reproducible.

- Grab and keep readers' attention.
- Signal the importance or organization of ideas.
- Illustrate or elaborate on key concepts.
- Provide needed context.
- Include additional information that would interrupt the flow of the main text.

The chart on the previous page defines and gives examples of three types of text features. When you read a complex text, you might not need to study every feature closely. Instead, you can *evaluate*, or judge, which are most useful. Focus first on the *key idea signals* and *important context* features. These will provide an overview of what you can expect from the text. Next, evaluate the *added information* features to decide which ones are relevant (see step 3 for more about this).

> To evaluate text features, ask yourself these questions.
> - Which features seem to highlight key ideas and how they are organized?
> - Which features tell me about who wrote the text and why they wrote it?
> - Which added information is relevant to my reading purpose?
> - Which features are just attention grabbers?

2. Activate Background Knowledge

As you preview the text features, consider your *background knowledge*—what you already know or think that connects with the ideas and information in the text. This will help you learn more from your reading. Even when the topic seems unfamiliar, you can still connect with what you know, think, believe, or wonder.

> To activate your background knowledge, ask yourself these questions.
> - What is this text about? What do I know about this topic or related topics?
> - Why is the topic important or interesting?
> - How does this text connect to my experiences, the world I know about, or other texts I have read?

3. Make a Reading Plan

Before you read a complex info-text, it is helpful to make a *reading plan*, deciding how you will read the text to meet your needs. You might decide to slowly read all the text, from top to bottom. If you know a lot about the topic and just need specific information, you might be able to skip or skim some parts. You might read just the main text, ignoring the added information (like inset boxes or hyperlinked sources), or you might explore some of those features.

If your teacher wants you to read the text in a specific way, you can still think through these questions to get the most out of your reading.

> To make a reading plan, ask yourself these questions.
> - What can I learn from the text?
> - What do I need to know? What do I need to do with what I learn?
> - How will I read the text to meet my needs?

REPRODUCIBLE | 101

Learning Guide: Determine the Text Structure

Text structure is how an author organizes the most important ideas and how those ideas connect with each other. Many informational texts are organized using one of five text structures: (1) *description*, (2) *sequence*, (3) *problem-solution*, (4) *cause-effect*, or (5) *compare-contrast*. You might have learned about text structure before. If so, you might have practiced identifying the structure of short, simple texts. This strategy helps you determine the structure of longer, more complex texts.

1. **Consider the author's purpose.**

2. **Review the key idea signals.**

3. **Assess organization issues.**

4. **Determine the top-level text structure.**

- **Why:** When you recognize the text structure of an info-text, you can build a more accurate *mental map*—how your mind remembers the text's key ideas and how they are organized. When you have a detailed and organized mental map of a text in your memory, you understand the text better and remember more about it later.

- **When:** You pause to determine the top-level text structure after you have previewed the text features. This strategy works best when it is combined with the Preview Texts strategy.

Strategy Steps

To determine the text structure before you read an info-text, follow these four steps.

1. Consider the Author's Purpose

Review the important context features (like the author's note and introduction) to help you determine why the author wrote the text. Then, use the following Possible Purposes for Common Info-Text Structures table to decide which text structure best fits the author's purpose.

Possible Purposes for Common Info-Text Structures

Description	Sequence	Problem-Solution	Cause-Effect	Compare-Contrast
• To provide definitions, facts, details, or examples • To describe characteristics or components	• To present a sequence of events • To describe steps in a process or stages of a cycle • To present an ordered list	• To explain a problem and potential or real solutions • To describe attempts to address the causes of a problem	• To explain causes and effects • To describe a chain reaction	• To describe similarities and differences • To compare two points of view on an issue • To consider benefits and drawbacks • To judge something or to compare features

2. Review the Key Idea Signals

Review the key idea signals (like the title and headings) for *signal words*, like those shown in the following Signal Words for Common Info-Text Structures table. Then scan the text for signal words. If the author uses the signal words only in one part of the text, they may have organized only one section with that structure.

page 1 of 2

Making Deep Sense of Informational Texts © 2025 Solution Tree Press • SolutionTree.com
Visit **go.SolutionTree.com/literacy/MDSIT** and enter the unique access code found on this book's inside front cover to access this reproducible.

Signal Words for Common Info-Text Structures

Description	Sequence	Problem-Solution	Cause-Effect	Compare-Contrast
• Describe, define, definition, facts, detail, example • Attribute, characteristic, quality, feature, property • Component, part • For example, for instance, specifically, such as, particular, namely	• Sequence, order, steps, timeline, stages, list, from _____ to _____ • First, second, initially, preceding, beginning, before • Next, following, after, at a later date • Finally, now, eventually	• Problem, issue, concern, challenge, crisis, decline, threat, risk • Solution, possible, possibility, address, consider, attempt	• Input, contribution, factor • Effect, consequence, result, outcome, product, cause • Because, thus, consequently, as a result • Leads to, produces, is caused by	• **Compare:** Share, same, similar, similarity, compare, comparison, common, commonality, resemble, resemblance • **Contrast:** Different, difference, differentiate, distinct, distinction, distinguish, in contrast, oppose, in opposition, instead, however, alternatively, whereas, despite, although • **Pros and cons:** Benefit, advantage, pro, positive, liability, drawback, disadvantage, negative, con • **Evaluation:** Prefer, more, less, better, worse, superior, inferior

3. Assess Organization Issues

Not all authors use text features and signal words to help readers figure out how they organize their ideas. Some info-text authors don't think much about organizing their ideas as they write, so their texts seem more like conversations. Others might organize their texts according to a different structure related to their genre (such as narrative or essay).

4. Determine the Top-Level Text Structure

Info-text authors often use one *top-level text structure* to communicate their *central idea*—the big idea that they discuss throughout the text. However, they might use a different structure to organize a section. Authors might begin the text with an interesting anecdote to engage the reader. They might interrupt the top-level structure to insert an example or important background information. We have to focus on the big picture.

To determine the top-level text structure, ask yourself these questions.

- How does the author organize the text to communicate their central idea?
- Do they communicate the top-level text structure with key idea signals? With signal words?

Deep Sense Approach Resource: Determine the Text Structure

This chart is designed to be used with the Determine the Text Structure strategy as part of the Deep Sense Approach.

Structure Variations	Possible Purposes	Common Signal Words	Question Stems
Description Entity or Process → Fact or Feature / Fact or Feature / Fact or Feature / Fact or Feature	• To provide definitions, facts, details, or examples • To describe characteristics or components	• Describe, define, definition, facts, detail, example • Attribute, characteristic, quality, feature, property • Component, part • For example, for instance, specifically, such as, particular, namely	• How is _____ defined? • What is an example? • What is _____ like? • What are the characteristics (distinguishing features)? • What are the components (parts)?
Sequence Event 1 → Event 2 → Event 3 Phase 1 → Phase 2 → Phase 3 → Phase 4 (cycle) Step 1 → Step 2 → Step 3 → Step 4	• To present a sequence of events • To describe steps in a process • To describe the stages of a cycle • To present an ordered list	• Sequence, order, steps, timeline, stages, list, from _____ to _____ • First, second, initially, preceding, beginning, before • Next, following, after, at a later date • Finally, now, eventually	• What is the sequence? • What is the order? • In what order did the events occur? • What are the steps in the process? • What are the stages of the cycle?
Problem-Solution Issue or Problem → Solution or Problem Reduction Problem → Solution / Better Solution Problem → Solution → Problem → Solution	• To explain a problem and potential or real solutions • To describe attempts to address the causes of a problem	• Problem, issue, concern, challenge, crisis, decline, threat, risk • Solution, possible, possibility, address, consider, attempt	• What has happened or is happening? • Why is it a problem? What are the consequences? What might happen if nothing is done? • What has been / is being / should be done? Who is trying to solve the problem?

page 1 of 2

Structure Variations	Possible Purposes	Common Signal Words	Question Stems
Cause-Effect Causes → Event or Situation → Effects Cause 1, Cause 2, Cause 3 → Event or Situation → Event or Situation → Effect 1, Effect 2, Effect 3 Initial Cause → Results in ___, Which Causes ___ → Results in ___, Which Causes ___ → Results in ___, Which Causes ___	• To explain the causes and effects • To describe a chain reaction	• Input, contribution, factor • Effect, consequence, result, outcome, product, cause • Because, thus, consequently, as a result • Leads to, produces, is caused by	• What event, situation, or phenomenon has happened or is happening? • Why did it happen? or Why is it happening? • What led to it? • What are the effects or consequences of it?
Compare-Contrast Entity, Option, or Process 1 / Entity, Option, or Process 2 (Venn diagram) Benefits / Drawbacks Standard 1, Standard 2, Standard 3 × Entity, Option, or Process 1 / Entity, Option, or Process 2	• To describe similarities and differences • To compare two points of view on an issue • To consider benefits and drawbacks • To judge something or to compare features	• **Comparison:** Share, same, similar, similarity, compare, comparison, common, commonality, resemble, resemblance • **Contrast:** Different, difference, differentiate, distinct, distinction, distinguish, in contrast, oppose, in opposition, instead, however, alternatively, whereas, despite, although • **Pros and cons:** Benefit, advantage, pro, positive, liability, drawback, disadvantage, negative, con • **Evaluation:** Prefer, more, less, better, worse, superior, inferior	• What is being compared? • How are _____ and _____ similar? • How are _____ and _____ different? • Which is better or more effective? • What are the pros and cons?

CHAPTER 9
Read Actively

Strategies in This Chapter

- Annotate Texts
- Check for Understanding
- Fix Confusion and Fill Gaps

In chapter 2 (page 19), I shared a definition of reading comprehension as a dynamic, active, and complex cognitive process. Students must slow down their reading process to engage actively, meaning teachers must also slow down and make time for students to pause, think, make notes, reread, look up information, and ask peers for their perspectives. Students can make deeper meaning of complex info-texts when they internalize this slower, effortful process.

Building on the metacognitive and discourse strategies introduced in chapter 7 (page 71) and the pre-reading strategies discussed in chapter 8 (page 85), this chapter introduces three strategies that work together to help students engage actively in their reading: (1) Annotate Texts, (2) Check for Understanding, and (3) Fix Confusion and Fill Gaps. When students use this trio of strategies, they interact physically and mentally with the text, assess their comprehension, and take action when they do not understand. Learning guides and instructional materials for all three strategies are available at the end of this chapter and online. (Visit **go.SolutionTree.com/literacy/MDSIT** and enter the unique code found on the inside front cover of this book to access these materials.)

The Annotate Texts Strategy

Annotation is one of the most useful strategies I teach my students because it can:

- Help readers actively engage with the text as they decide what to underline, when to jot a margin note, and how much to write
- Reveal to readers at what point in the text they disengaged or stopped understanding
- Leave behind a thought trail that students can return to as they prepare for a class discussion, write a summary, or answer a text-based question

Research confirms that annotation can improve comprehension when done thoughtfully (Castek & Beach, 2013; Fisher & Frey, 2019; Mariage, Englert, & Mariage, 2019; Zywica & Gomez, 2008). It is also a powerful "meta-strategy" that helps readers apply other strategies.

Annotation helps teachers, too. Because adolescents often mask their reading difficulties, a teacher might not notice a problem until they read a student's annotations. When a reader struggles to make sense of a text, their underlining often becomes random or sparse, and their margin notes begin to parrot the text.

Unfortunately, many secondary students express a strong negative view of annotation. They see it as an unnecessary school task imposed by teachers or even administrators, often as a formulaic test-taking strategy (Davis & Wilson, 2015). When required to annotate, teenage students can do so mechanically, without much thought. When they take a comprehension test away from their teachers' view, they might forgo the strategy altogether.

In response to students' resistance, I have adapted my approach to annotation over time. Students are often wary at first, but once they get the hang of this streamlined, flexible strategy, they often adopt it as their own.

The following sections detail steps for this strategy, guidance for teaching the strategy, and several suggestions to support assessment.

The Strategy Steps

The Annotate Texts strategy focuses less on how students mark and notate the text and more on the active thinking behind these actions. Students learn that *annotation* consists of capturing thoughts as one reads by adding marks and notes to a text. They then learn a few guidelines to help them get the most out of their annotating. The "Learning Guide: Annotate Texts" reproducible (page 115) includes examples of handwritten and digital annotation.

1. **Mark the text selectively as you read:** In this step, students learn to mark the text as they read to help them avoid going on autopilot. They underline or highlight *selectively*, choosing the important words and phrases rather than whole sentences (unless capturing a quote).

2. **Jot quick notes to capture your thinking:** Students learn to pause briefly to add quick notes to the text, documenting their thinking in a margin note or digital comment. These notes go beyond paraphrasing the text; students can add notes whenever they have an important connection, realization, or question. The learning guide offers students helpful sentence stems to jump-start their note making.

3. **Adjust annotation to fit your purpose:** This step emphasizes the flexibility of the annotation strategy. Students can take an all-purpose approach, marking important words and phrases and noting their thoughts, insights, and questions. But they can also more precisely target their underlining and note making as they annotate for specific purposes. For example, as they reread an article, they might mark evidence the author introduced to support a claim or details that help them answer a particular question. Students learn to vary their tools and techniques depending on their purpose for annotation. They can adjust the "thickness" of their annotations depending on how important the portion of text is to their reading purpose. Over time, students develop a sense of ownership over annotation as they decide how much and how they will annotate based on their reading purpose, their background knowledge, and the difficulty and format of the text.

How to Teach the Strategy

The following recommendations can help you present this updated annotation strategy to students who might have preconceived notions and habits.

- As you introduce the strategy using the "Learning Guide: Annotate Texts" reproducible, solicit and acknowledge students' views and experiences before beginning strategy instruction. If they express doubt or unwillingness, reassure them that this strategy is designed to help them make sense of difficult texts and use the information later. It can take a few rounds for students to buy into the updated approach.

- Walk students through the steps using the learning guide. When you introduce step 2 (jot quick notes to capture your thinking), point out the helpful annotation stems that students can use to begin their margin notes. Explain that when they are unsure about what to write, the stems can help prompt their thinking. These stems are especially useful when students are used to surface paraphrasing. Refer to the handwritten and digital annotation examples in the learning guide, pointing out how each step has been applied.

- With a text students have not yet read, model selectively marking up the text and making quick margin notes, thinking aloud as you go. Refer to the step 2 annotation stems and compose a note using one of the stems.

- Have students imitate your annotations on their copy of the text and then continue annotating the next section as they read. Circulate as they work, reviewing students' annotation efforts as they practice. (See the list of annotation habits later in this section.) You might need to pull the whole class back together to provide general feedback and then model again. If most students successfully apply the strategy, you can work with a small group or pause to work with individual students as you circulate.

- When a student has particular difficulties with this strategy, I find it helpful to annotate a passage alongside them, narrating my decisions. You can also have them look with you at a completed model and discuss what they notice. Students unused to metacognitive thinking might struggle at first to decide what to write. To scaffold note making, prompt them to use the step 2 annotation stems. As additional scaffolding, students might work with shoulder partners to decide what to annotate or to share their independent annotations with their team members.

- As the class engages with new texts, you can have students code their annotations using different colors or symbols to indicate different focuses. For example, you might have them mark surprising information with an exclamation point, key ideas with a star, and unclear ideas with a question mark. They might also vary their marks, such as circling unfamiliar vocabulary and double-underlining sentences that express key ideas.

- When students work with digital texts, have them use whatever tools are available to help them annotate. Web-based platforms designed for students often have point-of-use tools built in, such as highlighter and sticky note tools. You can import a text into a web-based platform like Kami (https://kamiapp.com) or Actively Learn (https://activelylearn.com). You can also experiment with browser add-ons like Diigo (https://diigo.com). See the Digital Resources guide (available at **go.SolutionTree.com/literacy/MDSIT**) for links to these and other tools and platforms.

- Continue to give students feedback on their annotations and coach as needed. Because students have so much previous experience with annotation, they can easily fall back into old methods. You can refer students to this strategy's learning guide or post an anchor chart to remind them of the strategy steps. Students commonly fall into the following habits.
  - *Annotation after reading*—Many students are in the habit of setting down their writing instruments and reading without annotating. Encourage them to keep their writing instrument in hand, marking and noting as they go.
  - *Thin annotations*—Students might have difficulty discerning the relative importance of ideas, or they might be sampling. You might share your annotations for a passage they under-annotated, explain your decisions, and ask them about theirs.
  - *Over-annotation*—Some students spend so long composing margin notes that they lose track of their reading or run out of time. Encourage them to be quick, brief, and even messy if needed.
  - *Parroting*—If a student's annotations just echo the text, work with the student one-on-one, explaining that you are most interested in their thoughts. If they continue to struggle to capture their thinking as they annotate, it can be a sign of a deeper comprehension issue. Check with colleagues and campus leadership team members to see if the student has an identified learning or language need. If not, this might be a sign that the team needs to initiate a response to intervention (RTI) process.
- Discussing annotations in pairs, teams, or whole classes can become a regular feature of your info-text studies throughout the year.

Assessment Suggestions

In this section, I first list key terms and questions to help you assess students' strategy knowledge. I also suggest how you might prompt students to reflect on their strategy uptake. Finally, to help you assess their success in applying the strategy while they read, I describe what to look for when you observe students as they annotate and review their annotations.

- **Key terms:**
  - *Annotating*—Capturing thoughts as one reads by adding marks and notes to a text
  - *Marking selectively*—Underlining or highlighting only the most important words and phrases
  - *Margin note*—A short note made in the white space of a text
- **Strategic knowledge questions:**
  - Why is it important to annotate as you read a complex info-text?
  - What are the components of annotation?
  - What do you need to keep in mind as you annotate?
  - How can you adapt annotation to meet your needs?
- **Self-assessment:** Once students have practiced using the strategy with a variety of texts, prompt them to reflect on how their thinking and practice have changed. You can ask them to complete the frame, "When it comes to annotation, I used to think _____, but now I think _____. When I used to annotate, I _____, but now I _____. It makes a difference because _____."

- **Evidence of mastery:** When students have mastered the Annotate Texts strategy, you will observe them quickly marking the text and making notes as they read. When you review their annotations, you will see evidence of their efforts to make sense of the text. They will have been selective in marking key ideas and information. Their comments and questions will reveal connections and insights. They will note points of confusion and how they worked to resolve them.

The Check for Understanding Strategy

Many secondary students do not consciously check for understanding as they read, absent a teacher's probes or the embedded questions in platforms like Newsela (https://newsela.com) and CommonLit (https://commonlit.org). Students can assess their comprehension by pausing and looking away from the text to paraphrase or self-question (Atwell, 1990). At first, they are often surprised to discover how little they recall about what they just read.

Studies have confirmed that monitoring one's understanding of text is essential for comprehension (Barth & Elleman, 2017). When readers check for understanding, they:

- Notice when and where they stopped making sense of the text
- Consolidate information so they can remember it later

The Check for Understanding strategy is a flexible approach to comprehension monitoring that students can use whenever they read a challenging text. It is intended as a companion to the Fix Confusion and Fill Gaps strategy, introduced later in this chapter.

The following sections detail steps for this strategy, guidance for teaching the strategy, and several suggestions to support assessment.

The Strategy Steps

The metacognitive work of checking for understanding can seem very mysterious for students who are still learning to harness their thoughts as they read. These four steps are designed to take the mystery out of this important strategy.

1. **Pause to paraphrase the gist:** In this step, students learn to regularly pause, look away from the text, and try to paraphrase the gist of the portion they just read using their inner voice. The learning guide gives students simple definitions of *paraphrase* (to state in your own words) and *gist* (the main point the author is making).

2. **Find the gaps:** This step prompts students to ask themselves the *reporter questions* (Who?, What?, When?, Where?, Why?, and How?) to narrow down what they do not understand. Students learn to look away from the text while answering their questions. They might not have noticed or remembered a detail, or the author might not have given that detail yet.

3. **Return to fill in details:** Next, students are prompted to return to the passage, rereading to identify the missing details. They then repeat step 1, again paraphrasing the gist.

4. **Note what you still need to know:** Finally, students are encouraged to note what they are still unclear about and what they still need to know. From this point, they move on to the Fix Confusion and Fill Gaps strategy.

How to Teach the Strategy

Consider the following suggestions as you plan to teach the Check for Understanding strategy.

- Before introducing the strategy, ask students to write a private response to the prompt, "When you read an article, webpage, or textbook chapter, are you aware of pausing to check for understanding? What do you do to make sure you are making sense of what you read?" Review students' responses to assess their awareness of checking for understanding.

- In light of what you learn, use the "Learning Guide: Check for Understanding" reproducible (page 117) to introduce the strategy. Quickly explain the strategy steps and check students' understanding of key terms.

- After introducing the strategy, you might walk students through the reproducible titled "An Example: How You Might Check for Understanding as You Read" (page 118) to provide a model of the strategy steps. The example references the Childress (2023) article introduced in figure 8.3 (page 88). If students have not been introduced to the article excerpt included in the "Learning Guide: Annotate Texts" reproducible, you can access the article electronically (https://theconversation.com/the-heroic-effort-to-save-floridas-coral-reef-from-extreme-ocean-heat-as-corals-bleach-across-the-caribbean-210974). Or you can model with any text you choose, narrating your thinking as demonstrated in the example.

- Once students are familiar with the strategy steps, you can have them practice with any text they haven't already read closely.

  - To practice step 1 (pause to paraphrase the gist), pause the class after they have begun annotating. Ask students to look away from the text and paraphrase the gist of the section they just read. You might have them do this verbally with partners before having them write their gist statements. Then, prompt them to work through the remaining steps.

  - To practice step 2 (find the gaps), have students pause after reading a section of the text and work with a partner to ask and answer the reporter questions.

  - After students complete step 4 (note what you still need to know), ask them to share with a partner what they recorded, and then debrief with the whole class, recording points of confusion and questions to which they still want the answers. (You will take up these questions again when the class practices the Fix Confusion and Fill Gaps strategy.)

- Until students are able to use the strategy independently, continue to prompt them to paraphrase, self-question, reread, and make note of what is still unclear as they read complex new texts. Encourage them to note their questions and confusion in their margin notes as they annotate. You might have them review this strategy's learning guide before they tackle a difficult new text or post an anchor chart with the steps.

- Keep in mind that highly proficient readers might think this strategy is unnecessary for them. They check for understanding so habitually that they are unaware of it. They might have few knowledge gaps and points of confusion to address. Privately explain to them that they are indeed using this strategy, but that they are so proficient in it they do it unconsciously. Ask if they encounter texts in any of their classes or online that are difficult to make sense of. If they acknowledge this, explain that these steps can help them with those texts.

Assessment Suggestions

In this section, I first provide key terms and questions to help you assess students' knowledge of the strategy. Then I make suggestions for helping students practice metacognition by self-assessing their strategy knowledge and use. Finally, I share signs that tell you students are mastering the strategy.

- **Key terms:**
  - *Check for understanding*—To pause while reading to paraphrase or self-question and assess how well one understood a text
  - *Paraphrase*—To state in one's own words
  - *Gist*—The main point the author is making
  - *Reporter questions*—A set of questions associated with journalism (Who?, What?, When?, Where?, Why?, and How?)
- **Strategic knowledge questions:**
  - Why is it important to check for understanding as you read?
  - Why is it important to look away from the text as you paraphrase the gist and ask yourself questions?
  - How does it help to ask yourself the reporter questions after you read a section?
  - What should you do when you realize you don't understand or know something mentioned in the passage?
- **Self-assessment:** You might observe students as they read a difficult section of a new text and then have them reflect on how they applied the strategy steps. After practicing the strategy with several texts, you can ask students to discuss or write about how paraphrasing and self-questioning have helped them understand what they read.
- **Evidence of mastery:** When students have mastered the Check for Understanding strategy, they will look away from the text, pausing to paraphrase and self-question. They will be able to accurately paraphrase a section of the text or answer the reporter questions. They will be able to pinpoint which questions they couldn't answer. Their annotations will include questions and comments specifically indicating what they do not know or understand.

The Fix Confusion and Fill Gaps Strategy

When readers pause to make margin notes or paraphrase the gist, they might realize they didn't really understand the text. They might not know the meaning of a term or be able to decipher a long, complicated sentence. They might not know about an event or concept that is mentioned in the text.

Strong comprehenders take action to address their confusion and gaps in their background knowledge when those affect their comprehension of key ideas. Defining every term and tracking down information about every unknown place, person, event, and idea would be impractical. So, based on their reading purpose, they decide whether to take immediate action, wait until later, or ignore the issue altogether.

Then, they decide what action to take. They might go back into the text to see if they missed a definition, reference, or explanation. When they realize they tuned out of a passage, they might reread just that section, annotating more intentionally. If the text does not yield an answer, they might ask a colleague for their insight or use a search engine to learn more (Botsas, 2017; Denton et al., 2015).

Readers who fix confusion and fill gaps:

- Build more detailed and accurate mental maps
- Carry their newfound word and world knowledge into future reading

Students might be unaware that the information they need is in the text. Many students learned in elementary school to look for context clues in the paragraph where they encountered a confusing word or detail. Years later, they might look no further for text-based information. The farther away the clue is from the point in the text that confused them, the less likely they will connect the dots (van der Schoot et al., 2012). Readers who struggle with comprehension also miss clues hiding in plain sight in inset boxes, charts, and other text features. Sometimes, the information a reader needs is not provided in the text. The author might have left out a definition, explanation, illustration, or context because they assumed the reader would already know.

Numerous studies have confirmed that background knowledge is critical to comprehension (Smith et al., 2021). Vocabulary instruction remains important across the disciplines in the secondary grades, but students encounter many more words and concepts than their teachers can preteach. They need to be able to build their own background knowledge when they need it.

Readers often have access to resources beyond the text that can help fill gaps in their background knowledge, but they might not think to use them. Even if dictionaries and other resources are available, teenage students might worry that their teachers and peers might judge them if they admit they don't know a word or fact. It takes coaching for students to consistently use these resources when they need them. Even when reading on an online platform with many point-of-use features (such as hyperlinked explanations and pop-up definitions), students might ignore the tools without practice and reminders.

The following sections detail steps for this strategy, guidance for teaching the strategy, and several suggestions to support assessment.

The Strategy Steps

Once students have applied the steps of the Check for Understanding strategy, they are ready to take action to fix their confusion and fill their knowledge gaps. These three strategy steps help them do this methodically.

1. **Decide when to make a repair:** In the last step of the Check for Understanding strategy (note what you still need to know), students noted details where they still lack clarity and need clarification. Now, they reflect on their reading purpose to decide whether and when to make a repair. They might decide to stop and immediately make the repair, wait until they have finished reading the section or the whole text, or not make the repair at all.

2. **Consult the text for clues:** This step prompts students to return to the text to answer their open questions. In the "Learning Guide: Fix Confusion and Fill Gaps" reproducible (page 119), they learn that a *context clue* is a hint within a sentence,

paragraph, or passage that helps define or explain something the author mentions in the text. They are introduced to context clues they might not have considered before, such as hyperlinks and cause-effect relationships. They learn that they might find a context clue several paragraphs away or in a text feature.

3. **Fill knowledge gaps:** When students determine that the information they need is not in the text, this step encourages them to use available resources, such as looking up information or consulting with a knowledgeable peer.

How to Teach the Strategy

The following suggestions will help you ensure that your students successfully take up the Fix Confusion and Fill Gaps strategy.

- Use the "Learning Guide: Fix Confusion and Fill Gaps" reproducible to introduce the strategy and walk students through the steps. Then guide them through practice with a text they have already previewed and annotated.

  - To practice step 1 (decide when to make a repair), you can review the reading purpose for the text—that is, what they need to know and what they will do with the information they glean. Then, have them work in teams or pairs to discuss their questions, section by section, and decide whether and when to make a repair. As you debrief their work, note students' questions and points of confusion.

  - To practice step 2 (consult the text for clues), you might draw students' attention to context clues they missed and discuss how and why the author placed the information where they did. Remind students that context clues might be found in text features or several paragraphs away from the detail they are trying to figure out. Then, have students continue to work in teams or pairs to review the text for other context clues. As you debrief with the class, identify information no one could find in the text.

  - To practice step 3 (fill knowledge gaps), you can invite the class to use a search engine to look up an unfamiliar concept, detail, or term mentioned in the text and share what they find. You might provide a few links to get them started on a mini-inquiry into an unfamiliar topic and then share their notes with the class. You can use a digital tool like Pear Deck to collect students' notes and then share them with the class.

- If a definition is nowhere to be found in an article, it can be frustrating for students to hunt in the haystack for a nonexistent needle. When you preview and annotate the text as part of your planning process, be sure to make note of missing information, confusing syntax, hard-to-find context clues, and words students are unlikely to know.

- You can share what you noticed as you work with students to preview and read the text. This can lead to a valuable discussion about the fallibility of info-text authors and the need to critically evaluate information. (Students learn more about this in the Evaluate Evidence strategy introduced in chapter 10, page 127.)

Assessment Suggestions

In this section, you will find key terms and questions to help you assess students' strategy knowledge, suggestions for students' self-assessment of the strategy, and evidence you can look for to know students can successfully use the strategy.

- **Key terms:**
    - *Meaning repair*—An action to address a point of confusion or fill a gap in background knowledge
    - *Context clue*—A hint within a sentence, paragraph, or passage that helps define or explain something the author mentions in the text (Check to make sure students can recognize examples of the context clues mentioned in the "Learning Guide: Fix Confusion and Fill Gaps" reproducible.)
- **Strategic knowledge questions:**
    - Why is it important for you to fix your confusion and fill knowledge gaps when you read?
    - What are some examples of context clues you might find as you read a complex text?
    - What do you need to keep in mind as you review the text to look for context clues?
    - What are some ways you can fill knowledge gaps from outside the text?
    - How do the Check for Understanding and Fix Confusion and Fill Gaps strategies work together?
- **Self-Assessment:** After students have learned and practiced this strategy, ask them to reflect on their use of the strategy with a new complex text. They can discuss with a partner or write a journal entry about how they approached addressing confusing points in the text and acquiring needed background knowledge.
- **Evidence of mastery:** When students have mastered the Fix Confusion and Fill Gaps strategy, you will observe them taking action as or after they read. They might ask to use a dictionary or look up something online. They might ask a peer what they know about a particular detail. You will see them flipping back through the text. They will be able to tell you what confused them in the text and what action they took. They will also be able to tell you about context clues that helped them understand something they were initially confused about. When you ask what information they still need, they will be able to tell you specifically.

Concluding Thoughts

The seven Deep Sense Approach strategies introduced so far are foundational, arming readers with the tools they need to construct an accurate mental map of a complex info-text. The next seven strategies help students apply and consolidate what they have learned from their reading. In chapter 10, I present four strategies students can use to analyze and evaluate argumentative texts. Then in chapter 11, I offer three strategies students can use to consolidate, synthesize, and share what they have learned.

| REPRODUCIBLE | 115 |

Learning Guide: Annotate Texts

Annotation is an essential tool as we read longer and more complex texts. College students and professionals annotate to help them understand and remember what they read. Many adults print out digital texts so they can annotate them. Apps and web-based platforms often include ways for us to annotate digital texts.

1. Mark the text selectively as you read.

2. Jot quick notes to capture your thinking.

3. Adjust annotation to fit your purpose.

To *annotate* is to capture thoughts as you read by adding marks and notes to a text.

- **Why:** The Annotate Texts strategy can help you stay focused on thinking about the text. It helps you pay closer attention to ideas as you read. Annotating helps you apply other Deep Sense strategies, too. After you read, you can return to your annotations to identify relevant text evidence, write summaries, and answer text-based questions.

- **When:** Annotate when you need to understand ideas and information in a complex info-text. Mark up the text and make notes as you read to help keep your mind focused. Add to your annotations as you continue to work with the text. Revisit your annotations as you complete text-based tasks.

Strategy Steps

Annotation is a powerful tool if your mind is actively involved. A few simple steps have helped many students get more out of annotating.

1. Mark the Text Selectively as You Read

It works best to mark the text by underlining or highlighting *as* you read (not after). With printed texts, it helps to hold your pen or pencil in your hand, underlining as you read. When you read digital texts, you can hover your cursor over the text and highlight it as you go.

Be *selective*, marking only important words and phrases, unless you want to capture a quote. If you begin underlining whole sentences or skipping whole paragraphs, reread that paragraph or section and mark more selectively.

2. Jot Quick Notes to Capture Your Thinking

Pause briefly to make quick *margin notes* or add a digital comment as you read. Do not just restate the text. Capture your thoughts, questions, insights, and connections.

Annotation Stems for Making Margin Notes

- "I think this means . . ."
- "Does this mean . . . ?"
- "This makes me think . . ."

- "This connects with . . ."
- "How is this connected to . . . ?"
- "I wonder if/why/how . . ."

Use the following example annotation as a guide.

page 1 of 2

Making Deep Sense of Informational Texts © 2025 Solution Tree Press • SolutionTree.com
Visit **go.SolutionTree.com/literacy/MDSIT** and enter the unique access code found on this book's inside front cover to access this reproducible.

116 | **REPRODUCIBLE**

> **Sample Print Annotation**
>
> *, Check where this is.* 2023
>
> Armed with scrub brushes, young scuba divers took to the waters of <u>Florida's Alligator Reef</u> in late July to <u>try to</u>
> *unusual*
> <u>help corals</u> struggling to survive 2023's <u>extraordinary marine heat wave</u>. They carefully scraped away <u>harmful</u>
> <u>algae</u> and <u>predators</u> impinging on <u>staghorn fragments</u>, under the supervision and training of interns from
> Islamorada <u>Conservation</u> and <u>Restoration</u> Education, or <u>I.CARE</u>. *Why are they scraping off algae?*
>
> *This is unusual.*
> *moving*
> <u>Normally</u>, I.CARE's <u>volunteer divers</u> would be <u>transplanting corals to</u> waters off the Florida Keys this time of
> *put back*
> year, as <u>part of a national effort</u> to <u>restore the Florida Reef</u>. <u>But this year, everything is going in reverse.</u>
>
> *I think he means they are usually moving corals to the reef to replace old ones? So now they're moving corals from the reef?*
>
> As <u>water temperatures spiked</u> in the <u>Florida Keys</u>, <u>scientists</u> from universities, <u>coral reef restoration groups</u>
> and <u>government agencies</u> launched a <u>heroic effort to save the corals</u>. Divers have been in the water every day,
> <u>collecting thousands of corals</u> from <u>ocean nurseries</u> along the Florida Keys reef tract and <u>moving them</u> to <u>cooler</u>
> <u>water</u> and into <u>giant tanks</u> on land. *` For baby corals?* *` Ok, so the heat is killing the new corals in the Florida reef.*

Source: Childress, M. (2023, August 9). The heroic effort to save Florida's coral reef from extreme ocean heat as corals bleach across the Caribbean. The Conversation. Accessed at https://theconversation.com/the-heroic-effort-to-save-floridas-coral-reef-from-extreme-ocean-heat-as-corals-bleach-across-the-caribbean-210974 on August 18, 2024.

3. Adjust Annotation to Fit Your Purpose

You can focus your annotations to help you with a specific task. For example, imagine you are rereading an article to identify the evidence the author gave to support their claim. You might double-underline the examples, quotes, and statistics the author included and focus your margin notes on how those pieces of evidence support the claim.

Adapt the strategy to meet your style and needs. Try color-coding or using symbols. Experiment with using different tools to annotate digital texts. When you cannot mark up a text, try making quick notes on a digital or paper sticky note as you read.

> **Sample Digital Annotation**
>
> Armed with scrub brushes, <u>young scuba divers</u> took to the waters of Florida's Alligator Reef in late July to try to help corals
> struggling to survive 2023's extraordinary marine heat wave. They carefully scraped away harmful algae and predators
> impinging on staghorn fragments,
>
> 📝
> A kind of coral?
>
> 📝
> How will this save the coral from the heat?

Source: Childress, M. (2023, August 9). The heroic effort to save Florida's coral reef from extreme ocean heat as corals bleach across the Caribbean. The Conversation. Accessed at https://theconversation.com/the-heroic-effort-to-save-floridas-coral-reef-from-extreme-ocean-heat-as-corals-bleach-across-the-caribbean-210974 on August 18, 2024.

Decide: Should my annotations be thick or thin? When you read a section that you need to understand thoroughly, you might mark more and make more or longer notes. You might annotate more lightly if you are already very knowledgeable about the topic, are reading just for background information, or are looking for particular information.

page 2 of 2

Making Deep Sense of Informational Texts © 2025 Solution Tree Press • SolutionTree.com
Visit **go.SolutionTree.com/literacy/MDSIT** and enter the unique access code found on this book's inside front cover to access this reproducible.

Learning Guide: Check for Understanding

We can easily get lost in all the words and details when we read challenging articles, chapters, and other info-texts. It helps to pause often to *check for understanding*.

We check for understanding by using our inner voice to try to remember the author's main point. We ask ourselves questions to see what we missed and return to the text for more details. Finally, we make note of what we still need to know.

| 1. Pause to paraphrase the gist. |
| 2. Find the gaps. |
| 3. Return to fill in details. |
| 4. Note what you still need to know. |

- **Why:** Checking for understanding helps you keep your mind focused as you read. It also helps you notice when and where you stopped making sense of the text. When you check for understanding, your comprehension of the text improves.
- **When:** Pause to ask yourself questions and paraphrase the gist as you read. As you annotate, mark words or details you don't understand and jot down your questions. This strategy pairs with the Fix Confusion and Fill Gaps strategy.

Strategy Steps

You can take four steps to check for understanding as you read.

1. Pause to Paraphrase the Gist

Pause regularly (maybe after several paragraphs or at the end of each section) to see what you can remember. Look away from the text and try to paraphrase the gist of that portion in your own words. Use your inner voice as if you are talking to a friend.

Key Terms
- To *paraphrase* means to state in your own words.
- The *gist* is the author's main point in that portion of the text.

To paraphrase the gist, ask yourself this question.
- What was this section mostly about?

2. Find the Gaps

Still looking away from the text, ask yourself the *reporter questions*. Notice which details you are missing. You might not have noticed the detail as you read, you might not remember it, or the author might not have provided that detail.

To find the gaps, ask the reporter questions.
- Who?
- When?
- Why?
- What?
- Where?
- How?

3. Return to Fill in Details

Reread or skim the passage to identify the key details you are missing. Then, look away to paraphrase the gist again, filling in the details you found.

4. Note What You Still Need to Know

Add an annotation or write in your notes to track what was unclear and what you still need to know. Return to these questions after you finish reading the whole text or when you make a repair. (In the learning guide for the Fix Confusion and Fill Gaps strategy, you will find suggestions for making meaning repairs.)

To note what you still need to know, ask yourself these questions.
- What am I unclear about?
- What do I still need to know?

Making Deep Sense of Informational Texts © 2025 Solution Tree Press • SolutionTree.com
Visit **go.SolutionTree.com/literacy/MDSIT** and enter the unique access code found on this book's inside front cover to access this reproducible.

An Example: How You Might Check for Understanding as You Read

Now that you have learned the four steps of the Check for Understanding strategy, this example will help you see how to apply the steps. Imagine you are checking for understanding as you read the first few paragraphs of an article about coral bleaching.

Step 1: Pause to Paraphrase the Gist

- You pause to look away from the text and ask yourself, "OK, so what was this section mostly about?"

- Next, you use your inner voice to paraphrase the gist, saying in your mind, "OK . . . this first section mainly says that volunteer divers used to move corals to somewhere, but now people are moving the corals away from there to cooler places."

Step 2: Find the Gaps

- You ask yourself the reporter questions and realize you don't remember some details. You think, "I can't remember *where* they were talking about. I also can't remember *who* was moving the corals. Was it the divers they mentioned or someone else? And *why* are they moving them?"

Step 3: Return to Fill In Details

- You return to review the text and fill in the missing details. As you read, you think, "Oh yeah, it's about Florida . . . the Alligator Reef. And later, they say the Florida Keys. It talked about volunteer divers moving the corals—both ways. And they mentioned an organization called I.CARE. I guess this is one of the coral reef restoration groups they mentioned. But they also listed university scientists and government agencies. I wonder who they are."

- You look away and try to paraphrase the gist again: "OK, so this first section mainly says that volunteer divers used to move corals to the Florida reef, but when the Florida water got hot, scientists, restoration groups, and government agencies moved the corals away from there to cooler water and tanks on the land."

Step 4: Note What You Still Need to Know

- You think through what you still don't understand: "I still don't know why the water got so hot. Where is the Alligator Reef, and what are the Florida Keys? I'm not sure which scientists and agencies were involved. I wonder if I.CARE is the only group helping. I don't know why the divers were scraping off algae. Didn't it say they were moving them?"

- You add to your annotations, circling unclear details and writing quick questions.

Learning Guide: Fix Confusion and Fill Gaps

When we annotate and check for understanding as we read, we might realize that we do not know the meaning of a word or we are confused about something the author said. When this happens, it is important to make a *meaning repair*—taking an action to fix our confusion and fill gaps in our background knowledge.

> **1. Decide when to make a repair.**
>
> **2. Consult the text for clues.**
>
> **3. Fill knowledge gaps.**

- **Why:** By fixing confusion and filling knowledge gaps, you will understand the text more deeply and build knowledge you can use later.

- **When:** Use the Fix Confusion and Fill Gaps strategy while you are reading or after you finish reading. It is especially important when you need to deeply understand a text. This strategy is a companion to the Check for Understanding strategy.

Strategy Steps

When you check for understanding as you read, you might find some details confusing or realize there are things you do not know. You can fix your confusion and fill those gaps by taking three simple steps.

1. Decide When to Make a Repair

When you realize you don't understand something, decide whether and when to make a repair. Think about your reading plan and what you need to learn from the text. Ask yourself how important the unfamiliar word, detail, or idea is to your understanding.

You can decide to stop and immediately make the repair, wait until you have finished a section or the whole text, or not make the repair at all.

> To decide when to make a repair, ask yourself these questions.
>
> - How important is this to my understanding?
>
> - Do I need to stop and figure this out now? Do I wait until I have finished the section or the whole text? Do I skip it?

2. Consult the Text for Clues

When you want to figure out an unfamiliar detail or confusing concept, the first place to look is in the text.

Sometimes, authors leave out information. They assume that the reader already knows the meaning of a term or is familiar with an event, person, place, or idea. But often, authors provide a *context clue*—a hint within a sentence, paragraph, or passage that helps define or explain something they mention in the text.

You might discover these context clues close to the unfamiliar word or detail, even in the same sentence. However, the information might be several paragraphs away or in a text feature.

To identify context clues, you might find it helpful to:

- Check your annotations to identify a section you need to reread more carefully

- Review the text features to see if you missed any clues

- Scan the text for related words

> When you consult the text for context clues, ask yourself these questions.
>
> - Did I miss a context clue?
>
> - Would it help to do any of the following?
>   - Reread a section.
>   - Review the text features.
>   - Scan for related words.

page 1 of 2

Making Deep Sense of Informational Texts © 2025 Solution Tree Press • SolutionTree.com
Visit **go.SolutionTree.com/literacy/MDSIT** and enter the unique access code found on this book's inside front cover to access this reproducible.

Types of Context Clues

Authors use context clues like the following.

- A brief explanation or definition
- An example (*like, such as, include*)
- A synonym (similar meaning) or paraphrase
- An antonym (opposite meaning) or contrast (*but, however, although*)
- A comparison
- A cause-effect relationship (*because, so, therefore, thus*)
- A hyperlink or footnote
- Information in an index or glossary

3. Fill Knowledge Gaps

If you consulted the text but did not find the information you need, you might be able to use available resources outside the text. Decide what you need to know and where you might find the information you need.

Once you have decided which resource to consult, it is time to take action to fill your knowledge gaps.

> To fill knowledge gaps, ask yourself these questions.
> - What do I need to know more about?
> - How can I get the information? Might I do one of the following?
>   - Look up a word.
>   - Consult another text.
>   - Ask someone.

- **Look up a word:** You might look up a word in a dictionary or search for it online. Some digital texts allow you to click on the word for a definition. Read through the definitions to make sure you choose the one that makes the most sense. Jot the definition in the margin or in your notes.

- **Consult another text:** If you don't recognize a concept, event, or person mentioned in the text, you can consult other texts or search for more information online. With most websites and digital texts, you can use the CTRL+F function to find all the mentions of a word or phrase.

- **Ask someone:** Finally, you can consult with an adult (such as a teacher, family member, or librarian) or knowledgeable peer to ask what they might know. Even if they do not know the answer, they might suggest a source you had not considered.

CHAPTER 10
Evaluate Arguments and Evidence

Strategies in This Chapter

- Trace the Reasoning
- Consider Perspectives
- Evaluate Evidence
- Analyze Rhetoric

Writers, speakers, and other content creators introduce arguments in a broad range of info-text genres and formats that touch on every academic discipline and are pervasive in adolescent students' lives outside of school as well (American Institutes for Research, 2017).

This chapter focuses on making deeper sense of evidence-based *arguments*—written or oral presentations that make a case for a specific position with reasoning and evidence (Newell, Beach, Smith, & VanDerHeide, 2011). Throughout the chapter, I use the word *text* to refer to traditional written texts and visual, audio, and multimedia texts. Regardless of the medium, I refer to the *author* or *writer* as shorthand for content creators. Writers introduce arguments in books, essays, columns, articles, letters, sermons, reports, and social media posts. Politicians, other public figures, and experts in various fields make speeches and presentations. Documentary filmmakers and podcasters often use their mediums to make arguments.

Because expository and argumentative texts can have similar structures and use many of the same elements, teenage students might not recognize arguments presented subtly in the guise of exposition. The arguments they see play out on social media are rarely subtle. Instead of reasoning and evidence, these disputes are often driven by intolerance, loaded language, and either-or thinking. Students who are not adept at evaluating such arguments can be swayed by manipulative language and flawed logic.

Across all academic disciplines and in their personal lives, students benefit from being able to:

- Recognize when an author moves from exposition to argumentation
- Trace an author's claims, reasoning, and evidence
- Recognize the uses and misuses of *rhetoric*—the use of language to influence how an audience thinks or feels

- Compare arguments presented on the same topic in multiple texts
- Understand multiple perspectives on important issues

In this chapter, I introduce four Deep Sense Approach strategies students can use to help them evaluate arguments: (1) Trace the Reasoning, (2) Consider Perspectives, (3) Evaluate Evidence, and (4) Analyze Rhetoric. You will find learning guides and instructional materials for these four strategies at the end of this chapter and online. (Visit **go.SolutionTree.com/literacy/MDSIT** and enter the unique code found on the inside front cover of this book to access these materials.) For an example of how these strategies can work together in the study of an argumentative text, explore the "Shared Info-Text Study (SITS) Example 2" reproducible in appendix B (page 177).

Before applying these strategies, students should preview, read, and annotate the text to form an accurate mental map. They can then return to the text to use each strategy in turn. After students get instruction in these strategies, they can practice applying them with a wide range of argumentative texts. The goal is for students to integrate these strategies into their evaluation of any argument they encounter, whether written or oral, in school or in their personal lives. Being able to evaluate arguments is also essential for writing argumentative texts.

The Trace the Reasoning Strategy

To successfully evaluate an argument, students need to be able to set aside the rhetoric long enough to see the bones of the argument. In this strategy, they learn to start their evaluation by examining the *logic*, or reasoning, of essays, speeches, and other argumentative texts. To establish the bones of a logical argument, the author:

- Defines the issue and explains its significance
- States their position clearly
- Gives valid reasons for their position
- Acknowledges counterarguments
- Gives explanations and evidence to support their claims

The following sections detail steps for this strategy, guidance for teaching the strategy, and several suggestions to support assessment.

The Strategy Steps

The "Learning Guide: Trace the Reasoning" reproducible (page 133) explains that effective arguments are more than disagreements. Students learn that evaluating an argument should come after previewing, reading, and annotating the text to ensure they understand the key ideas presented. They are then introduced to the following steps.

1. **Determine the issue and position:** In this step, students learn to ask questions that help them determine the issue at the heart of the argument, its significance, and the author's position. They also learn that the central claim often articulates the author's position in an argumentative text.

2. **Identify the author's reasons:** Students learn to look for the reasons the author gives for their position. They learn that reasons are stated as *claims*, defined as confident statements of belief that can be proven or disproven with reasoning and evidence.

Evaluate Arguments and Evidence 123

3. **Look for a counterclaim:** In this step, students learn definitions of *counterclaim*, *concession*, and *rebuttal* and how to look for them as they trace the author's reasoning.

4. **Note the explanations and evidence:** The learning guide explains that authors support their claims with explanations and evidence. The Evaluate Evidence strategy (page 127) gives information about the types of evidence and the qualities that make evidence more or less credible. Here, students are simply identifying how the author has supported their claims.

5. **Look for logical fallacies:** Students are introduced to logical fallacies and learn simple definitions for the false cause, slippery slope, sunk cost, false dilemma, and straw man fallacies. (The Analyze Rhetoric strategy, page 129, introduces additional logical fallacies that present emotional appeals in the guise of logic.)

How to Teach the Strategy

Consider the following suggestions as you plan to teach the Trace the Reasoning strategy.

- Lead students through the introduction and first four steps in this strategy's learning guide; then walk them through the school uniform example provided in the reproducible "An Example: Trace the Reasoning in a Student Column" (page 135). You can have them generate additional reasons to support the student's position, reasons for the opposite position, and additional explanations and evidence. (Britannica's ProCon.org website provides abundant resources to help students structure arguments on dozens of topics of interest.)

- Introduce students to the last strategy step (look for logical fallacies), and have them practice generating logical fallacies related to the uniform example. Teams might create an example for each fallacy introduced in this strategy's learning guide. You can also have students work with peers to generate logical fallacies relevant to a popular topic, such as banning cell phones or TikTok.

- For high school students, you might consider introducing them to the concept of cognitive biases alluded to in this strategy's learning guide. *Cognitive biases* are thinking mistakes resulting from how humans process and interpret information and make decisions and judgments. Psychology, cognitive neuroscience, and economics researchers have found evidence of numerous biases (Kahneman, 2011; Kizart, 2025; Tversky & Kahneman, 1974). Unconscious cognitive biases can make humans vulnerable to believing logical fallacies. If you want to work more with cognitive biases or logical fallacies, there are great online resources that you can use to explain and give more examples of each phenomenon. (I have included some of those in the Digital Resources guide available online at **go.SolutionTree.com/literacy/MDSIT**.)

- When students discuss argumentative texts and generate ideas with their peers, they can practice reasoned argumentation, focusing on the merits of the ideas and evidence. Emphasize the discussion guidelines introduced in the Talk About Texts strategy (chapter 7, page 71) since using tentative language, building on each other's arguments, and clarifying understanding are essential discourse skills for oral argumentation.

- You can also take advantage of online platforms that enable students to reason through arguments with peers. In addition to a discussion board that you might have available in your school's learning management system, several free or low-cost discussion platforms are available. See the Digital Resources guide (at **go.SolutionTree.com/literacy/MDSIT**) for links and descriptions.

- You can structure guided and independent practice around familiar argumentative texts the class has already studied, or you can use short essays, opinion columns, or letters to the editor on topics of interest to students. As they trace the reasoning in a text, students can work with a shoulder partner to discuss the questions introduced in this strategy's learning guide. It helps to have them mark and label the issue, significance, position, reasons, counterclaim, explanations, and evidence.

- With a new text, have students answer in writing the questions introduced in this strategy's learning guide. As an alternative, they can outline or diagram the reasoning of the text.

Assessment Suggestions

In this section, you will find several suggestions to consider as you plan for assessment. The listed key terms and questions will help you assess students' strategy knowledge. As you plan to assess students' application of the strategy, you can incorporate the suggestions for student self-assessment and the evidence of mastery.

- **Key terms:**
  - *Argument*—A written or oral presentation that makes the case for a specific position with reasoning and evidence
  - *Logic*—Reasoning
  - *Issue*—A topic or problem
  - *Significance*—Why an issue is important
  - *Position*—Where someone stands on an issue
  - *Claim*—A confident statement of belief that can be proven or disproven with reasoning and evidence
  - *Central claim*—The author's statement of their position on an issue
  - *Reason*—Why the author has taken a particular position
  - *Counterclaim*—A statement of a position that contrasts with the author's central claim
  - *Concession*—Acknowledgment that some aspects of the counterclaim are valid
  - *Rebuttal*—A refutation of the counterclaim explaining why it is invalid
  - *Explanation*—A statement that clarifies something or gives the reason for or cause of something
  - *Logical fallacy*—An error in reasoning that weakens an argument

- **Strategic knowledge questions:**
  - How is an effective argument different from a disagreement?
  - What are the components of an effective argument?
  - Why is it important to trace the reasoning in arguments you encounter in school and your personal life?
  - Why are logical fallacies a problem? What are some examples of logical fallacies?

- **Self-assessment:** After students have practiced this strategy with various texts, ask them to write in response to the prompt, "Now that you have learned and practiced the Trace the Reasoning strategy, how has your process changed for making sense of an author's argument?" As a scaffold, you might have them look through the strategy's learning guide to refresh their memory of terminology. You can also give them the frame, "When it comes to tracing the reasoning in an argumentative text, I used to _____, but now I _____. This helps because _____."

- **Evidence of mastery:** When students have mastered the Trace the Reasoning strategy, they will be able to identify the components of an argument in a written or oral text. They will be able to articulate the issue and its significance, the position, and the central claim. They will be able to summarize the author's reasoning.

The Consider Perspectives Strategy

I have noticed that when middle and high school students are introduced to an argumentative text, they often do not think to ask, "Who wrote this?" They might not think critically about the author's purposes, stake in the outcome, or expertise. They might take for granted that the author's assertions are true. It might not occur to them that the author might speak with more certainty than warranted. If readers are unfamiliar with the topic, they might not notice how the author treats other perspectives or that the author excludes other perspectives altogether. Finally, students might not examine their own perspective on the issue or assess whether they need to know more to have a well-informed position. As part of evaluating an argument, students need to learn to consider the author's perspective, the perspectives of other stakeholders, and their own perspectives.

In a strong argument that honors multiple perspectives, the author acknowledges:

- Their stake in the outcome
- The limitations of their argument or expertise
- Diverse stakeholders' concerns
- The valid aspects of other positions

The following sections detail steps for this strategy, guidance for teaching the strategy, and several suggestions to support assessment.

The Strategy Steps

Many secondary students practice identifying the author's central claim in argumentative texts like speeches or opinion essays, but they might not go beyond this first step to practice broader perspective taking. The three steps of the Consider Perspectives strategy help students investigate the author's and other stakeholders' points of view as well as their own.

1. **Analyze the author's point of view:** The "Learning Guide: Consider Perspectives" reproducible (page 136) introduces students to questions they can discuss or ask themselves to help them analyze the author's perspective. It also offers several considerations to help students infer the author's perspective when it is not explicitly stated.

2. **Consider other perspectives:** Students are encouraged to pay close attention to how the author treats other perspectives. They ask questions to help them think through the viewpoints of stakeholders discussed in the text and those the author leaves out.

3. **Reflect on your own point of view:** This step encourages students to think through their own position on an issue and determine whether they need to read more broadly before forming a confident position.

How to Teach the Strategy

Consider the following suggestions as you plan to teach the Consider Perspectives strategy.

- Introduce the discussion on perspective using a photograph or painting; have students discuss what they can infer about the artist's and the subjects' perspectives and then reflect on their perspectives as viewers.

- After assessing students' current understanding of perspective taking, introduce the strategy and walk through each step using this strategy's learning guide (page 136), giving salient examples and pausing for discussion. As you introduce step 2 (consider other perspectives), you can use the screen time and social media example introduced in the learning guide to discuss varied stakeholders' perspectives. For example, some teenage students might be concerned about social media's effect on their mood and acknowledge that sometimes they don't seem to control how long they stay on. Other teenage students might feel that social media is essential for their sense of connection and well-being and feel they can manage their use of the apps. Some teachers might feel responsible for limiting students' use of social media during school time, while others might believe it is silly even to try to control students' use. Administrators are often concerned about the risks of cyberbullying, cheating, and other inappropriate uses of social media. Researchers and experts disagree about how negative screen time is for adolescents and which factors actually are responsible for any harm caused.

- It is helpful to practice the steps of this strategy with a text that addresses a familiar issue that your students care about. For younger readers or those who struggle with inference, it might help to start with a shorter text or one they already know. They might also need additional direct instruction and applied practice in a small-group setting.

- You might lead students in a quick online inquiry to learn more about the perspectives under discussion. After doing this as a whole class, you can release students to do this verification in pairs and then independently whenever they read argumentative texts.

- Have students work with a new argumentative text, independently applying the three sets of questions in the learning guide. Continue to remind students to consider the author's perspective, other stakeholders' perspectives, and their own perspectives as they encounter new texts across disciplines and platforms, in school, and in their personal lives. This can be an ongoing conversation in the classroom, with students discussing diverse perspectives in arguments they encounter in their school reading, on social media, or in their personal lives.

- Analyzing perspectives is not just the purview of English class. Important debates in the disciplines of mathematics, science, social studies, and career and technical education lend themselves to the analysis modeled throughout this chapter.

Assessment Suggestions

Refer to the following recommendations as you plan to assess students' knowledge and application of the Consider Perspectives strategy. These include key terms and questions, suggestions for facilitating self-assessment, and evidence of mastery.

- **Key terms:**
  - *Perspective*—Point of view
  - *Blind spot*—A bias someone is unaware of
  - *Stake*—The interest in an outcome due to its personal impact
  - *Stakeholder*—A person with a specific interest in or concern about an issue
  - *False dilemma*—A logical fallacy driven by either-or thinking
- **Strategic knowledge questions:**
  - Why is it important to consider the author's perspective when evaluating an argument? What are some factors that can shape an author's point of view?
  - Why is it important to consider various stakeholders' perspectives? What can happen if the author dismisses or ignores other perspectives?
  - How does it help to reflect on your perspective on an issue? What questions should you ask yourself?
- **Self-assessment:** After students have practiced applying the strategy steps to varied texts, ask them to reflect on how considering perspectives—the author's, other stakeholders', and their own—has changed how they read, listen to, and make arguments.
- **Evidence of mastery:** Students who master the Consider Perspectives strategy can articulate the author's perspective, and they can make reasonable inferences based on evidence when it is not stated explicitly. They will be able to identify stakeholders who would have a stake in the issue. They will be able to summarize the perspectives of stakeholders discussed in the text and hypothesize the likely perspectives of other stakeholders. They will be able to articulate their own perspective and how they came to take that perspective.

The Evaluate Evidence Strategy

This strategy is helpful whether students evaluate the evidence presented in one text or multiple texts. It can also help students choose credible evidence to add to an argumentative essay. Students often take the evidence presented in an argument at face value. With some new information and ways of thinking, students can learn to think critically about what evidence the author offers, how the author presents the evidence, and the conclusions the author draws from the evidence.

In a strong argument that presents effective evidence, the author:

- Offers credible, authoritative evidence from varied sources
- Backs up each claim with relevant evidence
- Gives the context of the evidence
- Acknowledges the limitations of the evidence
- Draws reasonable conclusions that fit the evidence

The following sections detail steps for this strategy, guidance for teaching the strategy, and several suggestions to support assessment.

The Strategy Steps

These steps help students recognize a variety of supporting evidence in argumentative texts and discern the credibility and relevance of that evidence.

1. **Identify the supporting evidence:** In this step, students are encouraged to return to the text to categorize the supporting evidence. The "Learning Guide: Evaluate Evidence" reproducible (page 138) defines and gives examples of common types of supporting evidence: examples, facts, testimony, documentary evidence, statistics, research findings, and text evidence.

2. **Examine the author's approach to evidence:** This step teaches students to consider how the author presents their evidence. They learn that when an author uses evidence in good faith, they often disclose how, when, by whom, and for what purpose information was gathered. They acknowledge the limitations of their evidence and try to verify its validity.

3. **Judge the evidence:** Students are encouraged to review the evidence provided for each claim. They learn that an author might naturally notice and accept information that supports their position. Authors with a strong personal stake in their position might actively look for information that confirms their position, fail to search for information that contradicts their position, cherry-pick evidence, or dismiss credible information that does not support their view (News Literacy Project, n.d.). Students are encouraged to look up sources if they doubt the credibility of the sources the author relies on.

4. **Scrutinize the conclusions:** Students learn to pay attention to the conclusions an author draws based on the evidence they present, thinking about whether the evidence warrants the conclusions. They ask questions to help them notice overgeneralizations and assumptions.

How to Teach the Strategy

Consider the following suggestions as you plan to teach the Evaluate Evidence strategy.

- Introduce the strategy using the learning guide. Explain step 1 (identify the supporting evidence), and then engage students in helping you identify the supporting evidence in the text the class used for the Trace the Reasoning and Consider Perspectives strategies introduced earlier in this chapter. Continue with the other three steps, explaining each step and practicing applying them to the same text.

- With a different text, have students discuss each set of questions in the learning guide, capturing their responses in writing. Debrief students' responses, addressing misconceptions or disagreements. Reinforce concepts explained in the learning guide as needed.

- Whenever students read an argumentative text, whether in a shared text study, independent reading, or inquiry, you can encourage them to use this strategy to scrutinize the evidence the author offers to support their claims. You can also ask them to justify their choice of evidence when composing argumentative texts using the steps of the strategy.

Assessment Suggestions

This section includes several suggestions to help you assess students' strategy knowledge and application of the Evaluate Evidence strategy. You will find a list of key terms and strategic knowledge questions, suggestions for student self-assessment, and evidence of mastery.

- **Key terms:**
  - *Supporting evidence*—Information used to support or prove a particular claim
  - *Credible*—Believable
  - *Fact*—A verifiably true statement
  - *Context (of evidence)*—How, when, by whom, and for what purpose evidence was gathered
  - *Verify*—To confirm
  - *Conclusion*—A judgment or decision someone makes based on the evidence

  In addition to being able to recognize or produce accurate definitions of these key terms, students should be able to distinguish among the different types of evidence introduced in this strategy's learning guide: examples (such as anecdotes, narratives, and hypothetical examples), facts, testimony (eyewitness, expert, and peer), documentary evidence, statistics, research findings, and text evidence.

- **Strategic knowledge questions:**
  - What are common types of supporting evidence?
  - What are the different kinds of testimony?
  - How does it help an author's argument to offer a variety of evidence?
  - Why is it important for an author to give context for their evidence and acknowledge the limitations?
  - How can you check to ensure an author's evidence is credible?
  - Why is it important to examine the author's conclusions?

- **Self-assessment:** After students have evaluated supporting evidence in several argumentative texts, ask them to reflect on what they have learned. Have them write in response to the prompt, "How has the Evaluate Evidence strategy changed how you think about supporting evidence? Since you learned the strategy, what have you noticed about the evidence authors include in their arguments?" Allow them to refresh their memory by reviewing the learning guide as needed.

- **Evidence of mastery:** When students have mastered the Evaluate Evidence strategy, they will recognize the different types of supporting evidence introduced in the learning guide when they encounter them in a spoken or printed argument. You will hear them discussing the considerations articulated in this strategy's learning guide rather than just taking an author's evidence at face value. They will pause to look up sources they have questions about. They will select and explain their evidence more carefully in their argumentative writing.

The Analyze Rhetoric Strategy

Rhetoric refers to how an author or speaker uses language to influence how their audience thinks or feels about some aspect of an issue. Powerful rhetoric can obscure weaknesses in an argument or help the audience understand an issue or an author's position. In this strategy, students learn to consider tone and direct address as rhetorical elements. Then, students are introduced to several common misuses of rhetoric that they might encounter as they evaluate arguments.

It is beyond the scope of this chapter to explore the vast world of rhetorical devices in depth. Over time, scholars have come to give specific names to certain ways authors and speakers use language to influence their audience. (Some of these are also discussed as literary devices in narrative analysis.) Students are exposed to a number of rhetorical devices during their middle and high school education, including metaphors, similes, and analogies; personification; alliteration and onomatopoeia; satire, paradoxes, and irony; and various kinds of allusions. Great resources are available online to learn more about rhetorical devices; this book's Digital Resources guide (at **go.SolutionTree.com/literacy/MDSIT**) includes several of my favorites.

In a strong argument that utilizes effective rhetoric, the author:

- Uses language that is honest and clear
- Avoids manipulative emotional appeals, loaded language, and equivocation

The following sections detail steps for this strategy, guidance for teaching the strategy, and several suggestions to support assessment.

The Strategy Steps

By taking the steps described in the "Learning Guide: Analyze Rhetoric" reproducible (page 140), students learn to analyze several aspects of rhetoric, including tone, direct address, manipulative appeals, loaded language, and equivocation.

1. **Identify tone and direct address:** In this step, students learn to consider tone as an element of rhetoric, and they get an update on the concept of tone in the context of argumentation. They learn that an author might shift their tone in a more extended argument. Students also learn to look for uses of direct address and calls to action.

2. **Look for manipulative appeals:** Students learn about manipulative appeals that can masquerade as logic. The strategy's learning guide explains that authors can introduce logical fallacies while appealing to their audience's emotions or respect for authority. Students learn about four manipulative appeals that are logical fallacies: ad hominem attacks, bandwagon appeals, appeals to authority, and guilt by association to add to those they learned about in the Trace the Reasoning strategy.

3. **Look for loaded language:** This step provides students with a definition and example of loaded language. They learn how words and phrases with strong emotional connotations might be intentionally used in arguments.

4. **Look for equivocation:** This step introduces students to equivocation (the use of intentionally vague language; Shatz, n.d.) and provides questions they can ask to detect vague language.

How to Teach the Strategy

Consider the following suggestions as you plan instruction for the Analyze Rhetoric strategy.

- Use the learning guide to introduce the strategy and work through each step. As you go, ask students to identify social media examples of the misuses of rhetoric discussed in this strategy's learning guide. You can give students short scenarios to practice identifying manipulative emotional appeals, loaded language, and equivocation. You might also use commercials, especially political or special-interest commercials, for this purpose. Discussing the ethical aspects of using rhetoric to influence the audience's beliefs or feelings is important.

Evaluate Arguments and Evidence 131

- Once students understand the concepts, they can practice analyzing rhetoric in a familiar or short new text with a partner. They can refer to the questions introduced in this strategy's learning guide as they discuss and annotate the text.
- When students are ready to independently practice the strategy with a new text, you can have them write their answers to the strategy questions, discuss the questions with a partner, or summarize their findings in a video recording using Padlet or a similar web-based application. Your school's learning management system might include a discussion board tool that allows for text or video responses.

Assessment Suggestions

In this section, you will find suggestions to inform your strategy assessment plan. Refer to the listed key terms and questions as you plan to assess students' strategy knowledge. To assess students' application of the strategy, you can incorporate the suggestions for student self-assessment and the evidence of mastery.

- **Key terms:**
  - *Rhetoric*—How an author or speaker uses language to influence how their audience thinks or feels about some aspect of an issue
  - *Tone*—An author's use of language to communicate their attitude toward an issue or a particular viewpoint
  - *Diction*—The words and phrases an author uses
  - *Syntax*—How an author composes their sentences
  - *Direct address*—A rhetorical device in which the author speaks directly to the audience using *you* or includes the audience in their statements using *we*
  - *Manipulative appeal*—A statement intended to stir specific emotions, such as patriotism, compassion, belonging, guilt, or anger
  - *Call to action*—A rhetorical device in which the author asks or suggests that the audience should take a certain action
  - *Loaded language*—A word or phrase with a strong positive or negative connotation that provokes emotions and influences the audience
  - *Equivocation*—The intentional use of vague or multiple-meaning words to deceive the audience or avoid committing to a specific stance

  Also, check to make sure students can distinguish among the logical fallacies introduced in this strategy's learning guide: ad hominem attack, bandwagon appeal, appeal to authority, and guilt by association. You can give students short scenarios or text examples containing manipulative appeals to see how well they recognize the problem.
- **Strategic knowledge questions:**
  - Why is it important to identify an author's tone? How is tone conveyed? How might an author vary their tone in a more extended argument?
  - How might a direct address or call to action influence the audience?
  - Which logical fallacies might authors and speakers introduce when appealing to their audience's emotions? Their respect for authority?

- Why do some authors and speakers use loaded language? How can you guard against being influenced by loaded language?
- Why do some authors and speakers use vague language? How can you guard against being influenced by equivocation?

- **Self-assessment:** After students have worked with analyzing rhetoric in several argumentative texts, ask them to reflect on what they have learned. You might have them write or discuss using the frame, "When it comes to analyzing rhetoric, I used to _____, but now I _____." Ask them to respond to the prompt, "Since you learned the Analyze Rhetoric strategy, what have you noticed about how authors use rhetoric in their arguments?" Allow them to refresh their memory by reviewing the learning guide as needed.
- **Evidence of mastery:** When students have mastered the Analyze Rhetoric strategy, they can identify the author's tone and explain what text evidence led them to that inference. They can identify examples of direct address, manipulative appeals, loaded language, and vague language in written and oral texts.

Concluding Thoughts

Secondary teachers can attest that many students struggle to evaluate arguments and evidence in complex texts. Though it will take time and practice to help students integrate the four strategies introduced in the chapter, this effort will eventually bear fruit. Students will not just be able to engage more thoughtfully in academic tasks that call for them to analyze and evaluate an author's argument. You will also see growth in their ability to articulate and support their own evidence-based arguments. Finally, they will be better equipped to recognize false logic, invalid evidence, and manipulative rhetoric in the arguments they encounter in all aspects of their lives.

REPRODUCIBLE | 133

Learning Guide: Trace the Reasoning

Many social media arguments are characterized by hot takes and a win-lose mentality. Some influencers ride their outrage to great fame. These high-conflict arguments often sound reasonable, but we can see weaknesses when we look further.

An *effective argument* is more than a disagreement. It is a written, oral, or visual presentation that makes a clear case for a specific position with reasoning and evidence.

When we evaluate arguments, we focus first on the author's *logic*, or reasoning.

1. Determine the issue and position.

2. Identify the author's reasons.

3. Look for a counterclaim.

4. Note the explanations and evidence.

5. Look for logical fallacies.

- **Why:** It is important to trace the reasoning in arguments, whether in the texts you read in school or in those you encounter in your personal life. This practice can protect you from falling for arguments that are not valid.

- **When:** You can use this strategy when you read, view, or listen to any presentation of an argument. It is best to trace the reasoning after you have previewed, read, and annotated the text. Applying the Check for Understanding and Fix Confusion and Fill Gaps strategies helps you start out with an accurate mental map of the text.

Strategy Steps

You can add to your annotations or make separate notes as you practice these steps. You can also make an outline or diagram to trace the author's reasoning.

1. Determine the Issue and Position

In a strong argument, the author:

- Defines the *issue* (a topic or problem)

- Explains its *significance* (why the issue is important)

- Makes clear their *position* on the issue (where they stand)

In an argument, the author makes a series of claims. A *claim* is a confident statement of belief that can be proven or disproven with reasoning and evidence. The *central claim* is the author's statement of their position on the issue.

To determine the author's issue and position, ask yourself these questions.

- What is the central issue?

- Why does the author think it is significant?

- What is their position on the issue?

2. Identify the Author's Reasons

Look for the reasons the author gives for their position. In a strong argument, the author makes clear *why* they have taken a particular position on an issue. The reasons for the author's position are often stated as claims.

To identify the author's reasons, ask yourself this question.

- What reasons does the author give for their position?

page 1 of 2

Making Deep Sense of Informational Texts © 2025 Solution Tree Press • SolutionTree.com
Visit **go.SolutionTree.com/literacy/MDSIT** and enter the unique access code found on this book's inside front cover to access this reproducible.

3. Look for a Counterclaim

In a formal argument, the author often acknowledges an opposing argument. A *counterclaim* is a statement of a position that contrasts with the author's central claim. A *concession* acknowledges that some aspects of the counterclaim are valid. A *rebuttal* refutes the counterclaim and explains why it is invalid.

To identify a counterclaim, ask yourself these questions.
- Does the author offer a counterclaim?
- Do they make a concession?
- Do they offer a logical, well-supported rebuttal?

4. Note the Explanations and Evidence

In a strong argument, the author supports their claims with explanations and evidence. An *explanation* is a statement that clarifies something or gives the reason for or cause of something. A definition is a type of explanation. Evidence can take many forms. (You'll learn more about the types of evidence in the Evaluate Evidence strategy.)

To identify explanations and evidence, ask yourself this question.
- What explanations and evidence does the author give to support their claims?

5. Look for Logical Fallacies

Research in many fields has found that the human brain makes decisions in these ways.
- Quickly and often unconsciously
- Based on limited evidence
- To try to keep us safe

To identify logical fallacies, ask yourself this question.
- Are there logical fallacies in the author's argument?

This makes humans vulnerable to believing *logical fallacies*—errors in reasoning that weaken an argument. When dissecting an argument, it is important to look for logical fallacies that make it less convincing. Sometimes, authors make these errors in reasoning because of their own cognitive biases. Often, they intentionally introduce them because they know their audience is prone to believe them.

An Example: Trace the Reasoning in a Student Column

Consider this example of a column a tenth grader might write for their school paper.

Issue Definition

- **Issue:** *Many schools across the world require their students to wear uniforms.*
- **Significance:** *Families, children, and school staff all pay a price for uniforms.*
- **Position:** *Schools should enforce reasonable dress codes instead of requiring uniforms.*

Reasons

The student's key supporting ideas are the reasons they give to support their position. Each of the reasons is stated as a claim.

- **Reason 1:** *Uniforms are a significant financial burden for many families.*
- **Reason 2:** *Uniforms don't improve students' behavior.*
- **Reason 3:** *Dress codes can solve many of the problems uniforms were supposed to solve.*

Notice that the first two claims elaborate on the problem, while the third one supports the solution. Many arguments follow the problem-solution text structure.

Counterclaim, Concession, and Rebuttal

- **Counterclaim:** *School districts cite reports of decreased disciplinary problems and gang activity after introducing uniform policies.*
- **Concession:** *It might be true that after implementing uniform policies, some schools have had fewer violent incidents.*
- **Rebuttal:** *Research is inconclusive. Some studies dispute the causal link between uniforms and decreases in crime, while others show increased violent activity in some schools after uniform policies were implemented.*

Reasoning and Evidence

Let's look at how the student supports two of their claims against uniforms. You will see two types of evidence mentioned: an example and a research finding.

- **Reason 1:** *Uniforms are a significant financial burden for many families.*
  - Explanation—*Schools often change their policies yearly, forcing families to buy new clothes when last year's still fit.*
  - Evidence—*The schools in my area even insist families purchase shirts and jackets with logos, which are often more expensive than what they can find in discount stores.*
- **Reason 2:** *Uniforms don't improve students' behavior.*
  - Explanation—*Adults look at correlation studies as proof that uniforms somehow magically make students behave better, but other studies refute this assumption.*
  - Evidence—*A 2021 Ohio State University study found that uniforms did not affect the amount of bullying or social anxiety a student experienced.*

Making Deep Sense of Informational Texts © 2025 Solution Tree Press • SolutionTree.com
Visit **go.SolutionTree.com/literacy/MDSIT** and enter the unique access code found on this book's inside front cover to access this reproducible.

REPRODUCIBLE

Learning Guide: Consider Perspectives

Everyone has a *perspective*, or point of view. We see the world, ourselves, and specific issues through our unique lens. Our perspective is influenced by what we and others around us have experienced and learned.

> 1. **Analyze the author's point of view.**
>
> 2. **Consider other perspectives.**
>
> 3. **Reflect on your own point of view.**

- **Why:** If you do not consider the perspective of the person making an argument, it might be harder to see the weaknesses or limitations in their reasoning. You can fall into either-or thinking when you do not consider other perspectives.

- **When:** You can use this strategy whenever you read, view, or listen to any presentation of an argument. It helps to first preview, read, and annotate the text to make basic sense of it. Then, apply the Trace the Reasoning strategy to identify the issue, the central claim, and the reasons the author presents. Once you are familiar with the argument, you can step back to consider perspectives.

Strategy Steps

The three steps of the Consider Perspectives strategy help you analyze varied perspectives on issues discussed in argumentative texts and determine your own point of view.

1. Analyze the Author's Point of View

All writers have a perspective that shapes their understanding of issues and helps determine their position. As you analyze the author's point of view in an argumentative text, keep these considerations in mind.

- When someone speaks strongly and confidently, it does not mean they are right. Experts might speak tentatively and consider other points of view because they know how complex the issue is.

- A writer might have a *blind spot*—a bias they are unaware of. They might not realize how their assumptions, worldview, and beliefs have shaped their perspective. Or, they might have a misconception or gap in their background knowledge that affects their understanding of an issue.

- A writer might care deeply about the outcome because they stand to benefit or be harmed. They might have a stake in the issue because of their professional or personal interests. They might be paid to write content. They might also have biases that make them feel strongly about the issue.

- An author might write differently when addressing expert peers than when writing for readers new to the topic.

- An expository author might slip into argumentation when they care deeply about their topic.

> To analyze the author's point of view, ask yourself these questions.
>
> - Who is the author, speaker, or creator? What is their experience or expertise with the topic?
>
> - Why did they write this text? Is their purpose to inform, to convince, or both? Who is their primary audience?
>
> - What is their attitude toward the issue? What stake do they have in the outcome?
>
> - What beliefs does the author seem to have? What assumptions do they make?

page 1 of 2

Making Deep Sense of Informational Texts © 2025 Solution Tree Press • SolutionTree.com
Visit **go.SolutionTree.com/literacy/MDSIT** and enter the unique access code found on this book's inside front cover to access this reproducible.

2. Consider Other Perspectives

Think through other perspectives discussed in the text and other important perspectives that the author has left out. Think about the *stakeholders* who might be affected by the issue. (Stakeholders are people with a specific interest in or concern about an issue.)

For example, consider how different groups might differ on a hot topic: teens' screen time and social media usage. Parents, elementary school children, teenage students, teachers, administrators, psychologists, media companies, and researchers might all have different perspectives on the topic. Even within these groups there are varying viewpoints.

> To consider other perspectives, ask yourself these questions.
> - What other viewpoints does the author present? How does the author represent the viewpoints?
> - What viewpoints does the author not include that are important to consider?

Even if an author does not express a clear counterclaim, they might acknowledge other points of view by including quotes, explanations, examples, or data that challenge their central claim.

We should be cautious when we read or hear arguments that dismiss or ignore other perspectives. Such arguments might present a *false dilemma*, a logical fallacy driven by either-or thinking. In this case, consider exploring other texts that address the same issue from different points of view to better understand.

3. Reflect on Your Own Point of View

It's also important to think carefully about what you think, believe, and feel about the issue. This self-reflection helps you form a logical position on the issue. You might agree or disagree with the author or land somewhere in between. Sometimes, the best position is, "It depends on . . ." or "I'm not sure. I need to learn more."

However, we must remember that a position can feel true but be untrue. It helps to:

- Check the quality of the author's evidence and reasoning
- Check for our own assumptions, biases, and blind spots
- Do further inquiry to expand our understanding of the issue

> To reflect on your own point of view, ask yourself these questions.
> - What do I think, believe, and feel about the issue?
> - What is my view on the author's position?
> - What assumptions am I making? What blind spots or biases might influence my thinking? Do I have a stake in the outcome?
> - What do I need to know more about or understand better before I can form a clear point of view on this topic?

Learning Guide: Evaluate Evidence

Supporting evidence is the information used to support or prove a particular claim. In a strong argument, an author offers a variety of *credible* (believable) supporting evidence to help prove each of their claims. They are honest about the origins and limits of the evidence, and their conclusions fit with the evidence they give.

> 1. **Identify the supporting evidence.**
>
> 2. **Examine the author's approach to evidence.**
>
> 3. **Judge the evidence.**
>
> 4. **Scrutinize the conclusions.**

- **Why:** For each claim an author makes, they need to do more than define or explain it; they must provide credible evidence. Readers must carefully evaluate the supporting evidence to decide whether an argument is valid. If an author does not provide much credible evidence, they might not have a valid position.

- **When:** You can use this strategy when you read, view, or listen to a presentation of an argument. It helps to preview, read, and annotate the text first. Use this with the Trace the Reasoning strategy.

Strategy Steps

Practicing these steps will help you judge whether the author's evidence is credible and supports their claims.

1. Identify the Supporting Evidence

After identifying the author's claims, review the text to identify the supporting evidence they offer. There are a number of different types of supporting evidence.

> **Types of Supporting Evidence**
>
> - Examples
> - Facts
> - Testimony
> - Documentary evidence
> - Statistics
> - Research findings
> - Text evidence

- **Examples:** Authors use examples as illustrations of general claims. They might just quickly mention an example or offer an *anecdote*, a brief true story. They might include a *narrative*, a longer story referenced throughout the text. They might provide examples from their experience or other people's. They might mention specific events or phenomena. Authors might also offer a *hypothetical example*—an imagined though reasonable scenario.

- **Facts:** An author might provide a *fact*—a verifiably true statement. The fact might be a direct observation or a known, proven piece of information.

- **Testimony:** *Testimony* is a formal statement someone makes orally or in writing about what they saw or know. There are several kinds of testimony.

  - *Eyewitness (firsthand) testimony*—A statement from someone who was present at an event being discussed or who experienced something being discussed

  - *Expert testimony*—A statement from someone with formal knowledge, training, or methods related to the topic

  - *Peer testimony*—A statement from someone who is like those in the intended audience

  - *Informal expert opinion*—A quote from an email or phone call given by an expert

- **Documentary evidence:** This includes documents, correspondence, and financial records.

- **Statistics:** A *statistic* is a number generated from data analysis, such as an average, percentage, or probability.
- **Research findings:** This evidence is the result of a careful, planned investigation. For example, researchers might show correlations between two variables or find important patterns.
- **Text evidence:** The author might quote or paraphrase what another author wrote, especially if that author has expertise or authority on the topic.

> To identify the supporting evidence, ask yourself these questions.
> - What evidence does the author provide?
> - Which types of evidence do they rely on?

2. Examine the Author's Approach to Evidence

An author should give the *context* for the evidence: how, when, by whom, and for what purpose it was gathered. They should also acknowledge the limitations of their evidence. For example, the author might mention that some studies have contradicted the research findings they cite.

Reporters and editors must *verify*, or confirm, the information they get from their sources. They are expected to consult all relevant sources for a story. In other fields, authors are expected to verify the evidence they present.

> To examine the author's approach to evidence, ask yourself these questions.
> - Does the author give the context for the evidence?
> - Do they acknowledge the limitations of their evidence?
> - Do they share how they verified that their evidence is valid?

3. Judge the Evidence

An author might naturally notice and accept information that supports their position. They might fail to search for information that contradicts their position. They might even intentionally cherry-pick evidence or dismiss credible information that does not support their view.

Review the evidence presented for each claim. If you have doubts about the credibility of a source, try to look it up and decide for yourself how credible it is.

> To judge the evidence, ask yourself these questions.
> - Does the author seem to present only evidence to support their position, ignoring other evidence?
> - Does the author use questionable sources?

4. Scrutinize the Conclusions

Authors draw *conclusions*—judgments or decisions they make based on the evidence. When you reread these statements, consider whether you feel the author's conclusions are supported by the evidence they have provided. When someone makes an argument, they might be tempted to misrepresent or exaggerate what their evidence proves. If they give one example or quote one person, they might not be able to state with certainty that their conclusions are valid.

> To scrutinize the conclusions, ask yourself these questions.
> - What conclusions does the author draw? Do the conclusions logically follow from the evidence?
> - Do they overgeneralize or make assumptions about what the evidence proves?

Learning Guide: Analyze Rhetoric

The term *rhetoric* refers to how an author or speaker uses language to influence how their audience thinks or feels about an issue. When you read the speeches of renowned speakers like Abraham Lincoln, Martin Luther King Jr., and Malala Yousafzai, you can see how carefully they craft the language of a speech. Some lines read almost like poetry. These speakers weave in metaphors, personification, repetition, and alliteration like a novelist or poet would.

1. **Identify tone and direct address.**
2. **Look for manipulative appeals.**
3. **Look for loaded language.**
4. **Look for equivocation.**

Many argumentative writers and speakers use rhetoric to draw their audience's attention to their ideas. However, rhetoric can also hide a weak argument or manipulate the audience.

- **Why:** You must be alert to how authors use rhetoric in argumentative texts. They might use language to move or mislead you.
- **When:** You can use this strategy along with the Evaluate Evidence strategy. If possible, preview, read, and annotate the text first so you start with an accurate mental map of the text.

Strategy Steps

Use these strategy steps to analyze the rhetoric in the argumentative texts you read.

1. Identify Tone and Direct Address

Tone is the author's use of language to communicate their attitude toward an issue or a particular viewpoint. Tone is conveyed with the author's *diction* (the words and phrases they use), the details they choose to emphasize, how formal or informal their language is, and their *syntax* (how they compose their sentences).

An author might shift their tone in a longer argument. For instance, they might convey a concerned tone when discussing the general issue, an impassioned tone when discussing their position, and a cynical tone when discussing their opponent's position.

To identify tone and direct address, ask yourself these questions.

- What tone does the author take when discussing the issue? Their position? Their opponent's position?
- What evidence do I have?
- Does the author directly address the audience? Do they issue a call to action?

Common Tone Words

Assertive, concerned, critical, cynical, diplomatic, earnest, formal, humorous, impassioned, informative, ironic, optimistic, outraged, pessimistic, resigned, skeptical, thoughtful, urgent, virtuous

Make note of places where the author uses direct address—speaking directly to the audience using *you* or including the audience in their statements using *we*. Also, note whether the argument includes a call to action—asking or suggesting that the audience should take a certain action.

2. Look for Manipulative Appeals

Argumentative text often appeals to logic and expertise but might also appeal to the reader's emotions, such as patriotism, pride, compassion, belonging, guilt, and anger. Authors might mention well-known people to influence the audience. These appeals are not always misleading, but authors might introduce logical fallacies as they try to appeal to emotions or respect for authority.

To identify manipulative appeals, ask yourself these questions.

- Does the author appeal to the audience's emotions or respect for authority?
- Does the author resort to logical fallacies?

Manipulative Appeals That Are Logical Fallacies

- **Ad hominem attack:** Attacking the person rather than their position
- **Bandwagon appeal:** Suggesting that because something is popular, the audience should believe or do it
- **Appeal to authority:** Suggesting that since someone famous or powerful believes or does something, the audience should, too
- **Guilt by association:** Suggesting that since a certain person or group of people believes or does something, it must be bad

3. Look for Loaded Language

Loaded language is a word or phrase with a strong positive or negative connotation that provokes emotions and influences the audience. For example, a scientist might refer to mosquitoes as "fascinating members of the insect family," while someone attending an outdoor concert might refer to them as "pests and bloodsuckers."

Politicians and influencers might choose certain terms to describe a policy or position to provoke an emotional reaction in their audience. When an author uses loaded language, they might feel very strongly about their own position and have difficulty thinking objectively about other points of view.

To identify loaded language, ask yourself this question.

- Does the author use words and phrases that are meant to create strong feelings or associations in their audience?

4. Look for Equivocation

Equivocation means intentionally using vague or multiple-meaning words to deceive the audience or avoid committing to a specific stance. Authors might use equivocation when explaining a position their audience might disagree with.

Imagine a parent asking their teenager, "Did you stay up playing that video game again?" The teen might equivocate, saying, "Mom, I turned off the light and went to bed at ten just like you told me to." The teen never answered the question, but their parent might assume they did not play the video game.

To identify equivocation, ask yourself these questions.

- Does the author use unclear language?
- Do they change the way they use certain words over the course of an argument?
- Do they avoid directly addressing counterarguments or questions?

page 2 of 2

Making Deep Sense of Informational Texts © 2025 Solution Tree Press • SolutionTree.com
Visit **go.SolutionTree.com/literacy/MDSIT** and enter the unique access code found on this book's inside front cover to access this reproducible.

CHAPTER 11
Consolidate Learning

Strategies in This Chapter
- Summarize Texts
- Synthesize Across Texts
- Share Learning

For years, I wondered why so many of my students seemed to fake it when they summarized articles, wrote research reports, and created presentations. They wove together text snippets with words from the prompt and a bit of formulaic language. They changed a few words to keep from plagiarizing. *Voila!* They had a paragraph or a slide deck to submit, but their work just skimmed the surface of the text, lacking any real insight.

Now, I understand that for students to thoughtfully complete these tasks, they must be able to:

- Articulate the most important ideas
- See how those ideas are connected
- Ignore information that is irrelevant to their purpose
- Write in a scholarly voice separate from the author's
- Choose relevant evidence to support their points

Students are often surprised that they only vaguely remember a recently studied text. They might have formed an accurate mental map at the time, but if they do nothing with their newly gained knowledge, it can seem as if their memory has been wiped clean. Readers need to continue working with the ideas and information they have read about to ensure their mental maps are robust, flexible, and enduring. This occurs as they *consolidate* their learning, integrating the ideas and details into a coherent whole.

Several practices discussed in previous chapters help students consolidate new learning, including setting a reading purpose, connecting with background knowledge, checking for understanding, and rereading. Three additional strategies facilitate consolidation when they are done mindfully: summarizing a text, synthesizing it with additional texts on the same topic, and sharing one's learning with others (O'Reilly et al., 2015).

The final three Deep Sense Approach strategies help students consolidate what they have learned: (1) Summarize Texts, (2) Synthesize Across Texts, and (3) Share Learning. You will find learning guides and instructional materials for these strategies at the end of the chapter and online. (Visit **go.SolutionTree.com/literacy/MDSIT** and enter the unique code found on the inside front cover of this book to access these materials.)

The Summarize Texts Strategy

Summarization has been well documented to help improve comprehension (Solis et al., 2012; Stevens, Park, & Vaughn, 2019). A summary paragraph can also be an excellent indicator of how well a student understood the text.

Though many teenage students had instruction and practice with summarizing in earlier grades, the strategy becomes more important starting in middle school, when students are asked to read more complex info-texts and do more with them (Merchie & Van Keer, 2016). However, teenage students often focus on ensuring their summary is long enough and detailed enough rather than capturing the key ideas and how the author has organized them (Mateos et al., 2008).

Bewildered by the summation, students often resort to hunting for what they feel are relevant sentences and paraphrasing them (or, at least, "changing up the words," as my students might say). Years of being told to "find" the main idea might have given them the impression that summarizing involves patching together the author's words rather than creating a coherent representation of the text. Students need to learn that a strong summary has the following traits.

- It expresses the central idea.
- It includes key supporting ideas.
- It includes key details and terms.
- It might include examples or explanations.
- It is clearly organized to show how ideas are connected.
- It is written in the student's own scholarly voice.

Summarization works best after students have activated their background knowledge and determined the top-level structure (Hagaman, Casey, & Reid, 2016). It becomes much easier once students have read and marked up the text, returned to it for various purposes, and considered it from various perspectives.

The Strategy Steps

In this strategy, students learn a step-by-step process to help them write strong summaries. It consists of the following steps, which are explained in the "Learning Guide: Summarize Texts" reproducible (page 156).

1. **Compose a central idea statement:** This step encourages students to review the text features and their annotations as they confirm the top-level text structure identified using the Determine the Text Structure strategy (page 92). They are prompted to look away from the text as they try to state the central idea the author wants to communicate. They then draft a *central idea statement*, which becomes the topic sentence of their summary. They can use a sentence frame as a scaffold (see the following example), which prevents them from copying a sentence.

   In [type of text], [title], [author] [central idea stem] [central idea].

2. **Paraphrase key supporting ideas:** In this step, students learn to review the text section by section, focusing on text features and their annotations to help them determine the key supporting ideas that fit together to support the author's central idea. They learn that these ideas might be stated or implied. They are prompted to again look away from the text as they paraphrase each idea.

3. **Note key details and terms:** In this step, students review the text again, asking themselves the reporter questions to decide which key details and terms they need to add. They are encouraged to consider their reading purpose to help them decide whether they should include an example or explanation. As they learn in the strategy overview, the summary's length and level of detail depend on the purpose for which it is being written.

4. **Draft and revise your summary:** This step explains how to draft a summary by combining the central idea statement and key supporting ideas and adding key details and terms. Students are encouraged to review the text to ensure they have accurately represented it in their draft. Then, they are prompted to reread their draft to ensure their ideas flow logically. Finally, they revise to make ideas and connections clearer.

To support student understanding of these strategy steps, figure 11.1 (page 146) offers an example of the strategy applied to the Childress (2023) article on coral bleaching first introduced in the Preview Texts strategy (chapter 8, page 85). This example is organized with a problem-solution text structure, with different colors of highlighting applied to the first three strategy steps (dark gray = step 1, medium gray = step 2, and light gray = step 3).

How to Teach the Strategy

Consider the following suggestions as you plan for explicit strategy instruction and continued practice.

- Introduce the strategy using the "Learning Guide: Summarize Texts" reproducible (page 156). Have students reflect on their current process for composing an article or chapter summary. Debrief to assess their background knowledge and identify misconceptions. Acknowledge that they might have had a lot of instruction and practice with summarization but might need to update their strategy to work with more complex texts.

- To get a baseline of your students' current summarization practices, you can have them write a summary of a text you have worked with recently. Afterward have students review the traits of a strong summary in the learning guide. Then, return their benchmark summaries and have them self-assess their work using the criteria.

- Work through the learning guide with students step by step, explaining and demonstrating each step with a text the class has studied recently. Questions included for each step can guide the discussion. You might type the ideas generated for each step in a digital document projected on the screen to combine the elements when you model step 4 (draft and revise your summary). You might want to use a graphic organizer such as the one in figure 11.2 (page 147) to organize the ideas generated in each step.

Step 1: Central Idea Statement

In his 2023 scientific article, "The Heroic Effort to Save Florida's Coral Reef From Extreme Ocean Heat as Corals Bleach Across the Caribbean," ecologist Michael Childress explains the problem of coral bleaching and describes the efforts of scientists and volunteers to protect them.

Step 2: Key Idea Statements

1. Rising marine temperatures have damaged corals off the Florida Keys and in the Caribbean.
2. Scientists worked with volunteer divers to move heat-resistant corals to a Florida reef to replace the damaged ones.
3. The water got even hotter, making the coral bleaching even worse.
4. Scientists started working with volunteers to move the transplanted baby corals.
5. Organizations are taking other actions to save the corals.
6. Scientists are hopeful they can save the reef, but they need help.

Step 3: Key Details, Terms, Examples, and Explanations

Who	NOAA (National Oceanic and Atmospheric Administration)
When	2019 (NOAA started moving corals.)
	2023 (The water got so hot scientists had to move them again.)
Where	Florida Keys, Alligator Reef (They are moving the corals to cooler waters and marine labs.)
Why	They are moving corals again because the new transplants are now in danger.
(explanations)	The reef is important to the ecosystem and the local economy.
	Extreme heat causes corals to release the helpful algae that give them color.
What (examples)	Training divers to remove harmful algae and monitor bleaching

Step 4: Summary

In his 2023 scientific article, "The Heroic Effort to Save Florida's Coral Reef From Extreme Ocean Heat as Corals Bleach Across the Caribbean," ecologist Michael Childress explains the problem of coral bleaching and describes the efforts of scientists and volunteers to protect them. Since 2019, rising marine temperatures have damaged corals off the Florida Keys and in the Caribbean, causing them to release the helpful algae that give them color. Scientists with NOAA (National Oceanic and Atmospheric Administration) worked with volunteer divers to move heat-resistant corals to Florida's Alligator Reef to replace the damaged ones. In 2023, the water got even hotter, making the coral bleaching even worse and threatening the new transplants. In response, scientists began to work with volunteers to move the transplanted baby corals to cooler waters and marine labs. Organizations are taking other actions to save the corals, too, like training divers to remove harmful algae and monitor bleaching. Scientists are hopeful they can save the reef, which is critically important to the ecosystem and local economy, but they need help.

FIGURE 11.1: *Application of the Summarize Texts strategy.*

Central Idea Statement: _____

Key Supporting Ideas	Key Supporting Details (Who, What, When, Where, Why, and How)	Key Terms

FIGURE 11.2: Graphic organizer to organize notes for a summary.

*Visit **go.SolutionTree.com/literacy/MDSIT** for a free reproducible version of this figure.*

- Once you have explained step 3 (note key details and terms), you can have students work in pairs to identify key details and terms in the text. Consider posting a word cloud like the one shown in figure 11.3 to help them check their work. (This word cloud was generated in TagCrowd [https://tagcrowd.com] using Childress [2023] as the source info-text.) You can also use an application like AnswerGarden (https://answergarden.ch/create) and have students enter their key terms to make a custom word cloud.

algae areas **bleaching** care **corals** disease
divers effort **Florida** fragments **heat** help **keys** lab
marine normal nurseries **ocean** protect **reef** reports **restore**
risk **scientists** species **survive** symbiotic **temperatures**
training transplants **volunteers** **waters** weeks year

FIGURE 11.3: Word cloud generated from an info-text.

- After explaining step 4 (draft and revise your summary), you can walk students through the Childress (2023) example presented earlier using the "An Example: Apply the Summarize Texts Strategy With a Science Article" reproducible (page 158; color version online at **go.SolutionTree.com/literacy/MDSIT**). Then, model integrating the components in a draft paragraph. Ask students to help improve the draft, referring to the step 4 questions.

- Once students are familiar with the strategy, you can have them practice applying the steps with any text they have previewed, read, and annotated. At first, you might have them work in pairs to complete steps 1–3. Each student should record ideas separately, either by hand or in a digital document. Then, they can independently draft and use the step 4 questions to self-assess their work.

- To facilitate peer feedback and level setting, you can have students paste their summaries into the Short Answer platform (https://myshortanswer.com) and compare attempts two by two using the strong summary criteria. The class can then discuss one or two of the top-rated summaries, focusing on what each student did particularly well. Use student- or teacher-prepared exemplars to provide additional models for students who need more support with the strategy.

Note that the Digital Resources guide available online (at **go.SolutionTree.com/literacy/MDSIT**) provides links to the resources mentioned in this section. Following are some issues to look out for.

- **Grabbing interesting information:** If students write disjointed summaries, they might still be sampling (pulling lines from the text and lightly paraphrasing them). You can ask them to color-code the key supporting ideas in their drafts and then talk with you about how each connects with the central idea. Depending on their responses, you might have them review and annotate the text again and then document their work with each strategy step.

- **Making vague statements:** Students might have understood the key ideas but missed specific details. You can have them return to step 3 (note key details and terms) to generate specific details they would like to add. They might also need help determining which vague words need to be revised (such as pronouns with unclear antecedents and general labels like *people* or *things*).

Assessment Suggestions

In this section, you will find suggestions and information to help you assess the Summarize Texts strategy. Use the listed terms and questions to assess students' strategy knowledge. Refer to the self-assessment suggestions and evidence of mastery as you plan to assess how well students are able to apply the strategy with a complex text.

- **Key terms:**
  - *Central idea*—The big, important idea the author communicates in a text
  - *Central idea statement*—A sentence that summarizes the author's central idea
  - *Key*—Important, helping to clarify or support the central idea of a text
  - *Key supporting idea*—An important idea that supports the author's central idea
  - *Reporter questions*—A set of questions associated with journalism: Who?, What?, When?, Where?, Why?, and How?
  - *Key detail*—An important piece of information that helps the reader better understand the author's central idea
  - *Key term*—A word or phrase the reader needs to know to fully understand an important idea in the text
  - *Key example*—A specific instance that illustrates an important idea
  - *Key explanation*—A statement that clarifies something important related to the central idea
  - *Topic sentence*—A sentence that introduces the topic and main point of a paragraph
- **Strategic knowledge questions:**
  - What makes a strong summary? What should you include?
  - Why is it important to look away from the text as you summarize?
  - How do you compose a central idea statement?
  - How do you decide which key supporting ideas to include?
  - How do you decide which details and terms to add?
  - What do you need to consider as you revise your draft?

- **Self-assessment:** Once students have practiced writing summaries using the steps of the Summarize Texts strategy, have them use the list of qualities of a strong summary to self-assess their drafts. You can have them discuss or write about which qualities they have successfully demonstrated and which might need more work.

- **Evidence of mastery:** When students have mastered the Summarize Texts strategy, their summaries will demonstrate the strong summary traits introduced earlier.

The Synthesize Across Texts Strategy

The Synthesize Across Texts strategy is, in one sense, an application of the twelve Deep Sense strategies that come before it. When reading multiple texts, students benefit from evaluating text features to determine text structure, activate background knowledge, and establish a reading plan for multiple texts, as with a single text. They will understand more if they annotate, check their understanding, and repair confusion. They will understand even more deeply if they discuss the texts with others and themselves. If they are reading argumentative texts, they will benefit from tracing the reasoning, considering perspectives, and evaluating each author's use of rhetoric. They can evaluate the credibility of the evidence presented in each text. Finally, they can solidify their understanding by summarizing each text.

However, integrating texts into a coherent mental map makes additional demands on readers (Cho & Afflerbach, 2017). As they work to synthesize ideas and information across texts, they must continually assess the importance and relevance of the information they encounter and connect it with what they previously read (Crafton, 1982; O'Reilly et al., 2015). The cognitive and metacognitive demands multiply when students must choose their own texts and read them in a digital environment.

Unlike a traditional text set (such as a set of articles or books), the internet offers a dizzying volume of potential sources of information, each with its own structure, many linked to other texts. These texts are often nonlinear, forcing the reader to decide multiple times as they engage with a source whether to stick with one page or navigate to another link. Given how recently humankind has gained access to this way of retrieving information, it makes sense that adolescents would need help navigating online inquiry and synthesizing information across multiple online sources.

Helpful Context for the Challenging Aspects of Synthesis

Without explicit instruction and careful guidance, teenage students can easily fall into a mindless sampling habit when they have to make sense of multiple texts. In particular, they struggle with four aspects of multi-text synthesis.

1. **Evaluating the task:** When students analyze the task they must complete, they make more targeted reading plans and are able to focus on relevant information (Higgs et al., 2023). Though they should not just skim and grab information, they do need to be strategic about where they put their efforts.

2. **Evaluating sources:** When it comes to source evaluation, secondary students often struggle to discern the accuracy and reliability of sources in a sea of cloned websites, AI-generated content, and targeted disinformation (Macedo-Rouet et al., 2019; Sinatra & Lombardi, 2020). Without coaching, students might just enter a question

or a few keywords into a search bar and click on the first link. Many students do not understand how tech companies design search algorithms. They might take texts at face value, believing whatever they encounter. They might not wonder about the source of the information they read. They might have been told to avoid Wikipedia and *.com* domains, but Wikipedia can be an excellent starting point for inquiry, and anyone can now register any type of domain name. A number of excellent resources are designed to help students choose credible sources and avoid misinformation, but there is great value in adult modeling and guidance.

3. **Making organized, coded notes:** When students are left to their own devices, their note taking is often little more than a copy-and-paste operation. They can lose track of the source of information they copied. A notes template or format can be a helpful scaffold, but students also need to learn to organize and keep up with their note making throughout their inquiry.

- **Comparing and integrating information:** Without help, students might do little to process the information they collect in their notes. Students need to know how to tackle points of agreement and disagreement and questions for which their sources have no answer.

The Synthesize Across Texts strategy helps students with these challenging aspects of multi-text synthesis. In the following sections, I outline the strategy steps, offer guidance for teaching the strategy, and give several suggestions to support assessment.

The Strategy Steps

The four steps of this strategy tackle each of the challenges described in the preceding section. They are described in the "Learning Guide: Synthesize Across Texts" reproducible (page 160).

1. **Evaluate the task:** This step encourages students to familiarize themselves with the assignment or task and clarify their purpose for reading multiple texts. For example, they might be asked to compare the perspectives of several authors, gather additional information after reading an initial text, or verify information they previously encountered. Next, they assess their current knowledge and generate inquiry questions to focus their reading.

2. **Find credible, relevant sources:** This step explains that the information students encounter at the top of their search results might not be accurate, so they need to keep scrolling. They learn to ask themselves questions to evaluate each source's relevance, accuracy, perspective, and reliability. They learn to read laterally (Wineburg & McGrew, 2017) to double-check accuracy and reliability.

3. **Make organized, coded notes:** In this step, students ask themselves questions to decide on the format and organization of their notes; then they devise a system to track the source of each piece of information. They learn to distinguish among quotes, paraphrases, and their own comments and questions.

4. **Compare and integrate information:** Students learn to reread, reorganize, and add to their notes. They ask questions to identify points of agreement and disagreement across sources. They learn to paraphrase the consensus among sources and decide what to do in the face of conflicting information. They think about whether they need to return to the sources for further investigation or read additional sources.

How to Teach the Strategy

Consider the following suggestions as you plan for explicit strategy instruction and continued practice of the Synthesize Across Texts strategy.

- I have found it helpful to broach the topic of synthesis with empathy. The problems this strategy addresses challenge not just teenage students but all of us. Just because adolescents are frequently on digital screens does not mean they can easily discern accurate, relevant information and reliable sources.

- Introduce the strategy using the learning guide and explain and demonstrate the steps with your chosen topic.

- Students will most likely need ongoing guidance, additional modeling, and supported practice. Consider sharing the strategy information with grade-level colleagues so they can also support students in their classrooms.

- The News Literacy Project (https://newslit.org) provides a wealth of resources to help you teach students to better evaluate the accuracy of information and reliability of internet sources, including its Checkology curriculum (free to educators and their students). The Civic Online Reasoning curriculum (https://cor.inquirygroup.org/curriculum/?tab=collections), created by Stanford University researchers at the Digital Inquiry Group, provides lesson plans and student-facing materials on lateral reading and other aspects of information literacy. The Digital Resources guide (available at **go.SolutionTree.com/literacy/MDSIT**) provides links and descriptions for these resources.

- I encourage preselecting a set of sources for inquiry. You can have everyone read two or three of the sources and then choose several more. This allows you to check students' mental maps for a shared text and ensures they are starting with accurate information. If students will be finding their own sources, prompt them to use step 2 (find credible, relevant sources) to guide their work.

- Collaboration can be built into the inquiry process. I often have students work together on step 3 (make organized, coded notes), creating group notes in a shared digital document. It is important to monitor this collaborative process so students do not partition the work or, even worse, leave the work to one or two team members.

- Students should document the source for each piece of information and add meaning-making commentary and questions. When you scroll through their shared notes, you will be able to see which students are making meaning and which are just sampling.

- Have students review their shared notes for a particular purpose, with each student discussing their contribution. They can then work together through the step 4 (compare and integrate information) questions to help consolidate their learning.

Assessment Suggestions

The information and suggestions in this section can help you plan to assess the strategy. You can use the key terms and questions to assess students' strategy knowledge. The self-assessment suggestions and evidence of mastery support your assessment of students' application of the strategy.

- **Key terms:**
  - *Synthesize*—To combine and integrate elements into a coherent whole

- *Coherent*—Having all the parts fit together clearly
- *Relevant*—Applicable and useful
- *Accurate*—Correct in all details
- *Reliable*—Consistent, trustworthy
- **Strategic knowledge questions:**
  - Why is it important to evaluate your task before reading multiple sources?
  - What do you need to keep in mind when you search for sources on the internet? What do you need to consider when evaluating potential sources?
  - What do you need to decide when you set up notes?
  - What should you do when multiple sources agree on a point? What should you do when multiple sources disagree?
  - What should you do when you don't have information on a point?
- **Self-assessment:** Once students have practiced the strategy independently, ask them to reflect on their process. Ask them to review the steps in the learning guide and write or record their responses to the prompt, "How has practicing the Synthesize Across Texts strategy changed how you select and evaluate sources? How does the note-making process in this strategy differ from how you have made notes in the past? How has the strategy helped you? What do you still need more practice or support with?"
- **Evidence of mastery:** When students have mastered the Synthesize Across Texts strategy, you will see them scrolling deep into their search results and checking sources by reading laterally. They will choose reliable sources with accurate information and will be able to explain how they determined credibility. Their notes will be organized. The source of each piece of information will be clear. Their notes will make clear distinctions between quotes, paraphrases, and student-composed commentary. Their paraphrases and comments will show their thinking. In their written products or presentations, students will acknowledge points of disagreement among their sources where appropriate.

The Share Learning Strategy

In school, adolescent students are called upon to complete a wide variety of tasks to demonstrate and share their learning. They write essays and research papers, design slide decks, make solo and group presentations, and prepare creative responses, from podcasts to collages. In my years of assigning, facilitating, and assessing such assignments, I have found that many students take shortcuts. Sometimes, they run out of time and rush through the assignment, slapping something together that meets the minimum criteria. However, I have talked with many students who genuinely did not know more was expected than to zhuzh up quotes and paraphrases with some decorative elements.

It seems that many students believe teachers are looking for form over function. Even my undergraduate students focus on questions like the following.

- "How many words should it be?"
- "How many slides should it be?"
- "Should we use MLA or APA?"

Consolidate Learning   153

- "Should we use Google Docs or Microsoft Word?"
- "How many sources do we need?"

I find that many students expect to be rewarded with a high grade if they check the boxes on these formulaic aspects of an assignment.

Once students work through the Synthesize Across Texts strategy steps, many need help preparing to share their learning in a way that demonstrates deep comprehension. Tenaha O'Reilly and colleagues (2015) argue that "proficient students should not only be able to read and understand texts, but they should also be able to communicate, through writing or speaking, what they have read and learned (Deane et al., 2008; Deane, Sabatini, & O'Reilly, 2012)" (p. 13).

Though it is beyond the scope of this book to give specific guidance on the myriad assignments teachers use to assess students' learning, the Share Learning strategy emphasizes a handful of essential practices that are useful in many contexts. The following sections detail steps for this strategy, guidance for teaching the strategy, and several suggestions to support assessment.

The Strategy Steps

In this strategy, students learn that sharing what they have learned with others helps them check for understanding, comprehend the material more deeply, and form their own informed perspective. The strategy includes the following steps.

1. **Outline ideas and information:** This step encourages students to start with *task analysis*—determining the purpose, intended audience, and expected product or presentation. Then, they review the information they have gathered and outline the key ideas and information they want to share. They are prompted to reread or do further inquiry if they notice gaps in their understanding.

2. **Let content drive design:** The "Learning Guide: Share Learning" reproducible (page 162) introduces the idea that students should know what story they want to tell and which ideas and information they want to communicate before they start designing. They are encouraged to work with the material until they can clearly explain what they want to say.

3. **Streamline and emphasize:** In this step, students learn three principles of design that help them tap into and further consolidate their mental maps.

4. **Credit all contributions:** Students learn they are responsible for crediting all contributions to their product or presentation, not just quotes. They are advised to try to identify the origin of material they find on the web and find another source if they cannot. Finally, the "Learning Guide: Share Learning" reproducible provides specific guidance for using and crediting images they find on the Internet.

How to Teach the Strategy

Use the following suggestions to teach the Share Learning strategy.

- This strategy can be introduced immediately before students prepare a presentation or product to share what they have learned from reading multiple texts on a topic.

- Use this strategy's learning guide to introduce the strategy and explain step 1 (outline ideas and information). Then work with students to analyze your assigned task,

154 MAKING DEEP SENSE OF INFORMATIONAL TEXTS

focusing on the purpose, intended audience, and details of the product or presentation. Prompt students to work through the step 1 questions in pairs. (They should have annotations or notes to consult.)

- Refer to this strategy's example of a Power Notes outline, or model another outline format. (See the reproducible "An Example: A Power Notes Outline for a Presentation," page 164.) Once they understand the task, you can have students try their hand at reviewing the information they have gathered (in annotations or notes) to identify key ideas and information they want to highlight. You might work through this process for a while with younger students, projecting your outline as you review the material and begin adding points. Show students how to reorganize items in the outline and demote or promote levels.

- Introduce step 2 (let content drive design) and model how you would approach answering the questions. If students will be creating a slide presentation, show them how to start with an unformatted slide presentation. For example, using Microsoft PowerPoint, toggle to Outline mode via the View toolbar tab to demonstrate how to enter outline items and then add sections and summary slides.

- Consult the Digital Resources guide (at **go.SolutionTree.com/literacy/MDSIT**) for more guidance on outlining, presentation design, and source attribution.

Assessment Suggestions

In this section, you will find suggestions and information to help you assess the Share Learning strategy. Use the listed terms and questions to assess students' strategy knowledge. Refer to the self-assessment suggestions and evidence of mastery as you plan to assess how well students are able to apply the strategy as they prepare a product or presentation that synthesizes learning across multiple texts.

- **Key terms:**
  - *Streamline*—To make a text as concise as possible
  - *Outline*—An organized list that summarizes the key ideas and details of a text
  - *Credit*—To acknowledge the original source of quotes, ideas, images, or information generated by someone else or by artificial intelligence (AI)
  - *Copyright*—The legal ownership of written, visual, or recorded material, with the right to control how it is reproduced and distributed

- **Strategic knowledge questions:**
  - How does sharing your learning help you understand the material more deeply?
  - What do you need to do first when you get an assignment that asks you to share your learning?
  - How do you go about making an outline to prepare to share your learning?
  - When do you need to give credit in your product or presentation?
  - What should you do if you cannot find the source of an image or piece of information?

- **Self-assessment:** After students have prepared a product or presentation using the strategy, have them reflect on their process. Ask them to review the steps in the learning guide and write or record their responses to the prompt, "How has practicing the Share

Learning strategy changed how you prepare for a presentation (or product)? How is the presentation (or product) different from what you would have created before?"

- **Evidence of mastery:** When students have mastered the Share Learning strategy, their products and presentations will be relevant, organized, streamlined, and responsible, as defined by the following.
  - *Relevant*—Focused on the most important information and ideas related to the task
  - *Organized*—Telling a clear, coherent, logical story
  - *Streamlined*—Giving enough information to answer essential questions without getting lost in small details
  - *Responsible*—Crediting sources of information, quotes, and images and including only elements the student is authorized to use

Concluding Thoughts

Of all the text-based tasks we ask secondary students to complete, they tend to struggle most with those that ask them to summarize, synthesize, and share what they have learned from reading info-texts. The strategies introduced in this chapter turn those challenging tasks into continued learning opportunities as students work to integrate and communicate the ideas and details they have learned from reading challenging informational texts.

Learning Guide: Summarize Texts

Summarization is a powerful comprehension strategy. It is not just skimming the text and paraphrasing. To summarize well, you must return to the text to determine the *key*, or most important, ideas and information and how they fit together. It is harder to summarize a complex text, but this strategy gives you a step-by-step process to make it easier.

1. Compose a central idea statement.
2. Paraphrase key supporting ideas.
3. Note key details and terms.
4. Draft and revise your summary.

- **Why:** When you summarize a text, your mental map becomes more accurate, detailed, and memorable.
- **When:** Summarize after you preview, read, and annotate the text. This strategy builds on the Preview Texts, Determine the Text Structure, Annotate Texts, and Check for Understanding strategies.
- **What to know:** A strong summary exhibits the following traits.
  - It expresses the central idea.
  - It includes key supporting ideas.
  - It includes key details and terms.
  - It might include examples or explanations.
  - It is clearly organized to show how ideas are connected.
  - It is written in your own scholarly voice.

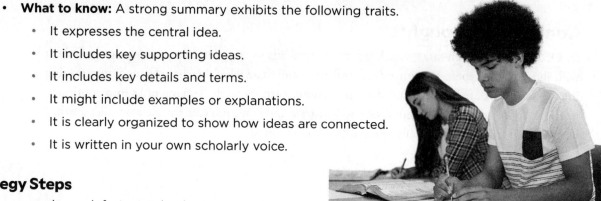

Strategy Steps

To summarize an info-text, take these steps.

1. Compose a Central Idea Statement

Return to the text, reviewing text features and annotations. Confirm the top-level text structure. Then, look away from the text and think about the *central idea*—the big, important idea the author communicates in the text. Decide which stem from the following suggested central idea stems list best reflects the top-level text structure.

To compose a central idea statement, ask yourself these questions.
- What is the central idea of the whole text?
- Which central idea stem fits with the top-level text structure?

Suggested Central Idea Stems

- **Description:** Described, described the features of, described how
- **Sequence:** Explained the process of, outlined steps to or of, described the series of events
- **Problem-solution:** Explained the issue or problem, discussed solutions or efforts
- **Cause-effect:** Explained the causes or effects of, explained why
- **Compare-contrast:** Discussed benefits and drawbacks of, compared, evaluated and recommended, argued for or against

Finally, draft a *central idea statement* using the following statement frame.

In [type of text], [title], [the author] [central idea stem] [central idea].

Two examples of central idea statements follow.

1. In a March 2022 editorial in the *Houston Post*, the editorial board evaluated four front-runners for the commissioner's race and recommended Terry Hemlock for the job.

2. In a September 2024 feature article on her university's website, gerontology expert Marina Herdéz described how research into aging has evolved in recent years.

2. Paraphrase Key Supporting Ideas

Review the text section by section. Determine the *key* (important) *supporting ideas* that fit together to support the author's central idea. These ideas may be stated, or you may have to infer them from your reading.

Look away from the text and paraphrase each idea in your own scholarly words.

> To paraphrase key supporting ideas, ask yourself these questions.
> - What does the author spend the most time talking about?
> - Which are the most important ideas?
> - Which ideas work together to support the central idea?

3. Note Key Details and Terms

Review the text again using the *reporter questions* (Who?, What?, When?, Where?, Why?, and How?) to identify key *details* (pieces of information) and *terms* (words and phrases) that will help your reader understand the author's central idea or key supporting ideas. Jot them down.

If you will be writing a more detailed summary, decide which examples or explanations can help you illustrate or clarify an important idea. Paraphrase the example or explanation.

> To note key details and terms, ask yourself these questions.
> - How detailed does the summary need to be?
> - Which details and terms are most important for me to add?
> - Are there examples or explanations that are really important to mention?

4. Draft and Revise Your Summary

To introduce the summary, use your central idea statement in step 1 as the topic sentence. Add the key supporting ideas you drafted in step 2 (paraphrase key supporting ideas). Weave in the details and terms you decided to add in step 3 (note key details and terms). Add examples (specific instances that illustrate a general idea) or explanations (clarifying statements) if you decide they will help your reader. The length and the level of detail of your summary depend on your purpose. You might write a detailed summary as part of an assignment or jot down a short informal summary in your notes.

Review the text you are summarizing to make sure your summary accurately represents the author's meaning. Read through your summary to make sure your ideas logically flow. Add transitions or combine sentences to show the connections between ideas. Revise sentences to make them clearer. Remove any unnecessary words.

> To draft and revise your summary, ask yourself these questions.
> - Does my draft make sense? Do I accurately represent the text?
> - Should I make connections between ideas clearer? Should I combine sentences? Should I add a transition?
> - Have I left anything out that I need to add? Have I included details that aren't important?
> - Can I improve my word choice to make my summary clearer and more scholarly?

Making Deep Sense of Informational Texts © 2025 Solution Tree Press • SolutionTree.com
Visit **go.SolutionTree.com/literacy/MDSIT** and enter the unique access code found on this book's inside front cover to access this reproducible.

An Example: Apply the Summarize Texts Strategy With a Science Article

In this example (color version available online at **go.SolutionTree.com/literacy/MDSIT**), you can see how the Summarize Texts strategy has been applied to a published scientific article. To read this article in full, visit its URL included in the source note at the end of this example.

Step 1: Central Idea Statement

In his 2023 scientific article, "The Heroic Effort to Save Florida's Coral Reef From Extreme Ocean Heat as Corals Bleach Across the Caribbean," ecologist Michael Childress explains the <u>problem</u> of coral bleaching and describes the <u>efforts</u> of scientists and volunteers to protect them.

Step 2: Key Idea Statements

1. Rising marine temperatures have damaged corals off the Florida Keys and in the Caribbean.
2. Scientists worked with volunteer divers to move heat-resistant corals to a Florida reef to replace the damaged ones.
3. The water got even hotter, making the coral bleaching even worse.
4. Scientists started working with volunteers to move the transplanted baby corals.
5. Organizations are taking other actions to save the corals.
6. Scientists are hopeful they can save the reef, but they need help.

Step 3: Key Details, Terms, Examples, and Explanations

Who	NOAA (National Oceanic and Atmospheric Administration)
When	2019 (NOAA started moving corals.)
	2023 (The water got so hot scientists had to move them again.)
Where	Florida Keys, Alligator Reef (They are moving the corals to cooler waters and marine labs.)
Why	They are moving corals again because the new transplants are now in danger.
(explanations)	The reef is important to the ecosystem and the local economy.
	Extreme heat causes corals to release the helpful algae that give them color.
What (examples)	Training divers to remove harmful algae and monitor bleaching

Step 4: Summary

In his 2023 scientific article, "The Heroic Effort to Save Florida's Coral Reef From Extreme Ocean Heat as Corals Bleach Across the Caribbean," ecologist Michael Childress explains the <u>problem</u> of coral bleaching and describes the <u>efforts</u> of scientists and volunteers to protect them. Since 2019, rising marine temperatures have damaged corals off the Florida Keys and in the Caribbean, causing them to release the helpful algae that give them color. Scientists with NOAA (National

---

page 1 of 2

Making Deep Sense of Informational Texts © 2025 Solution Tree Press • SolutionTree.com
Visit **go.SolutionTree.com/literacy/MDSIT** and enter the unique access code found on this book's inside front cover to access this reproducible.

Oceanic and Atmospheric Administration) worked with volunteer divers to move heat-resistant corals to Florida's Alligator Reef to replace the damaged ones. In 2023, the water got even hotter, making the coral bleaching even worse and threatening the new transplants. In response, scientists began to work with volunteers to move the transplanted baby corals to cooler waters and marine labs. Organizations are taking other actions to save the corals, too, like training divers to remove harmful algae and monitor bleaching. Scientists are hopeful they can save the reef, which is critically important to the ecosystem and local economy, but they need help.

Source: Childress, M. (2023, August 9). The heroic effort to save Florida's coral reef from extreme ocean heat as corals bleach across the Caribbean. The Conversation. Accessed at https://theconversation.com/the-heroic-effort-to-save-floridas-coral-reef-from-extreme-ocean-heat-as-corals-bleach-across-the-caribbean-210974 on August 18, 2024.

Learning Guide: Synthesize Across Texts

School assignments like research reports and presentations require you to read multiple informational texts. You might read other texts on a topic to check your understanding of an assigned text. You also read multiple texts for your own purposes—to learn more about a hobby or keep up with a topic.

1. Evaluate the task.
2. Find credible, relevant sources.
3. Make organized, coded notes.
4. Compare and integrate information.

- **Why:** It can be difficult to find quality sources, decide how to approach reading them, and keep track of the information you find. It is even more difficult to synthesize what you read, especially if sources have contradictory information or varied perspectives. When you *synthesize*, you combine and integrate elements into a *coherent* whole. When something is coherent, all the parts clearly fit together.

- **When:** This strategy is useful whenever you need to read multiple info-texts and synthesize the information. It builds on the other Deep Sense Approach strategies.

Strategy Steps

To synthesize information across multiple texts, follow these steps.

1. Evaluate the Task

Reread the assignment or think about your task. Consider your purpose for reading multiple texts.

Think about what you know, are unsure about, and need to know. Make a list of questions or specific information you need to know.

To evaluate the task, ask yourself these questions.
- What is the task? What is my purpose in reading multiple texts?
- What do I already know? What am I unsure about?
- What do I need or want to know?

2. Find Credible, Relevant Sources

To find sources, you can ask a teacher, librarian, or other knowledgeable person for suggestions. You might also use books and websites you already know about, or you can use an internet search engine.

When you type keywords in a search bar and hit Enter, you often get millions of results. (Use the Advanced Search function to narrow your search.) Try different keyword combinations as needed.

You might see AI-generated items at the top of your results, such as a "rich card" with summary information, questions with drop-down menus, and sponsored (paid) content and links. These items might not contain accurate information. Keep scrolling down.

To find credible, relevant sources, ask yourself these questions.
- Where can I get the information I need? Do I know some credible sources I can start with?
- Which individuals and organizations are known as experts on this topic?
- What keywords will help me get the search results I want?
- Is the source relevant? Is it accurate? Is it reliable?

Look at the URL of each search result to determine its source. Bookmark or copy the URLs for sources you want to evaluate further.

REPRODUCIBLE | 161

To evaluate the credibility of a source, assess its relevance, accuracy, and reliability (Coiro, 2017).

- **Relevance:** Is the source *relevant* (applicable and useful)? Can this source help me answer my questions or complete my task?

- **Accuracy:** Is the information *accurate* (correct in all its parts)? Is it factual and up-to-date? What are the author's sources of information? Are those sources credible? (Note that even reliable authors get it wrong sometimes.)

- **Reliability:** Is the source *reliable* (consistent and trustworthy)? Can I tell who the author is? (You might need to scroll to the bottom or visit a different page on the site.) Can I trust their work? Are they an expert in the field? What do others say about them? Is the publisher a legitimate organization, or did the author self-publish?

If you are unsure about a source, do some *lateral reading*. Open up a new tab and search for that person or organization. Look for reliable sites that help you determine their trustworthiness.

3. Make Organized, Coded Notes

If you don't have a required notes format, decide whether you will make notes on paper or digitally.

Set up your notes to help you complete your task. You might make notes for each source or organize them by topic or question.

Track the source for each piece of information with an in-text citation, URL, or number in parentheses. Distinguish between quotes, paraphrases, and your own comments and questions. (You might change your font style or color.)

> To make organized, coded notes, ask yourself these questions.
>
> - Will I make notes on paper or digitally?
> - How will I organize my notes?
> - How will I keep track of the source of each piece of information?
> - How will I distinguish among quotes, paraphrases, and my own comments and questions?

4. Compare and Integrate Information

Return to your notes and reread them. Add comments and questions. Reorganize information.

Look for points multiple sources agree on. Add a summary of the consensus view in your own words.

Look for points of disagreement. Decide whether you need to return to the sources to further evaluate them. Do the authors see the issue differently? Do they use different evidence? Is one text written more recently? Add comments in your notes.

Decide if you need to search for additional information to answer specific questions.

> To compare and integrate information, ask yourself these questions.
>
> - What points do sources agree on?
> - What points do sources disagree on? Do I need to review those sources or find additional ones?
> - Which points have I found in only one source? Am I sure they are accurate?
> - What do I now know for sure? What am I still unsure about? What information do I still not have?

Reference

Coiro, J. (2017, August 29). *Teaching adolescents how to evaluate the quality of online information*. Accessed at www.edutopia.org/blog/evaluating-quality-of-online-info-julie-coiro on September 27, 2024.

Making Deep Sense of Informational Texts © 2025 Solution Tree Press • SolutionTree.com
Visit **go.SolutionTree.com/literacy/MDSIT** and enter the unique access code found on this book's inside front cover to access this reproducible.

Learning Guide: Share Learning

You are often asked to share what you learned from your info-text reading. You might be asked to compose a report or make a slide presentation. Sometimes, you share your learning in blog posts, speeches, podcasts, and other creative expressions. Whatever the format, the purpose is to communicate what you learned.

1. Outline ideas and information.

2. Let content drive design.

3. Streamline and emphasize.

4. Credit all contributions.

- **Why:** Sharing what you learn from your reading helps you understand the material more deeply. You continue to think about the author's ideas and information. You catch gaps and points of confusion as you try to explain ideas. You also begin to form your own informed perspective. As you prepare, you might find it difficult to explain an important idea. This might be a sign you need to reread, consult with others, or do more research.

- **When:** Apply this strategy when you need to share with others what you have learned from reading info-texts. It should be used along with the Summarize Texts and Synthesize Across Texts strategies.

Strategy Steps

Use these steps to present what you have learned from reading info-texts.

1. Outline Ideas and Information

An *outline* is an organized list that summarizes the key ideas and details of a text. To make an outline for your product or presentation, do the following.

- Find out as much as you can about the purpose, intended audience, and expected product or presentation.

- Review all the information you have gathered in notes and annotations.

- Make an outline of key ideas and details. You might use the Power Notes method (AdLit, n.d.), the Outline view in PowerPoint, or the multilevel list feature in a digital document. Or you can use an outlining method or tool your teacher or you prefer.

- If you need to understand or know more, reread or do more research.

To outline key ideas and information, ask yourself these questions.

- What is the purpose? Who is my intended audience? What exactly am I supposed to prepare?

- What do I know so far? What are the most important ideas and information to communicate?

- What do I need to clarify? What other information do I need?

2. Let Content Drive Design

It is tempting to jump right in, but hold off on deciding the look or format until you know exactly what you want to say. Think through these questions without looking at your materials. If you cannot answer them, review your outline and, if needed, your notes and annotations. Continue until you have a clear idea of the story you want to tell and how you want to sequence that story.

If you are making a slide presentation, start with plain slides. Work out the organization and content of the slides. Then, use the program features to create sections and summary slides.

To create a content-focused design, ask yourself these questions.

- What story do I want to tell?

- What does my audience want or need to know?

- What ideas and information do I want to emphasize?

page 1 of 2

Making Deep Sense of Informational Texts © 2025 Solution Tree Press • SolutionTree.com
Visit **go.SolutionTree.com/literacy/MDSIT** and enter the unique access code found on this book's inside front cover to access this reproducible.

3. Streamline and Emphasize

To streamline and emphasize, do the following.

1. **Streamline the text:** Make the text as concise as possible by breaking up large chunks of text into digestible bites, using short sentences and phrases, and keeping quotes short.

2. **Make clear connections between ideas and information:** Use text features like headings, transition words, bulleted or numbered lists, diagrams, and arrows to show ideas and details are connected to each other. Create summary and section slides.

3. **Emphasize key ideas and information:** Each image, diagram, quote, and design detail should illustrate a specific point. Use visual text features like font changes, text boxes, and infographics to add emphasis. Crop images to just the relevant part.

Following is an example of a slide that presents streamlined information about red-tailed hawks. The heading and bullets signal how the information is connected, and the image is directly related to the content. The font changes help emphasize key ideas.

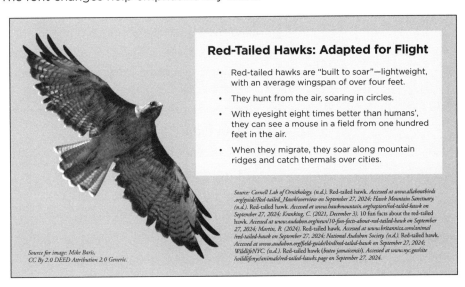

4. Credit All Contributions

Show your original thinking and work. If you use other people's quotes, ideas, images, or information, make sure to *credit* their work with a citation or other acknowledgment. If you paraphrase, you still need to give credit unless the information is very widely known. Because there is so much copied and AI-created content on the internet, it can be hard to find the original source for a quote, image, or piece of information, but it is important to try. If you can't verify where it came from, try to find something else that makes the same point.

Make sure images are available for use. Don't just right-click and copy them. In a Google search, you can click on Search by Image and then Find Image Source. The image might be copyright protected, meaning it is legally owned by someone who has control of how it is reproduced and distributed.

To credit contributions, ask yourself these questions.

- Do I know the origins of the information, quotes, and images I am using?
- Have I given credit for the ideas, information, and images in my product or presentation?

Reference

AdLit. (n.d.). *Power Notes*. Accessed at www.adlit.org/in-the-classroom/strategies/power-notes on November 13, 2024.

An Example: A Power Notes Outline for a Presentation

Sources

a. Cornell Lab of Ornithology. (n.d.). *Red-tailed hawk.* Accessed at www.allaboutbirds.org/guide/Red-tailed_Hawk/overview on September 27, 2024.

b. Hawk Mountain Sanctuary. (n.d.). *Red-tailed hawk.* Accessed at www.hawkmountain.org/raptors/red-tailed-hawk on September 27, 2024.

c. Kranking, C. (2021, December 3). *10 fun facts about the red-tailed hawk.* Accessed at www.audubon.org/news/10-fun-facts-about-red-tailed-hawk on September 27, 2024.

d. Martin, R. (2024). *Red-tailed hawk.* Accessed at www.britannica.com/animal/red-tailed-hawk on September 27, 2024.

e. National Audubon Society. (n.d.). *Red-tailed hawk.* Accessed at www.audubon.org/field-guide/bird/red-tailed-hawk on September 27, 2024.

f. WildlifeNYC. (n.d.). *Red-tailed hawk* (buteo jamaicensis). Accessed at www.nyc.gov/site/wildlifenyc/animals/red-tailed-hawks.page on September 27, 2024.

Power Notes: Red-Tailed Hawks—Masters of Adaptation

1 Thriving
- 2 most widespread hawk in N. Am. (a, b, c, d, e)
  - 3 estimated ½ m to 1 m (f)
- 2 numbers are stable or increasing (b, d)
- 2 range—almost all of N. Am. (d)
  - 3 migration map (see a or b)

1 Adaptable (f)
- 2 "partial migrants" (c, d, f)
  - 3 many "in the northern portion of the range" migrate south for winter (f)
  - 3 soar along mountain ridges, catch thermals over cities (f)
  - 3 migration decreasing with global warming
- 2 adapted for flight
  - 3 4+ ft avg. wingspan (c, d) but lightweight (a)
  - 3 hunt from the air, soaring in circles (b, c, f)
  - 3 eyesight 8x better than humans' (c)
    - 4 mouse at 100 ft
  - 3 courting: males perform aerial acrobatics (a, b, c, d)
- 2 apex predator with a widely varied diet
  - 3 mammals, reptiles, amphibians, bats, fish, insects (d f)

1 Can coexist with humans (f)
- 2 don't need forests
  - 3 can live in a wide variety of habitats (b)
    - 4 inc. scattered clearings, open grassland, or desert (b, e)
- 2 hunt along highways (c, f)
  - 3 perch-hunters—swoop down (b, f)
    - 4 prefer high perches (for example, telephone poles) (f)
    - 4 in open areas with patches of trees (d)
- 2 live in cities
  - 3 adapting to nesting in cities (b, d, e)
    - 4 in NYC—nest blocks from each other (c, e)
  - 3 Pale Male (NYC) (c)

Making Deep Sense of Informational Texts © 2025 Solution Tree Press • SolutionTree.com
Visit **go.SolutionTree.com/literacy/MDSIT** and enter the unique access code found on this book's inside front cover to access this reproducible.

CONCLUSION

In the introduction, I shared that the Deep Sense Approach and this book grew out of my concern for the millions of adolescent students whose comprehension skills are not developed enough to be able to make deep sense of the info-texts they must tackle daily. The four-pronged Deep Sense Approach introduced in this book can go a long way toward addressing the comprehension challenges that confront our secondary students.

Weak Info-Text Comprehension Is a Thorny Problem

Somewhere along the way, as reading demands got heavier and more serious, many of our students fell out of love with info-text reading, or at least with the kind of reading they are asked to do in school. I described in chapter 1 how secondary students slip into a negative feedback loop as they lose confidence in their comprehension skills and lose motivation to do the hard work of comprehending complex texts. They begin to hide their low self-efficacy with masks of indifference or apathy and perfect shortcuts like fake reading, sampling, and task avoidance.

It is important to remember that the great majority of secondary students can indeed read. When they focus on reading a text, they can usually state the gist, recognize a clearly stated central claim, and find answers to low-inference questions. These basic comprehension skills are sufficient for many tasks. The trouble comes when they need to interpret, infer, analyze, synthesize, or summarize, especially when the info-texts are not well organized.

The Solution Isn't Simple

The approach outlined in this book has made a true difference for my middle and high school students in building these deeper comprehension skills, and I believe it can make a difference for your students as well.

This is not a simple approach. It cannot be if it is to make a dent in the multi-pronged problem of shallow adolescent comprehension skills. If this problem were solvable with a workbook or a web-based computer program, I feel confident that we would have seen a substantial improvement in reading assessment results, since schools have invested billions of dollars and immeasurable time and effort trying to improve students' comprehension through those means.

165

We also cannot implement enough intervention classes, pull-outs, and after-school and weekend tutorials to fix the problem.

Motivation isn't enough. Strategy instruction isn't enough. Collaborative discussion isn't enough. Close reading isn't enough. However, when we combine these elements into a coherent approach enacted in general education classrooms across disciplines over time, the needle can start to move. My teaching experience and research support this conclusion. So does a large body of evidence from high-quality research conducted over decades.

Students Need a Four-Pronged Approach

I have designed this book to provide what you need to implement the four-pronged Deep Sense Approach: (1) building students' confidence and motivation, (2) explicitly teaching an updated set of info-text strategies, (3) providing meaningful context with text-centered discussions, and (4) reinforcing multiple strategies in shared info-text studies.

1. Building Students' Confidence and Motivation

In chapter 3, I discussed what research tells us about students' need to feel connected, competent, and in control of their reading and learning; then I detailed motivational practices that can be enacted in any classroom. In my instructional and assessment suggestions throughout the book, I have offered ideas for engaging secondary students in meaning making in a way that honors their background knowledge, their previous experiences, their insights, their interests, and their needs.

2. Explicitly Teaching an Updated Set of Info-Text Strategies

In chapter 2, I explained that strategy use is essential for comprehension and that strategies must evolve as texts and tasks get more complex. In chapter 4, I described what we know about effective comprehension strategy instruction from decades of research; then I laid out a flexible lesson sequence that can be adapted to varied strategies, students, and classrooms. In the chapters in part 3, I detailed each of the fourteen info-text comprehension strategies at the heart of the Deep Sense Approach and provided specific instructional and assessment guidance. In appendix A (page 169), I include a planning guide and sample lesson to further support your strategy instruction.

3. Providing Meaningful Context With Text-Centered Discussions

In chapter 5, I explained what research has revealed about the power of text-centered discussion and described the components of effective meaning-making discussions. Then in chapter 7, I detailed the Talk About Texts strategy, which teaches students how to engage in productive meaning-making discussions.

4. Reinforcing Multiple Strategies in Shared Info-Text Studies

In chapter 6, I presented the components of the shared info-text study (SITS), in which the class works together to make deep meaning of an interesting, complex text, increasing students' confidence, comprehension, and strategy knowledge along the way. For each strategy presented in part 3, I suggested ways to help students apply their new strategy knowledge as they work together with a complex text. In appendix B (page 177), I provide a planning guide and two sample SITS plans to help you make SITS a reality in your classroom.

Deep Sense Is a Partial Solution

Some secondary students continue to need support (sometimes intensive) to build their foundational literacy skills. For some, their skill gaps significantly interfere with their ability to comprehend. Though these students have sometimes been identified as having specific learning or language challenges, many have not.

- They may have inadequate phonics knowledge and decoding automaticity, especially with multisyllable and low-frequency words. They may skip long words altogether or stumble over or guess at their pronunciations. They may plow through decoding errors without recognizing that their substituted words make no sense.
- They may struggle with oral or silent reading fluency. They may read so slowly that they lose track of meaning. When they read aloud, they may pause frequently or misspeak. They may read aloud in a monotone voice, not pausing for phrasing or breath.
- They may struggle to make meaning of long sentences, especially those with multiple clauses, phrase insertions, passive voice, unclear antecedents, and other syntactic issues.
- They may have very limited background knowledge, including knowledge of word meanings, which affects their comprehension of info-texts and makes them less effective at inferencing.

We must address these issues, but for adolescent students, we do not have the luxury of treating these issues in a vacuum. In my experience, the Deep Sense Approach is broadly inclusive. The four components are useful for students who struggle with foundational issues. Too often, these students are excluded from the rich, collaborative, challenging literacy experiences recommended in this book. This exclusion does not benefit them; it isolates them. Secondary students deemed too low skilled for these experiences are fully aware of this negative perception of their capacity. With sufficient scaffolding, these students can grow from engaging with their peers in the experiences described in this book.

Deep Sense Is a Flexible, Grow-as-You-Go Approach

As I explained in the introduction and throughout the book, the Deep Sense Approach is designed to be flexible. Having spent seventeen years as a classroom teacher and many more in and around public secondary schools, I know the realities that cut into the best-laid plans of teachers and administrators.

Secondary teachers have many demands on their teaching time. If we are lucky, we have 180 hours scheduled each year for each class. In my last teaching assignment, I had 135. During those hours, most of us are required by our state or provincial government to address dozens of learning standards. We are not merely expected to introduce students to information, concepts, and skills. We are expected to teach to mastery. In addition to these curricular responsibilities, many of us are expected to prepare students for high-stakes assessments. Responding to the pressure teachers are under to produce satisfactory test scores, we learn to become strategic. Given our limited teaching time, we emphasize the knowledge and skills that will be assessed, and we adjust course at least some of the year to align our teaching to match the assessment. Though we may want to emphasize inquiry and exploration, we find ourselves dragging students through review, multiple-choice practice, and formulaic essays.

Beyond our responsibilities to teach the curriculum and prepare students for assessments, we must attend to dozens of "break-ins"—tasks required by our campus or district that eat up learning time. We administer district surveys or benchmark tests. We march our students to the cafeteria for assemblies. We evacuate the building for fire drills and hunker under counters for active shooter drills. We have unscheduled break-ins, too—an administrator drops by to speak to the class about a campus incident, or an argument demands the whole class's attention. Finally, we lose instructional time attending to the day-to-day exigencies of running our classroom, from attending to students' social-emotional needs to administering bureaucratic tasks.

Acknowledging these realities, I encourage you to start somewhere, start small, experiment, learn, tweak, and try again. I also encourage you not to go it alone. Though you certainly can implement the Deep Sense Approach just within your class, I have found that the issue of weak info-text comprehension is one that concerns teachers across grades and disciplines. In subject-area departments or grade-level teams, you might find kindred spirits who are willing to partner with you in the interest of collegial continuous improvement.

I have been working to understand more and grow in effectiveness in the area of comprehension instruction for most of my career. I still have much to learn. I encourage you to revisit this book as a reference and guide. Hopefully, it can inspire you to try again if a lesson, discussion, or text study doesn't go exactly as planned. This is a complex and difficult venture, and the teachers who do best with it are those brave enough to fail forward, trusting themselves and their students to improve with time. Just know that there are many others like you, working very hard to help students make deeper sense of what they read.

APPENDIX A

This appendix includes the following reproducible resources.

- "Strategy Instruction Planning Guide" (page 170)
- "Sample Strategy Lesson: Teaching the Annotation Strategy" (page 174)

Strategy Instruction Planning Guide

This planning guide is a supplement to chapter 4 (page 39) of *Making Deep Sense of Informational Texts*. As an example of a strategy instruction lesson, see the reproducible "Sample Strategy Lesson: Teaching the Annotation Strategy" (appendix A, page 174). Consult the relevant chapter in part 3 of this book for strategy-specific teaching and assessment suggestions. Learning guides and other instructional materials are available at the end of each strategy chapter. Resources are also available online (at **go.SolutionTree.com/literacy/MDSIT**).

The Strategy Instruction Planning Process

Preparation

- Identify learning standards.
- Prepare materials.

Strategy Lesson Components

1. Assess and activate background knowledge.
2. Explain and model.
3. Lead guided practice.
4. Facilitate independent practice.
5. Assess strategy knowledge and application.
6. Provide feedback and reteaching.

Preparation

Determine the learning standards you will address (including content and literacy-related objectives) and the resources and materials you will use (including the strategy learning guide, mentor texts, and technology tools).

- ☐ ***Identify learning standards.***

    - Alignment—*Which content and literacy standards align with the strategy?*

- ☐ ***Prepare materials.***

    - Learning guide—*Will I make copies of the strategy learning guide or have students access it digitally?*

    - Mentor text—*What text will I use to model and practice the strategy? Will I provide copies of the mentor text or have students access it digitally?*

    - Technology—*Will I need a projector, document camera, or laptop cart?*

Lesson Sequence

Plan for a gradual release of responsibility lesson, step by step. Consult the relevant chapter in part 3 for specific instructional and assessment suggestions for the strategy you are planning to teach.

1. Assess and Activate Background Knowledge

- ☐ **Ask low-stakes questions.**
  - Questions—*What open-ended question or questions will I ask to assess and activate students' background knowledge?*
  - Format—*Will I have students write their responses, discuss in pairs, or both?*
- ☐ **Observe practice.**
  - Options—*Will I observe students as they engage in a task independently or with peers?*
- ☐ **Honor background knowledge.**
  - Connections—*How can I help students connect with what they already know and do?*
  - Strengths—*How can I acknowledge their current strengths?*

2. Explain and Model

- ☐ **Introduce strategic information.**
  - Learning guide—*How will I use the strategy learning guide as I provide the overview and rationale for the strategy? How will students engage with the learning guide as I introduce each step?*
  - Student engagement—*What examples, stories, metaphors, or shared experiences might engage students and help them connect with the material?*
  - Questions—*What questions will I ask to check their understanding?*
- ☐ **Model each step.**
  - Sequence—*Will I explain all the steps and then model, or explain and model each step?*
  - Method—*Will I do a think-aloud, analyze a teacher- or student-created model, or demonstrate with an individual student or team?*
  - Questions—*If the learning guide includes questions, how will I use them in my modeling?*
  - Student input—*When can I invite students to give input on my modeling?*
- ☐ **Provide processing time.**
  - Chunk-and-chew—*When will I pause to have students discuss and process? Will students annotate their copies of the strategy learning guide, make notes, review the steps and check their understanding, or explain the steps to a peer?*

Note: If most of your students are already proficient in the strategy, you might move quickly through the explanation and modeling and then provide more focused instruction to a small group.

3. Lead Guided Practice

- ☐ **Lead whole-class practice.**
  - Sequence—*Will we practice strategy steps one at a time or altogether?*
  - Mentor text—*Will we practice the strategy with a familiar text, a new section of the text I modeled with, or a short new text on a familiar topic?*
  - Key terms—*How will students think about and use key terms?*

page 2 of 4

Making Deep Sense of Informational Texts © 2025 Solution Tree Press • SolutionTree.com
Visit **go.SolutionTree.com/literacy/MDSIT** to download this free reproducible.

□ ***Scaffold with discussion.***

- Questions—*If the strategy learning guide includes questions, how will I use them as we practice?*

- Constellations—*How can I engage students in discussion as a whole class and in teams and pairs?*

□ ***Release students to guided pair or team practice.***

- Timing—*When will I release students to practice with a partner or team?*

- Structure—*Will students work through the questions for a step with a partner or in their teams? Will they share their practice attempt with a peer and then give and receive feedback?*

- Scaffolding—*Will students refer to their strategy learning guide, anchor chart, written instructions, or a completed example? Will I circulate or work with a small group or an individual?*

□ ***Clarify as needed.***

- Approach—*What will I do if students aren't getting an aspect of the strategy?*

- Differentiation—*Which students might I expect to need more explanation and modeling? How can I build in extra support for them?*

4. Facilitate Independent Practice

□ ***Move from external to internal dialogue.***

- Questions—*If the strategy learning guide includes questions, will I have students answer those in writing as they work independently? Will I ask them to practice self-questioning without writing? If so, how will I assess their success?*

- Text—*Will I have students practice with a short, familiar text first before moving to a more challenging one?*

□ ***Structure and scaffold written tasks.***

- Instructions—*What instructions will I give? How will I give them? How will I ensure students understand them?*

- Standard setting—*Will I provide a rubric or checklist? Will I model? Will I provide a worked example?*

- Structured responses—*Will I have students complete a graphic organizer, paragraph frame, or sentence stems? Will I provide a word bank?*

- Consultation—*Will I allow students to consult with peers or resources like their strategy learning guide?*

- Extent—*Will I make scaffolds available to all students or just some students?*

5. Assess Strategy Knowledge and Application

□ ***Assess students' strategic knowledge.*** *(Strategy-specific assessment suggestions are available throughout part 3.)*

- Key terms—*How will I evaluate students' understanding of key terms introduced in the learning guide? Will I ask them to identify or produce a definition, combine the terms in a summary of the strategy, or use the terms during a team discussion?*

page 3 of 4

Making Deep Sense of Informational Texts © 2025 Solution Tree Press • SolutionTree.com
Visit **go.SolutionTree.com/literacy/MDSIT** to download this free reproducible.

| REPRODUCIBLE | 173 |

- Strategy questions—*What questions will I ask students to assess their uptake of strategic knowledge? In what format will I have them respond? Will they talk with peers or consult their strategy learning guide before or after they have tried to answer the questions? (You can use the following question stems to compose your own strategy questions.)*
  - *"Why is it important to . . . ?" or "How does it help to . . . ?"*
  - *"Which _____ do you think is most important?" or "Which _____ do you use the most?"*
  - *"What can you do when . . . ?"*
  - *"When is it important to . . . ?"*
  - *"What do you need to keep in mind when you . . . ?"*

☐ ***Assess students' strategy application.***
- Task and evidence of mastery—*Will I observe students, listen as they discuss in teams, or ask them to complete a written task? What evidence of mastery will I look for?*

☐ ***Make time for self-assessment.***
- Focus—*What open-ended question or questions will I ask?*
- Format—*Will I post a prompt, give an exit ticket, or use an online form? Will students discuss, write, or both?*
- Debrief—*Will I debrief with the class and synthesize what I learned from their reflections?*

6. Provide Feedback and Reteaching

☐ ***Provide precise feedback quickly.***
- Focus—*What will I focus my feedback on?*
- Format—*Will I give feedback individually or to the group? Will I do that in writing or verbally?*

☐ ***Compare and revise.***
- Standard-setting—*Will I refer to a rubric or checklist? Will I post examples of exemplary student work, a model I have created, or a published text? How will we analyze the model?*
- Effort comparison—*Will students compare their efforts with a partner or team? Will they compare their annotations, notes, graphic organizers, or drafts?*
- Revision—*Will they have an opportunity to revise after comparing their work with the model or their peers' work?*

☐ ***Reteach.***
- Method—*Will I explain differently, model with a different text, or have students analyze an exemplar with me?*
- Extent—*Will I reteach the material to the whole class, to a small group, or to individuals?*

page 4 of 4

Making Deep Sense of Informational Texts © 2025 Solution Tree Press • SolutionTree.com
Visit **go.SolutionTree.com/literacy/MDSIT** to download this free reproducible.

Sample Strategy Lesson: Teaching the Annotation Strategy

This sample lesson is an example of Deep Sense Approach strategy instruction aligned with the "Strategy Instruction Planning Guide" (appendix A, page 170). See chapter 4 (page 39) for a narrative description of Mr. Abara's lesson.

Teacher: Anthony Abara **Class:** Social Studies 7 **Strategy:** Annotate Texts

Date or Duration: Two class periods in the unit: Colonization of the Americas

Preparation

Standards

- **Content:**
    - "Explain how and where each empire arose and how the Aztec and Incan empires were defeated by the Spanish" (HSS-7.7.3; California Department of Education, 1998).
- **Literacy:**
    - "Determine the central ideas or information of a primary or secondary source" (RH.6-8.2; NGA & CCSSO, 2010).
    - "Read and comprehend history/social studies texts in the grades 6–8 text complexity band independently and proficiently" (RH.6-8.10; NGA & CCSSO, 2010).
    - "Draw evidence from informational texts to support analysis, reflection, and research" (W.9-10.9; NGA & CCSSO, 2010).

Resources and Materials

- Textbook excerpt, radio story, handouts (learning guide, Cortés letter, scholarly accounts, NPR transcript), speaker and screen, document projector, sticky notes, index cards
- Digital Inquiry Group. (n.d.). Moctezuma and Cortés. Accessed at https://inquirygroup.org/history-lessons/moctezuma-and-cortes on November 4, 2024.
- Fredrick, J. (2019, November 10). ≤ 500 years later, the Spanish conquest of Mexico is still being debated [Radio broadcast]. NPR. Accessed at www.npr.org/transcripts/777220132 on November 4, 2024.

Lesson Sequence

1. Assess and Activate Background Knowledge

- Have students do a think-write-pair-share (using sticky notes) with the prompt, "What does it mean to 'annotate' a text? What do you do when you annotate?"
- Emphasize that they will update their strategy to ensure it is useful for them as they read more complex texts in middle school, high school, and college.

2. Explain and Model

- Introduce the strategy and explain why and when it is useful for college students and professionals.
- Referring to the learning guide, introduce each step, and then pause for a turn-and-talk. Debrief and clarify.

page 1 of 3

Making Deep Sense of Informational Texts © 2025 Solution Tree Press • SolutionTree.com
Visit **go.SolutionTree.com/literacy/MDSIT** and enter the unique access code found on this book's inside front cover to access this reproducible.

REPRODUCIBLE | 175

- Give the pairs this prompt: "Without looking at the learning guide, review the strategy steps with your partner. What questions or concerns do you have?"
- Project an annotated textbook excerpt and ask students what they notice. Make connections with the steps.
- For the Cortés letter excerpt, instruct students to carefully observe the modeling. Read the first two paragraphs aloud, pausing to mark keywords and phrases and jot margin notes. Think aloud while deciding what to write, incorporating the step 2 stems from the strategy learning guide.
- Ask, "What did you notice during my modeling?" Engage students in a think-pair-share exercise.

3. Lead Guided Practice

- Pass out copies of Cortés's letter. Instruct students to imitate the model for the first two paragraphs and then finish annotating the passage. Circulate and coach.
- Have students compare annotations with shoulder partners and discuss the following questions.
  - What words and phrases did you mark? Why did you decide they were important?
  - What did you write—questions, connections, ahas, paraphrases?
- Circulate, check students' annotations, and listen to their conversations. Coach as needed.
- Project the teacher annotations. Briefly explain the decisions and ask students to add any underlines or margin notes they think would improve their annotations.
- Distribute copies of two scholarly accounts and discuss the authorship. Instruct students to use the strategy steps to annotate both passages. Model silently on the projector. Have students compare and discuss their annotations in pairs. Circulate and check their work, coaching as needed.

4. Facilitate Independent Practice

- Introduce the radio story. Instruct students to listen, keeping in mind the following focus questions.
  - What surprised you?
  - What did you already know?
  - What questions do you have?
- Afterward, have students discuss the focus questions in teams. Debrief and draw out connections.
- Distribute copies of the radio story transcript and instruct students to annotate it. Remind them they can refer to the strategy learning guide and use its step 2 stems if they get stuck. Circulate as they work. After most have finished, collect their annotated handouts.

5. Assess Strategy Knowledge and Application

- Review the annotations, looking for strategy application and evidence of meaning making.
- Post the terms <u>annotate</u>, <u>selective</u>, and <u>margin note</u>. Instruct students to write a sentence or two describing the Annotate Texts strategy, incorporating the terms.
- Ask students to write their responses to the following questions on an index card.
  - Why is it important to annotate as you read a complex info-text?
  - What do you need to keep in mind as you annotate?

page 2 of 3

Making Deep Sense of Informational Texts © 2025 Solution Tree Press • SolutionTree.com
Visit **go.SolutionTree.com/literacy/MDSIT** and enter the unique access code found on this book's inside front cover to access this reproducible.

- What surprised you about the Annotate Texts strategy?
- Instruct students to write a one-paragraph summary of the radio story without referencing the text. Post a reminder to include the central idea, key ideas, key details, and key terms (scaffold for select students: a paragraph frame).
- Read the summaries to assess whether students understood key ideas.

6. Provide Feedback and Reteaching

- As needed, model and lead small-group practice with a new text.
- Emphasize the selectiveness of underlining—important words and phrases only.
- Emphasize marking as you read.
- Practice using the stems to focus on thoughts, questions, insights, and connections.

References

California Department of Education. (1998). *California Content Standards: Historical and social sciences analysis skills*. Accessed at www2.cde.ca.gov/cacs/history on November 15, 2024.

National Governors Association Center for Best Practices & Council of Chief State School Officers. (2010). *Common Core State Standards for English language arts and literacy in history/social studies, science, and technical subjects*. Authors. Accessed at https://corestandards.org/wp-content/uploads/2023/09/ELA_Standards1.pdf on June 19, 2024.

APPENDIX B

This appendix includes the following reproducible resources.

- "Shared Info-Text Study (SITS) Planning Guide" (page 178)
- "Shared Info-Text Study (SITS) Example 1: A Middle School Science SITS" (page 183)
- "Shared Info-Text Study (SITS) Example 2: A Freshman English SITS" (page 188)

These resources are available online at **go.SolutionTree.com/literacy/MDSIT**.

Shared Info-Text Study (SITS) Planning Guide

This planning guide supplements chapter 6 (page 57) of *Making Deep Sense of Informational Texts*, distilling the suggestions and considerations in that chapter into a step-by-step planning process. Two sample SITS plans in appendix B (example 1 on page 183 and example 2 on page 188) help you envision possibilities for your SITS. The guide and sample plans are also available online (at **go.SolutionTree.com/literacy/MDSIT**). The relevant strategy chapters in part 3 of the book are great resources as you plan strategy instruction during the SITS. Feel free to adapt this planning process to fit your content, students, and teaching text.

SITS Components

- Shared study of a complex text
- Integrated strategy instruction
- A spiraled reading sequence
- Text-centered discussion
- Formative assessment, scaffolding, and stretching
- Emphasis on student agency

The SITS Planning Process

1. Select and evaluate texts.
2. Plan the reading sequence.
3. Plan strategy instruction.
4. Plan assessment.

----

1. Select and Evaluate Texts

☐ **Select a central text.**

- Time—*How much time can I devote to this SITS? Where does it fit into my instructional schedule? What else do I need to fit in? How might my colleagues support me?*

- Topic, ideas, tasks, and strategies—*Which topic or theme do I want to address? Which ideas and information do students need or want to learn? What do I want students to do with what they learn? What strategies do I want my students to practice?*

- Availability—*What sources of info-texts are available? Do I have instructional plans I can adapt?*

- Fit—*What other texts will students read before and after this text? What are students studying in other classes?*

☐ **Evaluate the central text.**

- Genre—*Is the text expository? Argumentative? Persuasive? Literary nonfiction? Procedural? Visual with text elements?*

- Central idea—*What is the central idea of the text? Is it explicitly stated? If not, how can readers determine it?*

- Author's purpose—*Why did the author write the text? Is the purpose explicitly stated? If not, how can readers determine it?*

- Text features and structure—*How did the author organize the text? Is the organization clearly signaled? What is the top-level text structure of the text?*

- Complexity—*How is the text complex? How might I support students in navigating complex aspects such as the following?*

  - *An unfamiliar topic requiring specialized background knowledge*
  - *Specialized vocabulary*
  - *Long, complicated sentence structures*
  - *Too few or misleading text features*
  - *Poor or unclear organization*
  - *A cluttered, cramped layout*

page 1 of 5

Making Deep Sense of Informational Texts © 2025 Solution Tree Press • SolutionTree.com
Visit **go.SolutionTree.com/literacy/MDSIT** to download this free reproducible.

- World and word knowledge—*How familiar are my students with the topic, concepts, and language in the text? What do students already know that will be helpful?*

- Style—*Is the text well written? Is the author's voice engaging? Are the diction and syntax scholarly? Will the text serve as a model for student writing?*

☐ **Select supporting texts.**

- Engagement—*Could I use an interesting video, photo, or short text to help set the tone and introduce the topic?*

- Filling gaps—*How can I use a text to fill in students' gaps in word and world knowledge?*

- Context—*Will it help students to learn more about the author, the topic, the text, or the context in which it was written?*

- Mentor texts—*Do I need to introduce a teacher- or student-prepared exemplar for a task?*

- Scaffolding and stretching—*Could students who need additional scaffolding or challenge benefit from working with a supporting text?*

- Inquiry—*Would students benefit from reading texts to compare and synthesize ideas?*

2. Plan the Reading Sequence

Chapters	Strategies	Pre-Reading	Round 1	Round 2	Round 3	Post-Reading	Beyond the Text
Chapter 7: Focus on Meaning Making	Focus Your Mind	●	●	●	●	●	●
	Talk About Texts	●	●	●	●	●	●
Chapter 8: Prepare to Read	Preview Texts	●					
	Determine the Text Structure	●					
Chapter 9: Read Actively	Annotate Texts			●			
	Check for Understanding		●	●			
	Fix Confusion and Fill Gaps		●	●			
Chapter 10: Evaluate Arguments and Evidence	Trace the Reasoning			●	●		
	Consider Perspectives				●		
	Evaluate Evidence				●		
	Analyze Rhetoric				●		
Chapter 11: Consolidate Learning	Summarize Texts					●	
	Synthesize Across Texts						●
	Share Learning					●	●

☐ *Plan pre-reading.*

- Key strategies—*Preview Texts, Determine the Text Structure*

- Introduction—*How will I introduce the text, provide context, and engage students?*

- Pre-reading routine—*How will students evaluate text features, determine text structure, activate background knowledge, and make a reading plan? What support do I need to give?*

- Background knowledge—*What additional word and world knowledge do students need? How will they acquire that knowledge?*

☐ **Plan reading round 1.**

- Key strategies—*Check for Understanding*

- Fluent reading model—*Will I read aloud or have students listen to a recording?*

- Focus questions—*What questions will I ask to ensure students focus on the gist, connections, and points of confusion?*

- Coding—*Will I have students code the text?*

- Chunk-and-chew—*Do we need to read the whole text for students to get the gist and make connections? Is the text long enough that I need to pause partway through for students to process?*

- Discussion—*What will I ask students to discuss in pairs, in teams, or as a whole class?*

- Notes capture—*Will students make notes before or after discussions? If so, in what format?*

☐ **Plan reading round 2.**

- Key strategies—*Annotate Texts, Check for Understanding, Fix Confusion and Fill Gaps*

- Reading—*Will students read independently or with a partner? Will they have access to audio?*

- Annotation—*Will students annotate what they think is important, or will I give a more specific focus? Will they annotate on paper or digitally? What modeling or guidance might they need?*

- Checking for understanding—*How will I help students paraphrase the gist and ask questions to check their own understanding? What do I need to make sure students understand? How will I assess their individual understanding of key ideas?*

- Fixing confusion and filling gaps—*Which context clues do students need to notice? Will they need access to outside resources (such as peers, a web search, or a dictionary)?*

- Discussion—*Which ideas or questions will students discuss in pairs, in teams, and with the class?*

- Scaffolding and stretching—*What additional scaffolding and support will students need? Will I provide this to some or all students?*

- Fluency practice or vocabulary study (optional)—*Will I engage students in fluency practice or do a word study with key terms? If so, will this happen as a whole class, in small groups, or individually?*

☐ *Plan reading round 3 (optional).*

- Key strategies—*Trace the Reasoning, Consider Perspectives, Evaluate Evidence, Analyze Rhetoric*

- Focused rereading—*For what purpose will students revisit the text? Do they need to reread the whole text, review the text for evidence, or revisit specific passages? Will they add to their annotations or make notes separately?*

page 3 of 5

Making Deep Sense of Informational Texts © 2025 Solution Tree Press • SolutionTree.com
Visit **go.SolutionTree.com/literacy/MDSIT** to download this free reproducible.

| REPRODUCIBLE | 181 |

- Task—*What work will students engage in during this round? How will I explain and model? What instructions do I need to give? How will the task be assessed? Will I include self-assessment or peer feedback? How will I provide additional support to students who need it?*
- Collaboration—*Will students complete a portion with a peer or check in with a peer afterward?*
- Discussion—*What should students discuss in pairs or teams? As a whole class? What prompts will guide these discussions?*
- Scaffolding and stretching—*What additional support or challenge will students need?*

☐ **Plan post-reading.**

- Key strategies—*Summarize Texts, Share Learning*
- Focus—*What should students focus on in this phase, given the text, their needs, and the target standards?*
- Shared learning—*How will students share what they have learned—individually, in pairs, or in teams?*
- Assessment—*How will I assess students' mastery of target standards? Text comprehension? Strategy knowledge and application?*
- Reflection—*How will students reflect on their learning, reading, and strategy use?*

☐ **Plan beyond the text (optional).**

- Key strategies—*Synthesize Across Texts, Share Learning*
- Comparison—*Will I have students read a second text and compare some aspect with the central text?*
- Inquiry—*Will students read further to learn more about the topic, an idea, or the author? (Consider the following questions.)*
  - *Will they generate their own inquiry questions, or will I set the focus?*
  - *Will students find their own sources, choose from a text set, or read a preselected group of texts?*
  - *Will students survey, interview, or observe to expand their understanding? Will they access visual, audio, or video resources as well?*
  - *How will students interact with peers during inquiry?*
  - *How will students record and share notes?*
- Synthesis—*What aspects will students compare or integrate? How will students synthesize across texts?*
- Shared learning—*How will students share what they have learned—individually, in pairs, or in teams?*

3. Plan Strategy Instruction

☐ **Plan explicit strategy instruction.**

Note: You can use the "Strategy Instruction Planning Guide" (page 170) to plan strategy instruction. Refer to the relevant strategy chapter and learning guide for specifics.

- Alignment—*Which Deep Sense strategy or strategies will students need to use to master the target standards, understand the text, and complete the planned tasks?*

page 4 of 5

Making Deep Sense of Informational Texts © 2025 Solution Tree Press • SolutionTree.com
Visit **go.SolutionTree.com/literacy/MDSIT** to download this free reproducible.

- Timing—*Will I introduce the strategy or strategies before or during the SITS? At what point?*
- Application—*How will I scaffold and support students' use of the strategy or strategies?*

☐ ***Build in practice with other strategies throughout the reading sequence.***

- Student needs—*Which Deep Sense strategies have my students already learned? Which do they need more practice with?*
- Timing—*When in the reading sequence does it make sense to build in strategy practice?*
- Review and reference—*How will students review and refresh their strategy knowledge? Will I post the learning guide and review with them? Will they refer to the learning guide as they work?*

4. Plan Assessment

☐ ***Decide what, when, and how you will assess.***

- Target standards—*Which standards do students need to master? What task will students engage in to demonstrate mastery? How will I assess their mastery?*
- Comprehension—*Which specific ideas, details, and terms do students need to understand in the central text? How will I assess their comprehension?*
- Mental maps—*Is it important for students to be able to show or explain how the author organized key ideas and information? If so, how will I assess the accuracy of their mental maps?*
- Strategy application—*Which strategy or strategies will I assess? What level of knowledge and skill do I expect students to achieve? How will I assess their application of the strategy?*
- Scaffolds—*How can I integrate clear instructions, assessment criteria, and models as I introduce the assessment task or tasks? How will I check for understanding before students begin work?*

Making Deep Sense of Informational Texts © 2025 Solution Tree Press • SolutionTree.com
Visit **go.SolutionTree.com/literacy/MDSIT** to download this free reproducible.

| REPRODUCIBLE | 183 |

Shared Info-Text Study (SITS) Example 1: A Middle School Science SITS

Betty Cho (a hypothetical teacher) teaches eighth-grade earth science in the port city of Wilmington, North Carolina. As part of a unit on the hydrosphere, the class has learned about the causes and impacts of rising ocean temperatures and sea levels. Though their city is no stranger to sea-level rise, students are struggling with some of the abstract concepts introduced in the unit.

Ms. Cho decides to devote time to a shared text study focused on the tangible consequences of rising marine temperatures. She knows that her students' proximity to the ocean has contributed to their interest in marine biology. After investigating various resources, she chooses a scientific article explaining how hotter ocean waters bleach coral reefs in Florida and the Caribbean. She likes that the article emphasizes both the dire problem and the heroic actions of scientists and volunteers to protect the corals. She will use the article as a springboard for an inquiry into local efforts to mitigate the consequences of sea-level rise closer to home, like saltwater encroachment and high-tide flooding.

She talks with her grade-level colleagues in their weekly team meetings. They have worked all year to improve their students' comprehension skills—a major push in their school-improvement plan. Roland Frazier, the English teacher, shares that he has introduced most of the Deep Sense strategies in the previous months, but students still need to practice using them together. Ms. Cho commits to reinforcing strategies throughout the shared text study and asks for his support in planning.

Here, you will find the SITS plan that Ms. Cho might create to guide a multiday text study of a science article that engages students in the Preview Texts and Determine the Text Structure strategies introduced in chapter 8 (page 85) and the Annotate Texts and Check for Understanding strategies introduced in chapter 9 (page 105). To create a SITS plan like Ms. Cho's, refer to the suggestions and considerations contained in the SITS planning guide (appendix B, page 177). The planning guide is a flexible template you can adapt to fit your context. A digital version of the planning guide is available online (at **go.SolutionTree.com/literacy/MDSIT**).

Teacher: Betty Cho   **Class:** Earth Science   **Unit or Topic:** Hydrosphere

Date or Duration: Three block classes

SITS Overview

Guiding Questions

- What are the impacts of rising ocean temperatures on marine ecosystems?
- What are individuals and groups doing to mitigate these impacts?

Target Standards

- "Use models to explain how temperature and salinity drive major ocean currents and how these currents impact climate, ecosystems, and the distribution of nutrients, minerals, dissolved gases, and life forms" (ESS.8.2.2; North Carolina Department of Public Instruction, 2023).

- "Analyze and interpret data to predict the safety and potability of water supplies in North Carolina based on physical and biological factors, including temperature, dissolved oxygen, pH, nitrates and phosphates, turbidity, and bio-indicators" (ESS.8.3.1; North Carolina Department of Public Instruction, 2023).

page 1 of 5

Making Deep Sense of Informational Texts © 2025 Solution Tree Press • SolutionTree.com
Visit **go.SolutionTree.com/literacy/MDSIT** and enter the unique access code found on this book's inside front cover to access this reproducible.

- "Engage in argument from evidence to explain that the good health of humans and the environment requires: monitoring of the hydrosphere, water quality standards, methods of water treatment, maintaining safe water quality, and stewardship" (ESS.8.3.2; North Carolina Department of Public Instruction, 2023).
- Literacy instruction components
  - Integrated discipline-specific vocabulary instruction
  - Questioning and reflection during and after reading
  - Application of newly learned strategies in all content areas
  - Question answering and note making
  - Structured whole-class and team discussions

Strategies

- **Pre-reading:** Preview Texts, Determine the Text Structure (review)
- **Reading round 2:** Annotate Texts, Check for Understanding (review)

Lesson Resources

- Copies of the article
- Laptop cart
- Google Classroom
- Science notebooks
- ELA folders (to access strategy learning guides)
- Copy paper (for foldables)
- Index cards (for exit tickets)

Central Text

Scientific article: expository, digital or printed

"The Heroic Effort to Save Florida's Coral Reef From Extreme Ocean Heat as Corals Bleach Across the Caribbean" (Childress, 2023)

- **Reading purpose:** Consolidate understanding of scientific concepts related to the hydrosphere.
- **Central idea:** Extreme marine temperatures are damaging corals off the Florida Keys, and scientists and volunteers are working hard to protect them.
- **Task:** Written responses to SITS questions (assessing comprehension of key ideas)

Supporting Texts

Maps from texts introduced previously (sea surface temperature distribution, ocean current circulation, and predicted salinity changes); map of the East Coast

- **Reading purpose:** Activate background knowledge and illustrate key ideas discussed in the article.
- **Tasks:** To respond to recall questions to activate background knowledge; to connect information in the maps with ideas in the article

Reading Sequence

Pre-Reading (~25 minutes)

- Work with students to review key concepts learned so far in the hydrosphere unit. Project maps we have examined during the unit. Project maps we've looked at previously (sea surface temperature distribution, ocean current circulation, and predicted salinity changes).

- Highlight the following key points.
  - Water in the subtropical zone (including North Carolina) is getting saltier and denser.
  - ↑ marine temperatures → ↑ evaporation → ↑ seawater salinity → ↑ seawater density.
  - ↑ seawater density in the subtropics (including North Carolina) affects the circulation of ocean currents.
  - Ocean currents control how water carries heat in the ocean and help regulate the climate.

- Explain that we will now study an article about the impact of rising ocean temperatures on the marine ecosystem in the Florida Keys to help students see an example of the processes we have been studying. Explain that we will also learn what people are doing to try to lessen those impacts.

- Post the SITS questions. Explain to students that they will be responsible for answering these questions with specific details from the article when we are done.

- Have students review the Preview Texts and Determine the Text Structure learning guides in their ELA folders. Project a map of the East Coast to orient students, pointing out Wilmington and the Florida Keys. Project the article online. Ask students what key idea signals they notice (title, headings). Refer to the text feature anchor chart as needed. Ask, "What do you think we will learn from this article based on the key idea signals?" Engage students in a think-pair-share and debrief (coral reefs, rising marine temperatures).

- Post step 2 questions from the Preview Texts learning guide: "What do I already know about this topic? Why is the topic important or interesting? What do I wonder?" Have students turn and talk.

- Post step 3 questions from the Preview Texts learning guide: "What can I learn from the article? What do I need to know? What do I need to do with what I learn?" Talk students through the process of making a reading plan.

- Point out the important context features, including the author's position at Clemson University. Ask, "Does his work relate to the topic?" Turn and talk. Click on the hyperlinked name. Read aloud the summary and show students the list of publications. Ask, "Does he seem to be an expert on this topic?"

- Ask, "Why might Dr. Childress have written this article?" (think time). Project the Possible Purposes chart from the Determine the Text Structure learning guide. Ask, "What purpose fits best with what we have learned so far?" (two-minute team discussion). Debrief. Explain that there are elements of cause-effect in the article, but the top-level structure is problem-solution. (Point out the words heroic, effort, emergency response, devastating, save, protecting, at risk, and rebuilding.)

Reading Round 1 (~30 minutes)

- Remind students that in the first reading round, they are just trying to get the big picture—the gist. Post the focus questions: "What does Dr. Childress want me to know? How can I connect this to my previous learning and experience? What confused me? What do I need to know more about?"

- Have students quickly make three-column foldables (labeled Key Ideas, Connections, and Questions) and copy the focus questions below the column headings. Distribute copies of the article. Explain that I will read aloud the first two pages as they follow along. (Encourage finger sweep.) Tell them I will pause so they can make notes.

- Read the first five paragraphs aloud (incorporate the text features). Pause. Have students make notes in their foldables. Continue reading the rest of the section aloud. Pause and have students continue to make notes. Have students share their thoughts in teams. Circulate. Call on several students to report highlights from their discussions.

Reading Round 2 (~55 minutes)

- Explain that students will now read and annotate the article. Remind them that their purpose is to be able to answer the two SITS questions. (Repost them.)

- Post a word cloud with the most frequently used words in the article. Read the terms aloud chorally. Explain that students will want to pay close attention to these terms as they read to understand how the author uses them and why they are important.

- Have students retrieve their ELA notebooks and review the Annotate Texts and Check for Understanding learning guides. Remind them that they will annotate their articles as they read, pause after each section to paraphrase the gist of the section, and use the reporter questions to check their understanding. Work with selected students in a small group to whisper-read.

- Ask pairs to review their annotations to identify lingering questions and then review their articles to see if they find answers to those questions. Ask students to share any questions they could not get the answers to. As needed, suggest where they might find the information in the article or do a quick look-up together.

- Project the word cloud again. Have students put away their articles and independently write a few sentences on an index card to capture the most important ideas in the article. Encourage them to try to incorporate the words in the word cloud (informal comprehension assessment: review with Mr. Frazier).

Post-Reading (~55 minutes)

- Have teams work together to make sure they can answer the following questions, referring to the text as needed: "How do rising marine temperatures cause coral bleaching? Why is coral bleaching a problem? What are scientists and volunteers doing to protect corals from the effects of bleaching?" Circulate as they discuss.

- Post the SITS questions and have students put away their articles. Instruct them to discuss both questions, letting them know we will do Numbered Heads Together. Call on groups to report out.

- Keep the SITS questions posted. Instruct students to write a paragraph response to each question (on notebook paper), referring to specific ideas and information from the article to illustrate their ideas.

Summative Assessment

- Examine students' written responses to SITS questions to assess comprehension.
- Look for the following.
  - *Impact:* Required: ↑ increasing ocean temperatures → cause coral bleaching. +: High heat leaves corals vulnerable. Extreme heat is even killing new transplants.
  - *Solutions (at least two):* Transplanting corals (+: specifically rescuing recent transplants), scraping algae, monitoring and reporting, and raising awareness

References

Childress, M. (2023, August 9). The heroic effort to save Florida's coral reef from extreme ocean heat as corals bleach across the Caribbean. *The Conversation*. Accessed at https://theconversation.com/the-heroic-effort-to-save-floridas-coral-reef-from-extreme-ocean-heat-as-corals-bleach-across-the-caribbean-210974 on August 18, 2024.

North Carolina Department of Public Instruction. (2023). *North Carolina standard course of study: K–12 science, eighth grade*. Accessed at https://www.dpi.nc.gov/documents/cte/curriculum/science/6-8-science-standards on December 10, 2024.

Shared Info-Text Study (SITS) Example 2: A Freshman English SITS

Rachel Zuniga (a hypothetical teacher) teaches ninth-grade ELA in a Grand Rapids, Michigan, high school. For two weeks, she and her students have explored the influences of media on their lives. She has planned a SITS centering on an article written by two psychiatric researchers that addresses the issue of teens' use of digital devices—a topic students have expressed a keen interest in, especially in light of recent moves by their parents and school administrators to limit screen time. She has chosen the article in part because it was written for a teen and tween audience. She also noticed that it has many elements of argumentation, though at first, it seemed like an expository text. She has a number of learning standards focused on analyzing and writing arguments, so she decides to focus on this aspect in the SITS.

She wishes her students could do a full-blown research project after studying the article, but she decides that given the instructional schedule, she will have teams do a brief inquiry with additional sources she has selected. Armed with information from their inquiry, students will articulate their own positions and prepare to share their reasoning and evidence in a formal class discussion.

Here, you will find the SITS plan that Dr. Zuniga might create to guide a multiday text study that engages students in three of the argumentation analysis strategies introduced in chapter 10 (page 121). To create a SITS plan like Dr. Zuniga's, refer to the suggestions and considerations contained in the SITS planning guide (appendix B, page 177). The planning guide is a flexible template you can adapt to fit your context. A digital version of the planning guide is available online (at **go.SolutionTree.com /literacy/MDSIT**).

Teacher: Rachel Zuniga   **Class:** ELA 9   **Unit or Topic:** Media Influence

Date or Duration: Four block classes

SITS Overview

Guiding Questions

- **Unit questions:** How do media influence us? How can we manage that media influence?

- **SITS questions:** Is screen time a problem for young people? How can we better manage our screen time?

Target Standards

- "Determine a central idea of a text and analyze its development over the course of the text, including how it emerges and is shaped and refined by specific details; provide an objective summary of the text" (RI.9-10.2; NGA & CCSSO, 2010).

- "Delineate and evaluate the argument and specific claims in a text, assessing whether the reasoning is valid and the evidence is relevant and sufficient; identify . . . fallacious reasoning" (RI.9-10.8; NGA & CCSSO, 2010).

- "Respond thoughtfully to diverse perspectives, summarize points of agreement and disagreement, and, when warranted, qualify or justify their own views and understanding and make new connections in light of the evidence and reasoning presented" (SL.9-10.1d; NGA & CCSSO, 2010).

- "Write arguments to support claims in an analysis of substantive topics or texts, using valid reasoning and relevant and sufficient evidence" (W.9-10.1; NGA & CCSSO, 2010).

- "Conduct short . . . research projects to answer a question" and "synthesize multiple sources, demonstrating understanding of the subject under investigation" (W.9-10.7; NGA & CCSSO, 2010).

REPRODUCIBLE | 189

Strategies

- **Pre-reading:** Determine the Text Structure (review)
- **Reading round 2:** Trace the Reasoning (review)
- **Reading round 3:** Trace the Reasoning, Consider Perspectives (review), Evaluate Evidence (introduction)
- **Post-reading:** Summarize Texts (review)
- **Beyond the text:** Synthesize Across Texts (preview)

Lesson Resources

- Resources in Canvas: Central article, learning guides, summary template, argument outline
- Digital tools: Student laptops, Diigo app
- Handouts: Evidence chart, summary graphic organizer
- Materials for process notes: Sticky notes, index cards, pens

Central Text

Scientific article: Argumentative, digital

"How Much Time Do Kids Spend on Devices—Playing Games, Watching Videos, Texting, and Using the Phone?" (Rosenberg & Szura, 2023)

- **Reading purpose:** Better understand the issue of teen screen time and how researchers are studying the issue.
- **Central idea:** The solution to the problems caused by teens' heavy screen use is to balance screen time with screenless activities.
- **Task:** Summary

Supporting Texts

Text set (research articles, scholarly essays, blog posts, and informative videos)

- **Reading purpose:** Synthesize diverse viewpoints; express an informed perspective on the issue.
- **Tasks:** Shared notes, argument outline, scored class discussion

Reading Sequence

Pre-Reading (~25 minutes)

- Remind students of the unit questions. Introduce the SITS questions.
- Post this question: "How much time do you think kids spend on tech devices each week (including playing games, watching videos, texting, and using the phone)?" Have each student print an estimate on a sticky note and hold it up. Have students scan the estimates around the room. Ask outliers to share their rationale. Ask, "Do you think kids spend more or less time on tech devices than adults?" (thumbs-up, thumbs-down, or thumbs-sideways).
- Project the article. Explain that the class will study and analyze this text to better understand the impact of technology use on teens, but they will also have an opportunity to explore other texts to gain diverse perspectives.
- Lead students in evaluating three types of text features (key idea signals, important context, and added information). (Key points are the title and introduction do not match the purpose of the article, author links show the authors work at the same university, the headings all emphasize solutions, the hyperlinks lead to evidence, and the videos are topical.)

page 2 of 7

Making Deep Sense of Informational Texts © 2025 Solution Tree Press • SolutionTree.com
Visit **go.SolutionTree.com/literacy/MDSIT** and enter the unique access code found on this book's inside front cover to access this reproducible.

190 | **R E P R O D U C I B L E**

- Project the Determine the Text Structure learning guide. Refer to the Possible Purposes chart. Have teams discuss, "Based on our preview, why do you think the authors wrote this article?" Debrief.

- Refer to the Signal Words chart in the learning guide. Point out that the signal words in the article are mostly cause-effect (effect, resulting, cause, because, leads to), but the headings emphasize a solution (Find the Right Balance, How to Avoid . . . , A Healthy Approach). (The key point is the authors seem to be using a problem-solution top-level structure, but they use the cause-effect structure in the first part of the article to discuss the causes and effects of teen screen use.)

- Walk students through the target standards and tasks they will be responsible for. Ask if they think they will need to read the whole article, given what they will be accountable for. Point out the hyperlinks, which we will navigate later. Point out the videos are nice but unnecessary for our purposes.

Reading Round 1 (~20 minutes)

- Remind students that in the first round, they will focus on getting the gist, making connections, and identifying points of confusion. Read the article aloud as students follow along in the digital text. Pause halfway through and prompt pairs to review what they have heard so far (without looking at the text).

- Ask students to each write their responses on an index card in three categories: (1) the gist of the article, (2) connections I made, and (3) questions I have. Have students share their thoughts with their teams. Collect the cards.

Reading Round 2 (~60 minutes)

- Explain that in order to make sure we understand the gist of the article, we will need to analyze the authors' argument. Display the Trace the Reasoning learning guide and ask students to review in their minds what the strategy steps entail. Explain they will apply steps 1–3 as they read in this round.

- Give instructions for students to read and annotate the article using the Diigo app.

  - Tell them, "First, as you read, highlight words and phrases related to the issue, significance, authors' position, and key claims. Second, pause to add digital comments with your insights and questions. Third, look away after each section to paraphrase the gist of the section in your mind."

  - Annotate on the screen to model; pause to circulate as students work. Support them as needed.

- Post the article with these research and medical terms highlighted in a different color from the other annotations: correlate, predict, MRI, abnormalities, impairment, addiction, sleep disruption. Have students highlight the terms. Give a synonym and brief explanation of each term, pointing out a context clue if available.

- Have teams work together to identify the text evidence that best captures the issue, significance, and authors' position. Encourage them to mark their texts and add a comment labeling the best evidence for each of these argument elements. Model on screen as they work. Debrief.

- Instruct teams to refer to their annotations as they make a list of the authors' claims. Reinforce the idea that a claim is an assertion that has to be proven or disproven with evidence and reasoning. Post the following questions to focus their work.

  - What do the authors claim are the consequences of heavy screen use?

  - What do the authors claim will address these consequences?

- Debrief. Address disagreements. Compile a consensus list of claims on chart paper and post it.

- Prompt students to work in teams to look for a counterclaim in the article (paragraph 8). Have them highlight and add a digital comment labeling the counterclaim.

page 3 of 7

Making Deep Sense of Informational Texts © 2025 Solution Tree Press • SolutionTree.com
Visit **go.SolutionTree.com/literacy/MDSIT** and enter the unique access code found on this book's inside front cover to access this reproducible.

| REPRODUCIBLE | 191 |

Reading Round 3 (~90 minutes)

- Explain now that we know the article pretty well, we will return to evaluate the authors' argument and evidence. Project step 5 of the Trace the Reasoning learning guide and review.

- Project the following statements from the article.
  - "These lonely feelings correlate with the rise in the use of digital media" (paragraph 5).
  - "But too much screen time can lead to problems" (paragraph 9).
  - "But spending too much time using digital devices can cause changes in the way you think and behave" (paragraph 10).
  - "The fear of missing out is pervasive, resulting in sleep disruption" (paragraph 12).
  - "Getting hooked on screens means missing out on healthy activities" (paragraph 14).

  Ask teams to review these statements in the article and discuss whether these statements constitute a false cause fallacy. Debrief. (The key point is this is a debatable issue, and they will need to examine the evidence more closely to decide whether the authors have made their case.)

- Have students access the Consider Perspectives learning guide and review step 1. Project and read aloud paragraph 6 in the article. Have students work with shoulder partners to discuss the step 1 questions focused on the authors' perspective. Debrief.

- Have students review step 2 of the learning guide. Ask, "Which stakeholders might be concerned with this issue?" Have pairs turn and talk. Debrief. (Possible answers are parents, students, doctors, educators, and tech companies.) Explain that they will express their own point of view after we read more widely.

- Introduce the Evaluate Evidence strategy using the learning guide. Walk students through steps 1–3, check for understanding, and address any questions.

- Distribute evidence charts. Explain that students will work in pairs to identify the evidence presented throughout the article, determine the type of evidence, and evaluate its credibility on a scale of 1 to 5 (1 being low and 5 being high).

Evidence From the Article *(Show the paragraph number.)*	**Type of Evidence**	**Credibility** *(Rate on a scale of 1–5, 1 being low and 5 being high.)*

- Have students access the learning guide and article digitally on Canvas. Point out that where there is a hyperlinked source, students should click it and scan the source to help them evaluate the credibility of the evidence. Circulate and coach.

- Discuss the following questions from steps 2 and 3 of the learning guide in a whole-class discussion. Pause after posing each question for students to review their texts and briefly discuss with their partners.
  - Do the authors give context for the evidence (how, when, by whom, and for what purpose it was gathered)?
  - Do they acknowledge the limitations of their evidence?
  - Do they share how they verified that their evidence is valid?
  - Do they seem to present only evidence to support their position, or do they provide other perspectives?

page 4 of 7

Making Deep Sense of Informational Texts © 2025 Solution Tree Press • SolutionTree.com
Visit **go.SolutionTree.com/literacy/MDSIT** and enter the unique access code found on this book's inside front cover to access this reproducible.

192 | **REPRODUCIBLE**

- Walk students through step 4 in the learning guide. Ask them to independently write their responses to the following prompt on an index card without referencing the text: "What conclusions do the authors draw? Are the conclusions supported by the evidence?" (Collect the cards as a formative assessment for standard RI.9-10.8.)

Post-Reading (~55 minutes)

- Distribute the summary graphic organizer.

Central Idea Statement: In their 2023 article, authors David Rosenberg and Natalia Szura . . .	
Key Supporting Ideas (Claims)	Key Details and Terms
Problem	
Solution	

- Project the Summarize Texts learning guide and review the steps. Explain that we will work through steps 1 and 2 together; then students will complete steps 3 and 4 independently.

- Lead the class through step 1 to compose a central idea statement that reflects the problem-solution structure. Have each student copy the sentence in their organizer.

- Reference the list of claims the class generated earlier. Talk through each claim with the class to make sure it is important enough to include in the summary. Cross out as needed. Have students add the claims to their organizers.

- Prompt students to review the article online, ask themselves the reporter questions to identify key details and terms, and add those details and terms to their organizers.

- Review step 4 in the learning guide. Remind students they can also reference the strategy example posted in Canvas. Instruct students to access the summary template in Canvas and draft a summary paragraph. Circulate. After most students are nearing completion of their drafts, post the step 4 questions and ask them to use them to guide their revision. Have them submit drafts.

Beyond the Text (~110 minutes)

- Explain that students will next investigate additional sources on the topic of teen screen use to better understand the range of perspectives on the issue and help them form their own informed arguments.

- Have students access the inquiry text set in Canvas and click each link to do a quick scan. Explain that the text set includes some of the articles Rosenberg and Szura refer to, as well as others. Introduce the following inquiry questions.

  - How do the new sources inform your understanding of the consequences of teen screen use?

  - How do the new sources inform your understanding of the best ways to address the problem?

- Have teams prepare for inquiry, giving the following instructions.

  - Choose four resources from the list. Decide who will read which article.

  - Have one team member create a Google Docs file and share it with their team members and me.

page 5 of 7

Making Deep Sense of Informational Texts © 2025 Solution Tree Press • SolutionTree.com
Visit **go.SolutionTree.com/literacy/MDSIT** and enter the unique access code found on this book's inside front cover to access this reproducible.

REPRODUCIBLE | 193

- Generate two or three more inquiry questions. Add the inquiry questions to the document.
- Decide on a font color for each team member. Decide how they will distinguish between direct quotes, paraphrases, and their own commentary and questions.

- As students read and make notes for their articles, check the shared notes files. Coach as needed. Remind them to look away and paraphrase and then add commentary and questions.

- Instruct teams to review their shared notes and discuss the following questions (from step 4 of the Synthesize Across Texts learning guide). Prompt them to annotate and add to their shared notes to capture key points from the discussion.
  - What points do sources agree on?
  - Which points do sources disagree on? Do we need to review those sources or find others?
  - Which points have we found in only one source? Are we sure they are accurate?

- Have students write individual responses on index cards to the following: "What do I now know for sure about the issue of teen screen use? What am I still unsure about? What information do I still not have?" Collect these as a formative assessment.

- Explain that students will now prepare an argument in response to the question, "Where do you stand on the issue of teens' screen use?" Present two extreme positions.
  a. "Teens' screen use is a disaster, clearly causing addiction and mental health issues. Teens' device use should be prohibited or severely limited."
  b. "The concerns about teens' screen use are all just hype. Adults just want to control kids. Sure, we use our screens a lot, but they help us way more than they hurt us."

- Prompt students to access the argument outline template in Canvas. Explain that students will prepare an outline of their position for a class discussion. Explain that they should include three or four reasons or claims to support their position, accurately paraphrase evidence, and cite sources.

Issue Definition:	Significance:
Position:	
My Reasoning (Own Words)	Key Evidence (Paraphrase, Cited)
Counterclaim:	Concession:
Rebuttal:	

- Explain that students will now engage in a scored discussion. Post the criteria. Remind them of the Talk About Texts discussion guidelines. Lead a class discussion to elicit students' positions, reasoning, and evidence. Pause to have students access their argument outlines. Mark the roster as students contribute. As needed, invite individuals to contribute. For students who did not contribute, offer an opportunity to discuss in a small group or one-on-one.

- After the discussion, prompt students to return to their argument outline and complete the counterclaim portion. They should summarize a reasonable counterclaim they heard during the discussion and add a concession and rebuttal. Have students submit their argument outlines.

page 6 of 7

Making Deep Sense of Informational Texts © 2025 Solution Tree Press • SolutionTree.com
Visit **go.SolutionTree.com/literacy/MDSIT** and enter the unique access code found on this book's inside front cover to access this reproducible.

Summative Assessment

- Summary

  - Assessment of RI.9-10.2, comprehension, application of the Summarize Texts strategy

  - Criteria: Gist captured, logical sequence of ideas, clear connections, inclusion of key details and terms

- Shared notes and index card response

  - Assessment of W.9-10.7 and RI.9-10.8

  - Criteria: Insightful paraphrases and commentary, valid inferences about the strength of evidence and reasoning presented in sources

- Class discussion

  - Assessment of SL.9-10.1d

  - Criteria: Respectful, meaningful contributions; warranted requests for clarification; valid reasoning and evidence; building on others' ideas; references to text evidence

- Argument outline

  - Assessment of W.9-10.1 and SL.9-10.1d

  - Criteria: Clear position, valid reasons, relevant and credible evidence, counterclaim discussed, valid concession and rebuttal

References

National Governors Association Center for Best Practices & Council of Chief State School Officers. (2010). *Common Core State Standards for English language arts and literacy in history/social studies, science, and technical subjects.* Authors. Accessed at https://corestandards.org/wp-content/uploads/2023/09/ELA_Standards1.pdf on June 19, 2024.

Rosenberg, D., & Szura, N. (2023, October 23). How much time do kids spend on devices—playing games, watching videos, texting, and using the phone? *The Conversation.* Accessed at https://theconversation.com/how-much-time-do-kids-spend-on-devices-playing-games-watching-videos-texting-and-using-the-phone-210118 on November 1, 2024.

REFERENCES AND RESOURCES

AdLit. (n.d.). *Power Notes*. Accessed at www.adlit.org/in-the-classroom/strategies/power-notes on November 13, 2024.

Afflerbach, P., Pearson, P. D., & Paris, S. G. (2008). Clarifying differences between reading skills and reading strategies. *The Reading Teacher, 61*(5), 364–373. https://doi.org/10.1598/RT.61.5.1

Almasi, J. F., & Fullerton, S. K. (2012). *Teaching strategic processes in reading* (2nd ed.). New York: Guilford Press.

Almasi, J. F., Garas-York, K., & Shanahan, L. (2006). Qualitative research on text comprehension and the report of the National Reading Panel. *The Elementary School Journal, 107*(1), 37–66. https://doi.org/10.1086/509526

Alvermann, D. (2009). Sociocultural constructions of adolescence and young people's literacies. In L. Christenbury, R. Bomer, & P. Smagorinsky (Eds.). *Handbook of Adolescent Literacy Research* (pp. 14-28).

Alvermann, D. E., & Moje, E.B. (2013). Adolescent literacy instruction and the discourse of "Every teacher a teacher of reading." In Alvermann, D.E., Unrau, N.J., & Ruddell, R.B. (Eds.). *Theoretical Models and Processes of Reading* (6th ed., pp. 1072-1103). Newark, DE: International Reading Association.

American Institutes for Research. (2017, January). *Reading framework for the 2017 National Assessment of Educational Progress*. Washington, DC: National Assessment Governing Board. Accessed at www.nagb.gov/content/nagb/assets/documents/publications/frameworks/reading/2017-reading-framework.pdf on June 19, 2024.

Applebee, A. N., Langer, J. A., Nystrand, M., & Gamoran, A. (2003). Discussion-based approaches to developing understanding: Classroom instruction and student performance in middle and high school English. *American Educational Research Journal, 40*(3), 685–730. https://doi.org/10.3102/00028312040003685

Atwell, N. (Ed.). (1990). *Coming to know: Writing to learn in the intermediate grades*. Portsmouth, NH: Heinemann.

Bandeira de Mello, V., Rahman, T., & Park, B. J. (2018). *Mapping state proficiency standards onto NAEP scales: Results from the 2015 NAEP reading and mathematics assessments* (NCES 2018-159). Washington, DC: National Center for Education Statistics. Accessed at https://nces.ed.gov/nationsreportcard/pubs/studies/2018159.aspx on June 19, 2024.

Barth, A. E., & Elleman, A. (2017). Evaluating the impact of a multistrategy inference intervention for middle-grade struggling readers. *Language, Speech, and Hearing Services in Schools, 48*(1), 31–41.

Beach, R. (2019). Leading the call: Engaging students in shared inquiry. *Voices From the Middle, 26*(3), 9–13. https://doi.org/10.58680/vm201930008

Boardman, A. G., Roberts, G., Vaughn, S., Wexler, J., Murray, C. S., & Kosanovich, M. (2008). *Effective instruction for adolescent struggling readers: A practice brief.* Portsmouth, NH: Center on Instruction. Accessed at https://files.eric.ed.gov/fulltext/ED521836.pdf on June 19, 2024.

Botsas, G. (2017). Differences in strategy use in the reading comprehension of narrative and science texts among students with and without learning disabilities. *Learning Disabilities: A Contemporary Journal, 15*(1), 139–162. Accessed at https://files.eric.ed.gov/fulltext/EJ1141985.pdf on June 19, 2024.

Brown, D. F., & Knowles, T. (2014). *What every middle school teacher should know* (3rd ed.). Portsmouth, NH: Heinemann.

Bruner, J. S. (1985). Vygotsky: A historical and conceptual perspective. In J. V. Wertsch (Ed.), *Culture, communication, and cognition: Vygotskian perspectives* (pp. 21–34). New York: Cambridge University Press.

California Department of Education. (1998). *California Content Standards: Historical and social sciences analysis skills.* Accessed at www2.cde.ca.gov/cacs/history on November 15, 2024.

Carlson, S. E., van den Broek, P., & McMaster, K. L. (2022). Factors that influence skilled and less-skilled comprehenders' inferential processing during and after reading: Exploring how readers maintain coherence and develop a mental representation of a text. *The Elementary School Journal, 122*(4), 475–501. https://doi.org/10.1086/719477

Carr, N. (2020). *The shallows: What the internet is doing to our brains.* New York: Norton.

Cartwright, K. B. (2015). *Executive skills and reading comprehension: A guide for educators.* New York: Guilford Press.

Castek, J., & Beach, R. (2013). Using apps to support disciplinary literacy and science learning. *Journal of Adolescent and Adult Literacy, 56*(7), 554–564. https://doi.org/10.1002/JAAL.180

Center on the Developing Child at Harvard University. (n.d.). *Executive function and self-regulation.* Accessed at https://developingchild.harvard.edu/science/key-concepts/executive-function on September 22, 2024.

Childress, M. (2023, August 9). The heroic effort to save Florida's coral reef from extreme ocean heat as corals bleach across the Caribbean. *The Conversation.* Accessed at https://theconversation.com/the-heroic-effort-to-save-floridas-coral-reef-from-extreme-ocean-heat-as-corals-bleach-across-the-caribbean-210974 on August 18, 2024.

Cho, B.-Y. (2013). Adolescents' constructively responsive reading strategy use in a critical internet reading task. *Reading Research Quarterly, 48*(4), 329–332. https://doi.org/10.1002/rrq.49

Cho, B.-Y., & Afflerbach, P. (2017). An evolving perspective of constructively responsive reading comprehension strategies in multilayered digital text environments. In S. E. Israel (Ed.), *Handbook of research on reading comprehension* (2nd ed., pp. 109–134). New York: Guilford Press.

Coiro, J. (2017, August 29). *Teaching adolescents how to evaluate the quality of online information.* Accessed at www.edutopia.org/blog/evaluating-quality-of-online-info-julie-coiro on September 27, 2024.

Cornell Lab of Ornithology. (n.d.). *Red-tailed hawk.* Accessed at www.allaboutbirds.org/guide/Red-tailed_Hawk/overview on September 27, 2024.

Costa, A. L. (Ed.). (2001). *Developing minds: A resource book for teaching thinking* (3rd ed.). Arlington, VA: ASCD.

Costa, A. L., & Garmston, R. J. (2002). *Cognitive coaching: A foundation for renaissance schools* (2nd ed.). Norwood, MA: Christopher-Gordon.

Crafton, L. K. (1982). Comprehension before, during, and after reading. *The Reading Teacher, 36*(3), 293–297.

Croninger, R. M. V., Li, M., Cameron, C., & Murphy, P. K. (2018). Classroom discussions: Building the foundation for productive talk. In P. K. Murphy (Ed.), *Classroom discussions in education* (pp. 1–29). New York: Routledge.

Davis, D. S., & Wilson, A. (2015). Practices and commitments of test-centric literacy instruction: Lessons from a testing transition. *Reading Research Quarterly, 50*(3), 357–379. https://doi.org /10.1002/rrq.103

Deane, P., Odendahl, N., Quinlan, T., Fowles, M., Welsh, C., & Bivens-Tatum, J. (2008). *Cognitive models of writing: Writing proficiency as a complex integrated skill* (Research Report No. RR-08-55). Princeton, NJ: Educational Testing Service. http://dx.doi.org/10.1002/j.2333-8504.2008.tb02141.x

Deane, P., Sabatini, J., Feng, G., Sparks, J., Song, Y., Fowles, M., et al. (2015). Key practices in the English language arts (ELA): Linking learning theory, assessment, and instruction. *ETS Research Report Series, 2015*(2), 1–29. https://doi.org/10.1002/ets2.12063

Deane, P., Sabatini, J., & O'Reilly, T. (2012). *English language arts literacy framework.* Princeton, NJ: Educational Testing Service. Accessed at www.academia.edu/83775593/English_Language_Arts _Literacy_Framework on September 27, 2024.

Denton, C. A., Wolters, C. A., York, M. J., Swanson, E., Kulesz, P. A., & Francis, D. J. (2015). Adolescents' use of reading comprehension strategies: Differences related to reading proficiency, grade level, and gender. *Learning and Individual Differences, 37*(1), 81–95. https://doi.org/10.1016 /j.lindif.2014.11.016

Denton, C. A., York, M. J., Francis, D. J., Haring, C., Ahmed, Y., & Bidulescu, A. (2017). An investigation of an intervention to promote inference generation by adolescent poor comprehenders. *Learning Disabilities Research and Practice, 32*(2), 85–98. https://doi.org/10.1111/ldrp.12134

Digital Inquiry Group. (n.d.). *Moctezuma and Cortés.* Accessed at https://inquirygroup.org/history -lessons/moctezuma-and-cortes on November 4, 2024.

Donovan, S. A., Stoll, A., Bradley, D. H., & Collins, B. (2022, March 31). *Skills gaps: A review of underlying concepts and evidence* (R47059). Washington, DC: Congressional Research Service. Accessed at https://crsreports.congress.gov/product/pdf/R/R47059 on June 19, 2024.

Duke, N. K., & Martin, N. M. (2019). Best practices in informational text comprehension instruction. In L. M. Morrow & L. B. Gambrell (Eds.), *Best practices in literacy instruction* (6th ed., pp. 250–270). New York: Guilford Press.

Duke, N. K., Ward, A. E., & Pearson, P. D. (2021). The Science of Reading comprehension instruction. *The Reading Teacher, 74*(6), 663–672. https://doi.org/10.1002/trtr.1993

Filderman, M. J., Austin, C. R., Boucher, A. N., O'Donnell, K., & Swanson, E. A. (2022). A meta-analysis of the effects of reading comprehension interventions on the reading comprehension outcomes of struggling readers in third through 12th grades. *Exceptional Children, 88*(2), 163–184. https://doi .org/10.1177/00144029211050860

Firth, J. A., Torous, J., & Firth, J. (2020). Exploring the impact of internet use on memory and attention processes. *International Journal of Environmental Research and Public Health, 17*(24), Article 9481. https://doi.org/10.3390/ijerph17249481

Fisher, D. (2008). *Effective use of the gradual release of responsibility model* [Monograph]. Accessed at http://srhscollaborationsuite.weebly.com/uploads/3/8/4/0/38407301/douglas_fisher.pdf on November 1, 2024.

Fisher, D., & Frey, N. (2019). Best practices in adolescent literacy instruction. In L. M. Morrow & L. B. Gambrell (Eds.), *Best practices in literacy instruction* (6th ed., pp. 150–172). New York: Guilford Press.

Fisher, D., & Frey, N. (2021). *Better learning through structured teaching: A framework for the gradual release of responsibility* (3rd ed.). Arlington, VA: ASCD.

Fisher, D., Frey, N., & Shanahan, T. (2012). The challenge of challenging text. *Educational Leadership, 69*(6), 58–62.

Fredrick, J. (2019, November 10). < *500 years later, the Spanish conquest of Mexico is still being debated* [Radio broadcast]. NPR. Accessed at www.npr.org/transcripts/777220132 on November 4, 2024.

Garas-York, K., & Almasi, J. F. (2017). Constructing meaning through discussion. In S. E. Israel (Ed.), *Handbook of research on reading comprehension* (2nd ed., pp. 500–518). New York: Guilford Press.

García, J. R., García-Serrano, M., & Rosales, J. (2022). Exploring the relation between the structure strategy and source attention in single expository text comprehension: A cross-sectional study in secondary education. *Reading and Writing, 36*(4), 195–221.

Goldman, S. R., & Varma, S. (1995). CAPping the construction-integration model of discourse comprehension. In C. A. Weaver III, S. Mannes, & C. R. Fletcher (Eds.), *Discourse comprehension: Essays in honor of Walter Kintsch* (pp. 337–358). Hillsdale, NJ: Erlbaum.

Gonzalez, V. (2019, March 27). *QSSSA: More than turn and talk* [Blog post]. Accessed at https://seidlitzblog .org/2019/03/27/qsssa-more-than-turn-talk on June 19, 2024.

Graesser, A. C., & Clark, L. F. (1985). *Structures and procedures of implicit knowledge.* Norwood, NJ: Ablex.

Greenleaf, C., Schoenbach, R., Friedrich, L., Murphy, L., & Hogan, N. (2023). *Reading for understanding: How reading apprenticeship improves disciplinary learning in secondary and college classrooms* (3rd ed.). San Francisco: Jossey-Bass.

Guthrie, J. T. (Ed.). (2008). *Engaging adolescents in reading.* Thousand Oaks, CA: Corwin Press.

Guthrie, J. T., & Klauda, S. L. (2014). Effects of classroom practices on reading comprehension, engagement, and motivations for adolescents. *Reading Research Quarterly, 49*(4), 387–416.

Hagaman, J. L., Casey, K. J., & Reid, R. (2016). Paraphrasing strategy instruction for struggling readers. *Preventing School Failure: Alternative Education for Children and Youth, 60*(1), 43–52. https://doi .org/10.1080/1045988X.2014.966802

Hall, C. S. (2015). Inference instruction for struggling readers: A synthesis of intervention research. *Educational Psychology Review, 28*(1), 1–22. https://doi.org/10.1007/s10648-014-9295-x

Hall, L. A. (2016). "I don't really have anything good to say": Examining how one teacher worked to shape middle school students' talk about texts. *Research in the Teaching of English, 51*(1), 60–83. https://doi.org/10.58680/rte201628685

Hanson, S., & Padua, J. F. M. (2011). *Text features.* Honolulu, HI: Pacific Resources for Education and Learning. Accessed at https://files.eric.ed.gov/fulltext/ED585193.pdf on June 19, 2024.

Harvey, S., & Goudvis, A. (2017). *Strategies that work: Teaching comprehension for understanding, engagement, and building knowledge, grades K–8* (3rd ed.). Portland, ME: Stenhouse.

Hawk Mountain Sanctuary. (n.d.). *Red-tailed hawk.* Accessed at www.hawkmountain.org/raptors/red -tailed-hawk on September 27, 2024.

Hebert, M., Bohaty, J. J., Nelson, J. R., & Brown, J. (2016). The effects of text structure instruction on expository reading comprehension: A meta-analysis. *Journal of Educational Psychology, 108*(5), 609–629. https://doi.org/10.1037/edu0000082

Higgs, K. P., Santuzzi, A. M., Gibson, C., Kopatich, R. D., Feller, D. P., & Magliano, J. P. (2023). Relationships between task awareness, comprehension strategies, and literacy outcomes. *Frontiers in Psychology, 14,* Article 1056457. https://doi.org/10.3389/fpsyg.2023.1056457

International Reading Association. (2012). *Adolescent literacy* [Position statement] (Rev. ed.). Newark, DE: Author.

Kagan, S., & Kagan, M. (2009). *Kagan cooperative learning.* San Clemente, CA: Kagan.

Kahneman, D. (2011). *Thinking, fast and slow.* New York: Farrar, Straus and Giroux.

Kamil, M., Borman, G. D., Dole, J., Kral, C. C., Salinger, T., & Torgesen, J. (2008). *Improving adolescent literacy: Effective classroom and intervention practices* (NCEE No. 2008-4027). Washington, DC: National Center for Education Evaluation and Regional Assistance. Accessed at https://ies.ed.gov /ncee/wwc/Docs/PracticeGuide/adlit_pg_082608.pdf on June 19, 2024.

Kelley, M. J., & Clausen-Grace, N. (n.d.). *Guiding students through expository text with text feature walks.* Accessed at www.readingrockets.org/topics/comprehension/articles/guiding-students-through -expository-text-text-feature-walks on June 19, 2024.

Kintsch, W. (1988). The role of knowledge in discourse comprehension: A construction-integration model. *Psychological Review, 95*(2), 163–182.

Kintsch, W. (2009). Learning and constructivism. In S. Tobias & T. M. Duffy (Eds.), *Constructivist instruction: Success or failure?* (pp. 223–241). New York: Routledge.

Kintsch, W., & Welsch, D. M. (1991). The construction-integration model: A framework for studying memory for text. In W. E. Hockley & S. Lewandowsky (Eds.), *Relating theory and data: Essays on human memory in honor of Bennet B. Murdock* (pp. 367–385). Hillsdale, NJ: Erlbaum.

Kizart, C. C. (2025). *Beyond implicit and explicit bias: Strategies for healing the root causes of inequity in education.* Bloomington, IN: Solution Tree Press.

Klauda, S. L., & Guthrie, J. T. (2014). Comparing relations of motivation, engagement, and achievement among struggling and advanced adolescent readers. *Reading and Writing, 28*(2), 239–269. https:// doi.org/10.1007/s11145-014-9523-2

Kranking, C. (2021, December 3). *10 fun facts about the red-tailed hawk.* Accessed at www.audubon .org/news/10-fun-facts-about-red-tailed-hawk on September 27, 2024.

Langer, J. A. (2009). Contexts for adolescent literacy. In L. Christenbury, R. Bomer, & P. Smagorinsky (Eds.), *Handbook of adolescent literacy research* (pp. 49–64). New York: Guilford Press.

Macedo-Rouet, M., Potocki, A., Scharrer, L., Ros, C., Stadtler, M., Salmerón, L., et al. (2019). How good is this page? Benefits and limits of prompting on adolescents' evaluation of web information quality. *Reading Research Quarterly, 54*(3), 299–321. https://doi.org/10.1002/rrq.241

Mancini-Marshall, A. (2014). *A new approach to middle school reading intervention balancing self-determination and achievement* [Doctoral dissertation, University of Nebraska–Lincoln]. DigitalCommons@University of Nebraska–Lincoln. http://digitalcommons.unl.edu/teachlearnstudent/46

Mariage, T. V., Englert, C. S., & Mariage, M. F. (2019). Comprehension instruction for Tier 2 early learners: A scaffolded apprenticeship for close reading of informational text. *Learning Disability Quarterly*, *43*(1), 29–42. https://doi.org/10.1177%2F0731948719861106

Martin, R. (2024). *Red-tailed hawk*. Accessed at www.britannica.com/animal/red-tailed-hawk on September 27, 2024.

Mateos, M., Martín, E., Villalón, R., & Luna, M. (2008). Reading and writing to learn in secondary education: Online processing activity and written products in summarizing and synthesizing tasks. *Reading and Writing*, *21*(7), 675–697. https://doi.org/10.1007/s11145-007-9086-6

Maybin, J., Mercer, N., & Stierer, B. (1992). "Scaffolding" learning in the classroom. In K. Norman (Ed.), *Thinking voices: The work of the National Oracy Project* (pp. 186–195). London: Hodder Arnold H&S.

McNamara, D. S., Kintsch, E., Songer, N. B., & Kintsch, W. (1996). Are good texts always better? Interactions of text coherence, background knowledge, and levels of understanding in learning from text. *Cognition and Instruction*, *14*(1), 1–43. https://doi.org/10.1207/s1532690xci1401_1

Medaille, A., & Usinger, J. (2020). "That's going to be the hardest thing for me": Tensions experienced by quiet students during collaborative learning situations. *Educational Studies*, *46*(2), 240–257. https://doi.org/10.1080/03055698.2018.1555456

Mehan, H. (1979). "What time is it, Denise?": Asking known information questions in classroom discourse. *Theory Into Practice*, *18*(4), 285–294.

Mercer, N., Wegerif, R., & Dawes, L. (1999). Children's talk and the development of reasoning in the classroom. *British Educational Research Journal*, *25*(1), 95–111.

Merchie, E., & Van Keer, H. (2016). Stimulating graphical summarization in late elementary education: The relationship between two instructional mind-map approaches and student characteristics. *The Elementary School Journal*, *116*(3), 487–522. https://doi.org/10.1086/684939

Meyer, B. J. F., Brandt, D. M., & Bluth, G. J. (1980). Use of top-level structure in text: Key for reading comprehension of ninth-grade students. *Reading Research Quarterly*, *16*(1), 72–103.

Meyer, B. J. F., & Ray, M. N. (2011). Structure strategy interventions: Increasing reading comprehension of expository text. *International Electronic Journal of Elementary Education*, *4*(1), 127–152.

Miller, M., Nevado-Montenegro, A. J., & Hinshaw, S. P. (2012). Childhood executive function continues to predict outcomes in young adult females with and without childhood-diagnosed ADHD. *Journal of Abnormal Child Psychology*, *40*(5), 657–668. https://doi.org/10.1007/s10802-011-9599-y

Moje, E. B. (2008). Foregrounding the disciplines in secondary literacy teaching and learning: A call for change. *Journal of Adolescent and Adult Literacy*, *52*(2), 96–107. https://doi.org/10.1598/JAAL.52.2.1

Murphy, P. K., Wilkinson, I. A. G., Soter, A. O., Hennessey, M. N., & Alexander, J. F. (2009). Examining the effects of classroom discussion on students' comprehension of text: A meta-analysis. *Journal of Educational Psychology*, *101*(3), 740–764. https://doi.org/10.1037/a0015576

National Assessment of Educational Progress. (n.d.a). *The Nation's Report Card—Main data explorer. Data tools: NAEP data explorer*. Accessed at https://www.nationsreportcard.gov/ndecore/landing on September 18, 2024.

National Assessment of Educational Progress. (n.d.b). *NAEP Report Card: Reading—National achievement-level results, grade 8, as of 2022*. Accessed at www.nationsreportcard.gov/reading/nation/achievement/?grade=8 on September 18, 2024.

National Assessment of Educational Progress. (n.d.c). *NAEP Report Card: Reading—National achievement-level results, grade 12, as of 2019*. Accessed at www.nationsreportcard.gov/reading/nation/achievement/?grade=12 on September 18, 2024.

National Assessment of Educational Progress. (n.d.d). *Data tools: Item maps (Reading, Grade 8, 2022)*. The Nation's Report Card. Accessed at www.nationsreportcard.gov/itemmaps/?subj=RED&grade=8&year=2022 on September 18, 2024.

National Audubon Society. (n.d.). *Red-tailed hawk*. Accessed at www.audubon.org/field-guide/bird/red-tailed-hawk on September 27, 2024.

National Center for Education Statistics. (n.d.a). *School Pulse Panel: Surveying high-priority, education-related topics*. Accessed at https://nces.ed.gov/surveys/spp/results.asp on September 20, 2024.

National Center for Education Statistics. (2023a). *Data tools: Item maps (reading, grade 8, 2022)*. Accessed at www.nationsreportcard.gov/itemmaps/?subj=RED&grade=8&year=2022 on June 19, 2024.

National Center for Education Statistics. (2023b). *Highlights of the 2022 U.S. PISA results web report* (NCES 2023-115). Accessed at https://nces.ed.gov/surveys/pisa/pisa2022 on June 19, 2024.

National Center for Education Statistics. (2023c). *NAEP Report Card: Reading, grade 4 as of 2022*. Accessed at www.nationsreportcard.gov/reading/nation/achievement/?grade=4 on June 19, 2024.

National Center for Education Statistics. (2024). *Highlights of the 2023 U.S. PIACC results web report* (NCES 2024-202). Accessed at https://nces.ed.gov/surveys/piaac/2023/national_results.asp on December 10, 2024.

National Governors Association Center for Best Practices & Council of Chief State School Officers. (2010). *Common Core State Standards for English language arts and literacy in history/social studies, science, and technical subjects*. Authors. Accessed at https://corestandards.org/wp-content/uploads/2023/09/ELA_Standards1.pdf on June 19, 2024.

National School Reform Faculty. (n.d.). *NSRF protocols and activities . . . from A to Z*. Accessed at https://nsrfharmony.org/protocols on June 19, 2024.

Newell, G. E., Beach, R., Smith, J., & VanDerHeide, J. (2011). Teaching and learning argumentative reading and writing: A review of research. *Reading Research Quarterly, 46*(3), 273–304. https://doi.org/10.1598/RRQ.46.3.4

News Literacy Project. (n.d.). *In brief: Confirmation bias and motivated reasoning*. Accessed at https://newslit.org/educators/resources/in-brief-confirmation-bias-motivated-reasoning on June 19, 2024.

Niemiec, C. P., & Ryan, R. M. (2009). Autonomy, competence, and relatedness in the classroom: Applying self-determination theory to educational practice. *Theory and Research in Education, 7*(2), 133–144. https://doi.org/10.1177/1477878509104318

North Carolina Department of Public Instruction. (2024). *North Carolina standard course of study: K-12 science, eighth grade*. Accessed at https://www.dpi.nc.gov/documents/cte/curriculum/science/6-8-science-standards on December 10, 2024.

Nussbaum, E. M. (2002). The process of becoming a participant in small-group critical discussions: A case study. *Journal of Adolescent and Adult Literacy, 45*(6), 488–497.

Nystrand, M. (1997). *Opening dialogue: Understanding the dynamics of language and learning in the English classroom*. New York: Teachers College Press.

O'Reilly, T., Deane, P., & Sabatini, J. (2015, December). *Building and sharing knowledge key practice: What do you know, what don't you know, what did you learn?* (Research Report No. ETS RR-15-24). Princeton, NJ: Educational Testing Service. Accessed at https://files.eric.ed.gov/fulltext/EJ1109314 .pdf on June 19, 2024.

Paris, S. G. (2005). Reinterpreting the development of reading skills. *Reading Research Quarterly, 40*(2), 184–202.

Pauloski, G. J. (2020). *A mixed-methods exploration of scaffolded co-constructive interactions with informational texts in a middle-grades classroom* [Doctoral dissertation, University of Houston]. University of Houston Institutional Repository. https://uh-ir.tdl.org/items/e33aca78-bc44-47ae -a5da-3b759e4bedeb

Pearson, P. D., & Gallagher, M. C. (1983). The instruction of reading comprehension. *Contemporary Educational Psychology, 8*(3), 317–344. https://doi.org/10.1016/0361-476X(83)90019-X

Perrone-Bertolotti, M., Kujala, J., Vidal, J. R., Hamame, C. M., Ossandon, T., Bertrand, O., et al. (2012). How silent is silent reading? Intracerebral evidence for top-down activation of temporal voice areas during reading. *Journal of Neuroscience, 32*(49), 17554–17562. https://doi.org/10.1523 /JNEUROSCI.2982-12.2012

Pew Internet & American Life Project. (2012). *The rise of e-reading: Part 2—The general reading habits of Americans.* Washington, DC: Pew Research Center. Accessed at www.pewresearch.org /internet/2012/04/04/part-2-the-general-reading-habits-of-americans on June 19, 2024.

Plane, S., Bazerman, C., Rondelli, F., Donahue, C., Applebee, A. N., Boré, C., et al. (Eds.). (2017). *Research on writing: Multiple perspectives.* Fort Collins, CO: WAC Clearinghouse. https://doi.org/10.37514 /int-b.2017.0919

Proctor, C. P., Daley, S., Louick, R., Leider, C. M., & Gardner, G. L. (2014). How motivation and engagement predict reading comprehension among native English-speaking and English-learning middle school students with disabilities in a remedial reading curriculum. *Learning and Individual Differences, 36*(1), 76–83.

Reninger, K. B., & Rehark, L. (2009). Discussions in a fourth-grade classroom: Using exploratory talk to promote children's dialogic identities. *Language Arts, 86*(4), 268–279.

Ritchey, K. D., Palombo, K., Silverman, R. D., & Speece, D. L. (2017). Effects of an informational text reading comprehension intervention for fifth-grade students. *Learning Disability Quarterly, 40*(2), 68–80. https://doi.org/10.1177/0731948716682689

Roehling, J. V., Hebert, M., Nelson, J. R., & Bohaty, J. J. (2017). Text structure strategies for improving expository reading comprehension. *The Reading Teacher, 71*(1), 71–82. https://doi.org/10.1002 /trtr.1590

Rogoff, B. (1990). *Apprenticeship in thinking: Cognitive development in social context.* New York: Oxford University Press.

Rosen, L. M. (1992). "Afloat on a sea of talk." *Language Arts Journal of Michigan, 8*(1), Article 2. https:// doi.org/10.9707/2168-149X.1618

Rosenberg, D., & Szura, N. (2023, October 23). How much time do kids spend on devices—playing games, watching videos, texting, and using the phone? *The Conversation.* Accessed at https://theconversation .com/how-much-time-do-kids-spend-on-devices-playing-games-watching-videos-texting-and-using-the -phone-210118 on November 1, 2024.

Ryan, R. M., & Deci, E. L. (2000a). Intrinsic and extrinsic motivations: Classic definitions and new directions. *Contemporary Educational Psychology, 25*(1), 54–67. https://doi.org/10.1006 /ceps.1999.1020

Ryan, R. M., & Deci, E. L. (2000b). Self-determination theory and the facilitation of intrinsic motivation, social development, and well-being. *American Psychologist, 55*(1), 68–78. https://doi.org/10.1037/0003-066X.55.1.68

Ryan, R. M., & Deci, E. L. (2002). Overview of self-determination theory: An organismic-dialectical perspective. In E. L. Deci & R. M. Ryan (Eds.), *Handbook of self-determination research* (pp. 3–33). Rochester, NY: University of Rochester Press.

Ryan, R. M., & Deci, E. L. (2017). *Self-determination theory: Basic psychological needs in motivation, development, and wellness.* New York: Guilford Press.

Santa, C. M., Havens, L. T., Franciosi, D., & Valdes, B. J. (2012). *Project CRISS: Creating independence through student-owned strategies* (4th ed.). Dubuque, IA: Kendall Hunt.

Shanahan, T., & Shanahan, C. (2008). Teaching disciplinary literacy to adolescents: Rethinking content-area literacy. *Harvard Educational Review, 78*(1), 40–59. https://doi.org/10.17763/haer.78.1.v62444321p602101

Shatz, I. (n.d.). *Equivocation and the equivocation fallacy.* Accessed at https://effectiviology.com/equivocation on June 19, 2024.

Shkedy, G., Shkedy, D., Sandoval-Norton, A. H., Fantaroni, G., Castro, J. M., Sahagun, N., et al. (2021). Visual Communication Analysis (VCA): Implementing self-determination theory and research-based practices in special education classrooms. *Cogent Psychology, 8*(1), Article 1875549. https://doi.org/10.1080/23311908.2021.1875549

Short, K. G., & Harste, J. C. (1996). *Creating classrooms for authors and inquirers* (2nd ed.). Portsmouth, NH: Heinemann.

Shuai, L., Daley, D., Wang, Y.-F., Zhang, J.-S., Kong, Y.-T., Tan, X., et al. (2017). Executive function training for children with attention deficit hyperactivity disorder. *Chinese Medical Journal, 130*(5), 549–558. https://doi.org/10.4103/0366-6999.200541

Sinatra, G. M., & Lombardi, D. (2020). Evaluating sources of scientific evidence and claims in the post-truth era may require reappraising plausibility judgments. *Educational Psychologist, 55*(3), 120–131. https://doi.org/10.1080/00461520.2020.1730181

Smith, R., Snow, P., Serry, T., & Hammond, L. (2021). The role of background knowledge in reading comprehension: A critical review. *Reading Psychology, 42*(3), 214–240. https://doi.org/10.1080/02702711.2021.1888348

Snow, C. E. (2002). *Reading for understanding: Toward an R & D program in reading comprehension.* Santa Monica, CA: RAND. Accessed at www.rand.org/pubs/monograph_reports/MR1465.html on June 19, 2024.

Solis, M., Ciullo, S., Vaughn, S., Pyle, N., Hassaram, B., & Leroux, A. (2012). Reading comprehension interventions for middle school students with learning disabilities: A synthesis of 30 years of research. *Journal of Learning Disabilities, 45*(4), 327–340. https://doi.org/10.1177/0022219411402691

Soter, A. O., Wilkinson, I. A. G., Murphy, P. K., Rudge, L., Reninger, K. B., & Edwards, M. (2008). What the discourse tells us: Talk and indicators of high-level comprehension. *International Journal of Educational Research, 47*(6), 372–391. https://doi.org/10.1016/j.ijer.2009.01.001

Stephane, M., Dzemidzic, M., & Yoon, G. (2021). Keeping the inner voice inside the head, a pilot fMRI study. *Brain and Behavior, 11*(4), Article e02042. https://doi.org/10.1002/brb3.2042

Stevens, E. A., Park, S., & Vaughn, S. (2019). A review of summarizing and main idea interventions for struggling readers in grades 3 through 12: 1978–2016. *Remedial and Special Education, 40*(3), 131–149.

Sukovieff, A., & Kruk, R. S. (2021). Reading difficulty and socio-emotional adjustment: Internalizing patterns depend on age of identification. *Cogent Education, 8*(1), Article 191016. https://doi.org/10.1080/2331186X.2021.1910162

Tan, A. (1989). *The joy luck club*. New York: Putnam's.

Tatum, A. W. (2009). *Reading for their life: (Re)building the textual lineages of African American adolescent males*. Portsmouth, NH: Heinemann.

Texas Education Agency. (2023a). *STAAR released test questions*. Accessed at https://tea.texas.gov/student-assessment/testing/staar/staar-released-test-questions on June 19, 2024.

Texas Education Agency. (2023b). *Statewide item analysis reports, STAAR*. Accessed at https://tea.texas.gov/student-assessment/testing/student-assessment-results/statewide-item-analysis-reports on June 19, 2024.

Texas Education Agency. (2023c). *Statewide summary reports, STAAR*. Accessed at https://tea.texas.gov/student-assessment/testing/staar/staar-statewide-summary-reports on June 19, 2024.

Tovani, C. (2000). *I read it, but I don't get it: Comprehension strategies for adolescent readers*. Portland, ME: Stenhouse.

Tovani, C. (2020). *Why do I have to read this? Literacy strategies to engage our most reluctant students*. Portsmouth, NH: Stenhouse.

Trabasso, T., & van den Broek, P. (1985). Causal thinking and the representation of narrative events. *Journal of Memory and Language, 24*(5), 612–630.

Troyer, M. (2017). A mixed-methods study of adolescents' motivation to read. *Teachers College Record, 119*(5), 1–48.

Tucker, N. (2021, January 21). Inauguration stories: Lincoln's 1865 "With Malice Toward None" speech [Blog post]. *Timeless Stories from the Library of Congress*. Accessed at https://blogs.loc.gov/loc/2021/01/inauguration-stories-lincolns-1865-with-malice-toward-none-speech on November 15, 2024.

Tversky, A., & Kahneman, D. (1974). Judgment under uncertainty: Heuristics and biases. *Science, 185*(4157), 1124–1131.

van den Broek, P., & Helder, A. (2017). Cognitive processes in discourse comprehension: Passive processes, reader-initiated processes, and evolving mental representations. *Discourse Processes, 54*(5–6), 360–372.

van de Pol, J., Mercer, N., & Volman, M. (2019). Scaffolding student understanding in small-group work: Students' uptake of teacher support in subsequent small-group interaction. *Journal of the Learning Sciences, 28*(2), 206–239. https://doi.org/10.1080/10508406.2018.1522258

van de Pol, J., Volman, M., & Beishuizen, J. (2010). Scaffolding in teacher–student interaction: A decade of research. *Educational Psychology Review, 22*(3), 271–296. https://doi.org/10.1007/s10648-010-9127-6

van der Schoot, M., Reijntjes, A., & van Lieshout, E. C. D. M. (2012). How do children deal with inconsistencies in text? An eye fixation and self-paced reading study in good and poor reading comprehenders. *Reading and Writing, 25*(7), 1665–1690. https://doi.org/10.1007/s11145-011-9337-4

van Dijk, T. A., & Kintsch, W. (1983). *Strategies of discourse comprehension*. New York: Academic Press.

van Lier, L. (2004). *The ecology and semiotics of language learning: A sociocultural perspective*. Boston: Kluwer Academic.

Vygotsky, L. S. (1978). *Mind in society. The development of higher psychological processes.* Cambridge, MA: Harvard University Press.

Wade, S. E. (1990). Using think alouds to assess comprehension. *The Reading Teacher, 43*(7), 442–451.

Walqui, A. (2006). Scaffolding instruction for English language learners: A conceptual framework. *The International Journal of Bilingual Education and Bilingualism, 9*(2), 159–180. https://doi.org/10.1080/13670050608668639

Walsh, J. A., & Sattes, B. D. (2016). *Quality questioning: Research-based practice to engage every learner* (2nd ed.). Thousand Oaks, CA: Corwin Press.

Watson, A. (2023, December 18). *Reading habits in the U.S.—statistics and facts.* Accessed at www.statista.com/topics/3928/reading-habits-in-the-us/#topicOverview on June 19, 2024.

Webb, S., Massey, D., Goggans, M., & Flajole, K. (2019). Thirty-five years of the gradual release of responsibility: Scaffolding toward complex and responsive teaching. *The Reading Teacher, 73*(1), 75–83. https://doi.org/10.1002/trtr.1799

Wei, L., & Murphy, P. K. (2018). Teacher and student roles: Walking the gradually changing line of responsibility. In P. K. Murphy (Ed.), *Classroom discussions in education* (pp. 30–53). New York: Routledge.

Wei, L., Murphy, P. K., & Firetto, C. M. (2018). How can teachers facilitate productive small-group talk? An integrated taxonomy of teacher discourse moves. *The Elementary School Journal, 118*(4), 578–609. https://doi.org/10.1086/697531

Wharton-McDonald, R., & Erickson, J. (2017). Reading comprehension in the middle grades: Characteristics, challenges, and effective supports. In S. E. Israel (Ed.), *Handbook of research on reading comprehension* (2nd ed., pp. 353–376). New York: Guilford Press.

Wijekumar, K., Meyer, B. J. F., & Lei, P. (2017). Web-based text structure strategy instruction improves seventh graders' content area reading comprehension. *Journal of Educational Psychology, 109*(6), 741–760. https://doi.org/10.1037/edu0000168

WildlifeNYC. (n.d.). *Red-tailed hawk* (buteo jamaicensis). Accessed at www.nyc.gov/site/wildlifenyc/animals/red-tailed-hawks.page on September 27, 2024.

Wilkinson, I. A. G. (2020, Fall). Talking to learn 2.0. *The Journal of Reading Recovery, 20*(1), 33–48.

Wineburg, S., & McGrew, S. (2017, September). *Lateral reading: Reading less and learning more when evaluating digital information* (Working Paper No. 2017-A1). Stanford, CA: Stanford History Education Group. https://doi.org/10.2139/ssrn.3048994

Wolf, M. (2018). *Reader, come home: The reading brain in a digital world.* New York: Harper.

Wood, D.J., Bruner, J.S., & Ross, G. (1976). The role of tutoring in problem-solving. *Journal of Child Psychiatry and Psychology, 17*(1), pp. 89-100.

Zhang, J., Niu, C., Munawar, S., & Anderson, R. C. (2016). What makes a more proficient discussion group in English language learners' classrooms? Influence of teacher talk and student backgrounds. *Research in the Teaching of English, 51*(2), 183–208. https://doi.org/10.58680/rte201628873

Zywica, J., & Gomez, K. (2008). Annotating to support learning in the content areas: Teaching and learning science. *Journal of Adolescent and Adult Literacy, 52*(2), 155–165. https://doi.org/10.1598/JAAL.52.2.6

INDEX

A

added information (AI), 87, 91, 99, 100
adolescent literacies, 32
Alexander, J., 42
AllRecord RoundRobin structure, 54
Alvermann, D., 32
Analyze Rhetoric Strategy
 directions for, 129–132
 reproducibles for, 140–141
Annotate Texts Strategy
 directions for, 105–109
 reproducibles for, 115–116, 174–176
argumentative texts. *See also* info-texts (information texts)
 about, 14, 36
 Analyze Rhetoric Strategy and, 140, 141
 Consider Perspectives Strategy and, 125, 126, 136
 Evaluate Evidence Strategy and, 128
 evaluating arguments and evidence and, 24, 121, 122
 Four As protocol and, 54
 Synthesize Across Texts Strategy and, 149
 Trace the Reasoning Strategy and, 122, 123, 124, 125
arguments and argumentation. *See* evaluating arguments and evidence
assessments. *See also* formative assessments
 for the Analyze Rhetoric Strategy, 131–132
 for the Annotate Texts Strategy, 108–109
 assessing strategy knowledge and application, 43–44
 for the Check for Understanding Strategy, 111
 for the Consider Perspectives Strategy, 126–127
 for the Determine the Text Structure Strategy, 97
 for the Evaluate Evidence Strategy, 128–129
 example of a strategy lesson, 45, 46–47
 for the Fix Confusion and Fill Gaps Strategy, 114
 for the Focus Your Mind Strategy, 75–76
 for the Preview Texts Strategy, 91–92
 for the Share Learning Strategy, 154–155
 Shared Info-Text Studies and, 66–67
 for the Summarize Texts Strategy, 148–149
 for the Synthesize Across Texts Strategy, 151–152
 for the Talk About Texts Strategy, 78–79
 for the Trace the Reasoning Strategy, 124–125
autonomy, 29, 30

B

background knowledge
 example of a strategy lesson and, 45
 explicit strategy instruction and, 40–41
 meaning-making discussions and, 52
 Preview Texts Strategy and, 89, 90
 text-centered discussions and, 49
bias, cognitive biases, 123
Block Party protocol, 55

C

cause-effect, 92, 96
Center on the Developing Child at Harvard University, 72
central ideas
 central idea statements, 144
 finding the main idea versus determining the central idea, 22
Check for Understanding Strategy
 directions for, 109–111
 Fix Confusion and Fill Gaps Strategy and, 112
 reproducibles for, 117, 118
cognitive biases, 123
compare-contrast, 92, 95
competence, 29, 30
comprehension, strategic approaches to
 about, 19
 comprehension strategies, evolution of, 21–22
 concluding thoughts, 25
 Deep Sense Approach and, 23–25
 info-texts and unique strategies, 22–23

207

making sense of texts, 19–20
skills and strategies, strong comprehenders' use
of, 20–21
Consider Perspectives Strategy
directions for, 125–127
reproducibles for, 136–137
consolidating learning
about, 143–144
concluding thoughts, 155
Deep Sense Approach and, 23, 24, 25, 68
reproducibles for, 156–164
Share Learning Strategy, 152–155
Summarize Texts Strategy, 144–149
Synthesize Across Texts Strategy, 149–152
context, important context (IC), 87, 91, 99, 100
context clues, 112
counterclaims, 123
COVID-19, impact of, 50

D

Daley, S., 31
Deane, P., 9
Deep Sense Approach. *See also specific strategies for*
about, 6–7
comprehension, strategic approaches to, 23–25
Deep Sense Approach info-text strategies, list of, 68
as a flexible approach, 167–168
impetus for, 2–3
as a partial solution, 167
students' need for, 166
where it fits in, 8–9
descriptions, 92, 95
Determine the Text Structure Strategy
directions for, 92–97
reproducibles for, 101–102, 103–104
discussions. *See also* text-centered discussions
independent practice and, 43
planning for varied structured discussions, 53–55
qualities of meaning-making discussions, 51–52
scaffolding with, 43
Shared Info-Text Studies and, 59
distractions and Focus Your Mind Strategy, 73

E

equivocation, 130
Evaluate Evidence Strategy
directions for, 127–129
reproducibles for, 138–139
evaluating arguments and evidence
about, 121–122
Analyze Rhetoric Strategy, 129–132
concluding thoughts, 132
Consider Perspectives Strategy, 125–127
Deep Sense Approach and, 23, 24–25, 68

Evaluate Evidence Strategy, 127–129
reproducibles for, 133–141
Trace the Reasoning Strategy, 122–125
evidence of mastery. *See* assessments
executive skills, 72
experiences, respecting and sharing, 32–33
explaining and modeling
example of a strategy lesson, 45–46
explicit strategy instruction and, 41–42
explicit instruction
about, 39–40
concluding thoughts, 47
Deep Sense Approach and, 6, 166
example of a strategy lesson, 45–47
recommendations for explicit strategy
instruction, 40–45
expository texts, 14, 36, 92. *See also* info-texts
(information texts)

F

fake reading, 16–17
false dilemmas, 123, 127, 137
feedback
example of a strategy lesson, 47
providing feedback and reteaching, 44–45
recitation and, 50
finding the main idea versus determining the central
idea, 22
Fix Confusion and Fill Gaps Strategy
directions for, 111–114
reproducibles for, 119–120
Flajole, K., 40
Focus Your Mind Strategy
directions for, 71–76
reproducibles for, 80–81
focusing on meaning making
about, 71
concluding thoughts, 79
Deep Sense Approach and, 23, 24, 68
Focus Your Mind Strategy, 71–76
reproducibles for, 80–83
Talk About Texts Strategy, 76–79
formative assessments. *See also* assessments
assessing strategy knowledge and application, 43–44
Shared Info-Text Studies and, 59
Four As protocol, 54

G

Gardner, G., 31
Goggans, M., 40
gradual release of responsibility model, 40
guided pairs, 42–43
guided practice, 42–43, 46
Guthrie, J., 29–30

H

Helder, A., 19
helping adolescent students regain their reading confidence. *See* reading confidence, helping adolescent students regain
Hennessey, M., 42

I

important context (IC), 87, 91, 99, 100
inclusion, quietly insisting on, 34–35
independent practice, 43, 46. *See also* practice, guided and independent
info-texts (information texts)
about, 1–2
complexity of, 14–16
Deep Sense Approach info-text strategies, 24, 68
problem of weak comprehension, 165
types of, 14
unique strategies, requirements and, 22–23
where secondary students are stuck, 3–6
info-texts, resistance to
about, 13
complexity of info-texts, 14–16
concluding thoughts, 18
difference between info-texts and literary texts, 13–14
masking and coping strategies for, 16–18
secondary students and confidence and motivation, 16
inner voices, 73
instruction and Shared Info-Text Studies (SITS), 58–59, 66
integrating strategy instruction that works. *See* explicit instruction
International Reading Association, 21
introduction
about info-texts, 1–2
about the Deep Sense Approach, 6–7
about this book, 7–8
impetus for a Deep Sense Approach, 2–3
where secondary students are stuck, 3–6
where the Deep Sense Approach fits in, 8–9

K

key idea signals (KIS), 87, 91, 95, 99, 100, 101
Klauda, S., 29–30

L

leading guided practice, 42–43
leading text-centered discussions. *See* text-centered discussions
Leider, C., 31
literacy rates, where secondary students are stuck, 3–6
literary nonfiction, 14, 36. *See also* info-texts (information texts)

literary texts versus informational texts, 13–14
loaded language, 130
logical fallacies
Analyze Rhetoric Strategy and, 130, 141
Consider Perspectives Strategy and, 127, 137
Trace the Reasoning Strategy and, 123, 124, 133, 134
Louick, R., 31
low-stakes questions, 40–41

M

main idea, finding the main idea versus determining the central idea, 22
manipulative appeals, 130, 131, 140, 141
masking and coping strategies for info-texts, 16–18
Massey, D., 40
meaning-making discussions, qualities of, 51–52. *See also* discussions; focusing on meaning making
mental maps, 19, 20
metacognition, 72, 75, 80, 109, 111
Mix-Pair-Share, 55
Moje, E., 32
motivation, managing motivation, 72–73
motivational practices to help students build their confidence. *See also* reading confidence, helping adolescent students regain
about, 30
experiences, respecting and sharing, 32–33
inclusion, quietly insisting on, 34–35
normalizing growth and struggle, 31–32
shifting perspective, 30–31
treating students as competent contributors, 33–34
Murphy, P., 42

N

National Assessment of Educational Progress (NAEP), 3–5
National Center for Education Statistics (NCES), 5
normalizing growth and struggle, 31–32
Numbered Heads Together structure, 54

O

open-ended questions
planning open-ended questions, 52–53
post-reading and, 65
O'Reilly, T., 9, 153

P

pair discussions, 55. *See also* discussions
paraphrasing
Check for Understanding Strategy and, 109–111, 117, 118
Fix Confusion and Fill Gaps Strategy and, 111
info-text comprehension and, 6

Shared Info-Text Studies and, 193
Summarize Texts Strategy and, 145, 156–157
Synthesize Across Texts Strategy and, 150, 152, 161
perspectives. *See* Consider Perspectives Strategy
persuasive texts, 14, 36. *See also* info-texts
(information texts)
post-reading sequence, 62, 65
Power Notes, 154, 164
practice, guided and independent, 41, 42–43
preparing to read
about, 85
concluding thoughts, 98
Deep Sense Approach and, 23–24, 68
Determine the Text Structure Strategy, 92–97
Preview Texts Strategy, 86–92
reproducibles for, 99–104
pre-reading sequence, 62–63
Preview Texts Strategy
directions for, 86–92
reproducibles for, 99–100
problem-solutions and Determine the Text Structure
Strategy, 92, 96
procedural texts, 14, 36. *See also* info-texts
(information texts)
Proctor, C., 31

Q

QSSSA structure, 55
questions
asking low-stakes questions, 40–41
open-ended questions, 52–53, 65
QSSSA structure, 55
strategy questions, 44

R

RAND, 15
reading. *See also* preparing to read
fake reading, 16–17
planning reading sequences, 61–66
spiraled reading sequences, 59
strategic readers, 17
reading actively
about, 105
Annotate Texts Strategy, 105–109
Check for Understanding Strategy, 109–111
concluding thoughts, 114
Deep Sense Approach and, 23, 24, 68
Fix Confusion and Fill Gaps Strategy, 111–114
reproducibles for, 115–120
reading confidence, helping adolescent students regain
about, 29–30
concluding thoughts, 35
Deep Sense Approach and, 6, 166
motivational practices for, 30–35
reproducibles for, 36–37

reading plans
pre-reading and, 62
Preview Texts Strategy and, 86, 89, 90, 91, 99, 100
Synthesize Across Texts Strategy and, 149
recitation, 50–51
reinforcing strategies with Shared Info-Text Studies.
See Shared Info-Text Studies (SITS)
relatedness, 29, 30
reporter questions, 109
reproducibles for
Deep Sense Approach resource: determining the
text structure, 103–104
example: apply the Summarize Texts Strategy
with a science article, 158–159
example: how you might check for understanding
as you read, 118
example: Power Notes outline for a
presentation, 164
example: Trace the Reasoning in a student
column, 135
learning guide: Analyze Rhetoric, 140–141
learning guide: Annotating Texts, 115–116
learning guide: Check for Understanding, 117
learning guide: Consider Perspectives, 136–137
learning guide: Determine the Text Structure,
101–102
learning guide: Evaluate Evidence, 138–139
learning guide: Fix Confusion and Fill Gaps,
119–120
learning guide: Focus Your Mind, 80–81
learning guide: Preview Texts, 99–100
learning guide: Share Learning, 162–163
learning guide: Summarize Texts, 156–157
learning guide: Synthesize Across Texts, 160–161
learning guide: Talk About Texts, 82–83
learning guide: Trace the Reasoning, 133–134
overview: making deep sense of info-texts, 36–37
sample strategy lesson: teaching the annotation
strategy, 174–176
Shared Info-Text Study (SITS) example 1, 183–187
Shared Info-Text Study (SITS) example 2, 188–194
Shared Info-Text Study (SITS) planning guide,
178–182
strategy instruction planning guide, 170–173
reteaching, 44–45, 47
rhetoric, 121, 131. *See also* Analyze Rhetoric Strategy
Rosen, L., 53

S

Sabatini, J., 9
sampling, masking and coping strategies for
info-texts, 17–18
scaffolding
facilitating independent practice and, 43
leading guided practice and, 42
Shared Info-Text Studies and, 59

scanning and skimming, masking and coping strategies for info-texts, 17
self-assessments, 44. *See also* assessments
self-efficacy, 16, 31
sequences
    Determine the Text Structure Strategy and, 92, 95
    planning reading sequences, 61–66
    spiraled reading sequences, 59
Share Learning Strategy
    directions for, 152–155
    reproducibles for, 162–163, 164
Shared Info-Text Studies (SITS)
    about, 57
    components of, 58–59
    concluding thoughts, 67
    Deep Sense Approach and, 6, 166
    my experience with, 57–58
    planning for, 59–67
    reading sequences, planning, 61–66
    reproducibles for, 178–194
    texts, selecting and evaluating, 60–61
shifting perspective, 30–31
Socratic seminars, 55
Soter, A., 42
source materials
    Evaluate Evidence Strategy and, 127, 128, 139
    Share Learning Strategy and, 153, 154, 155, 163
    Synthesize Across Texts Strategy and, 149–152, 160–161
    texts, tasks, and context and, 15
spiraled reading sequences, 59
strategic approach to improving comprehension. *See* comprehension, strategic approach to
strategic knowledge/strategy knowledge and application, 43–44. *See also* assessments
strategic readers, 17
stretching, 59
student agency, 59
students
    helping adolescent students regain their reading confidence. *See* reading confidence, helping adolescent students regain
    respecting students' experiences, 32–33
    secondary students and confidence and motivation, 16
    target students, 51
    treating students as competent contributors, 33–34
    where secondary students are stuck, 3–6
Summarize Texts Strategy
    directions for, 144–149
    reproducibles for, 156–157, 158–159

Synthesize Across Texts Strategy
    directions for, 149–152
    reproducibles for, 160–161

T

Talk About Texts Strategy
    directions for, 76–79
    reproducibles for, 82–83
target students, 51
task analysis, 153
team discussions, 54–55. *See also* discussions
team practice, 42–43. *See also* practice, guided and independent
tentative language, 33–34
text features
    evaluation of, 88
    Preview Texts Strategy and, 86–89, 90
    types of, 87–88
text-centered discussions. *See also* discussions
    about, 49–50
    concluding thoughts, 55–56
    Deep Sense Approach and, 6, 166
    explicit instruction and, 39
    motivational practices and, 33, 34
    qualities of meaning-making discussions and, 51–52
    Shared Info-Text Studies and, 59, 65, 178
    Talk About Texts Strategy and, 76, 82
    text-centered discussion planning, 52–55
    what gets in the way, 50–51
texts. *See also* Determine the Text Structure Strategy; Talk About Texts Strategy
    selecting and evaluating, 60–61
Text Rendering Experience protocol, 54
    text structure variations on complex texts, 94
Trace the Reasoning Strategy
    directions for, 122–125
    reproducibles for, 133–134, 135

V

van den Broek, P., 19
visual representations with text elements, 14. *See also* info-texts (information texts)

W

Webb, S., 40
whole-class discussions, 55. *See also* discussions
whole-class practice, 42. *See also* practice, guided and independent
why and how secondary students resist reading info-texts. *See* info-texts, resistance to
Wilkinson, I., 42

Their Stories, Their Voices
Kourtney Hake and Paige Timmerman
Though personal narrative writing has taken a backseat to other forms of writing in the classroom, this format enables students to send a message, answer questions, fight for change, and reflect on experiences. Kourtney Hake and Paige Timmerman share a step-by-step, build-your-own framework that helps students excel in writing, showing how personal narrative harnesses students' natural urge to tell stories.
BKG173

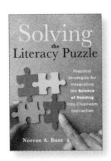
Solving the Literacy Puzzle
Norene A. Bunt
While there is growing awareness of the efficacy of the science of reading, teachers may feel overwhelmed by the volume of research on literacy. Using graphic organizers, assessments, and reflection questions, unpack *five* core components of literacy instruction within the science of reading framework. This comprehensive guide prepares teachers to confidently implement effective literacy instruction in their classrooms.
BKG158

Inspiring Lifelong Readers
Jennifer McCarty Plucker
Research shows that secondary students need daily opportunities to engage in reading, writing, and communicating to improve reading success. *Inspiring Lifelong Readers* equips teachers with literacy strategies that achieve lasting results. Grounded in practices that promote adolescent literacy, inquiry, motivation, inspiration, and engagement, this book offers tried-and-true, evidence-based strategies that support students in becoming competent, confident, and engaged readers.
BKF947

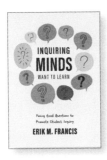
Inquiring Minds Want to Learn
Erik M. Francis
Quality questions, directed inquiry, and authentic literacy are important tools that enhance students' comprehension, knowledge, and application of what is taught. Learn how to phrase and pose good questions that will ignite inquiring minds and enrich student learning. Author Erik M. Francis shares a framework for engaging students' interest and then guiding students down four pathways of inquiry and questioning that make learning stick.
BKG102

Rigor Redefined
Michael McDowell
High-quality teaching balances knowing, connecting, and applying core knowledge. This enables students to take ownership of their learning process. Using ten research-supported learning habits paired with practical tools and relevant templates, teachers can implement rigorous instruction in small and doable ways that drive student learning and create a lasting impact. Discover how to connect the dots between surface learning, deep learning, and transfer learning.
BKG193

Solution Tree | Press

a division of Solution Tree

Visit SolutionTree.com or call 800.733.6786 to order.

Quality team learning **from authors you trust**

Global PD Teams is the first-ever **online professional development resource designed to support your entire faculty on your learning journey.** This convenient tool offers daily access to videos, mini-courses, eBooks, articles, and more packed with insights and research-backed strategies you can use immediately.

 GET STARTED
SolutionTree.com/**GlobalPDTeams**
800.733.6786